THE EXCELLENT MRS FRY

The Excellent Mrs Fry

Unlikely Heroine

Anne Isba

continuum

Published by the Continuum International Publishing Group
The Tower Building 80 Maiden Lane
11 York Road Suite 704
London New York
SE1 7NX NY 10038

www.continuumbooks.com

copyright © Anne Isba, 2010.

First published 2010

British Library Cataloguing-in-Publication Data
A catalogue record for this book is available from the British Library.

ISBN 978–1847–25039–1

Typeset by Pindar NZ, Auckland, New Zealand
Printed and bound by MPG Books Group Ltd

To the memory of my parents

Contents

List of illustrations   ix

Foreword   x

Introduction   xiv

PART ONE: AN UNLIKELY HEROINE

1   A Norfolk childhood   3

2   Awakenings   11

3   Marriage and ministry   29

PART TWO: THE NEWGATE EXPERIMENT

4   Howard's inheritor   49

5   'Hell above ground'   59

6   Exiles to a distant land   81

7   Celebrity and crash   99

PART THREE: SPREADING THE WORD

8   A manifesto for reform   121

9   Recovery   133

10 Continental campaigns   149

PART FOUR: THE FINAL YEARS

11 Nursing before Nightingale   177

12 'Into the valley of old age'   187

13 Epilogue   199

Chronology   207

Notes   211

Bibliography   221

Acknowledgments   227

Index   229

List of illustrations

1   Elizabeth Fry and friend Mary Sanderson entering Newgate women's prison (after a painting by Henrietta Ward).

2   Female prisoners at Newgate, from Knapp and Baldwin's *Newgate Calendar*.

3   Elizabeth Fry, an engraving by Cochrane from an 1823 painting by C. R. Leslie, when Fry was 43.

4   Joseph Fry, Elizabeth's husband, by C. R. Leslie.

5   Samuel Gurney, Elizabeth's brother (artist unknown).

6   Joseph John Gurney, Elizabeth's brother, from a watercolour by George Richmond.

7   The *Rajah* quilt, sewn by Newgate women convicts travelling on the ship of that name from England to Van Diemen's Land (Tasmania) in 1841. The women embroidered on the quilt a dedication of thanks to Fry's convict committee who provided the materials.

8   Statue of Fry in the Grand Hall of the Central Criminal Court at the Old Bailey in London, the original site of Newgate prison.

Credits: photographic images 1, 3, 4, 5, 6 are reproduced courtesy of The Religious Society of Friends in Britain. (Paintings 1, 3, 4 and 6 are in private collections.) Image 7, the *Rajah* quilt, is reproduced courtesy of the National Gallery of Australia, Canberra.

Foreword

I was five or six years old when my mother came home one day with a new comic she had bought for me. Not only that, but she had ordered a regular copy from our local newsagent. This was an extravagance almost unheard-of in post-war Carlisle. The comic was called *Girl* and it was the companion publication to the popular *Eagle* comic for boys. It was delivered every Friday, I think, and its arrival marked for me a high point in the week, rivalled only by the *Beano* being delivered for me at my grandfather's house on a Thursday. Looking back, *Girl* seems a strange sort of read. It was all jolly hockey-sticks and boarding school japes, alongside instructions on how to become a pilot, knit a glove puppet or grow a hyacinth for Christmas, plus profiles of film stars and prima ballerinas.

But there was one feature that captured my imagination. The back page – as I remember it – was given over every week to a cartoon strip depicting the lives of famous women. These were women like Florence Nightingale, Gladys Aylward, Mary Slessor, Queen Esther, Marie Curie and Grace Darling: women who had devoted their lives – or risked them in an instant – for the benefit of their fellow citizens. Elizabeth Fry was one of them. When I saw the picture of Fry entering Newgate women's prison for the first time, armed with only a Bible and a nose-gay, believing that faith and kindness could change people's lives for the better, I was transfixed. She has remained a heroine of mine, and I have been interested in prison reform ever since.

I first went into a prison in 1964. I was an exchange student in the USA before attending university, and our high school choir put on a summer concert for the inmates of the Concord Reformatory in Massachusetts. Our captive audience was far more appreciative of our efforts than I suspect our young talents deserved, and we were a great success. I have been in other prisons since then, and I am always impressed and humbled by how much a little kindness and mutual respect can contribute.

There are many biographies of Elizabeth Fry and at times I wondered whether the world needed another. There has not yet been a biography that gives almost exclusive centre stage to her work. I therefore made a conscious decision to depart from the traditional biographical format, by making Fry's career, rather than the woman herself, the hero of the piece.

The main sources of information on Fry's life are the 46 volumes of her diaries, and the two volumes of memoirs – comprising edited diary extracts, selected correspondence, and connecting narrative – that were published by her two eldest daughters two years after Fry's death. (In order to avoid repetitive endnotes, I have not duplicated references to these sources where the dating in the text makes the chronology perfectly clear.)

My aim has been to unpick the tapestry of Fry's life as presented in her diaries and her daughters' memoirs; and then to weave the main strands of her prison reform activities back into a simpler narrative, but one that, I hope, provides a more powerful impression of the enormous impact of her work in Western Europe and beyond. To reinforce this, I have introduced additional material from the memoirs of those who travelled with her on the campaign trail, including her brothers Joseph and Samuel, and her niece Elizabeth; as well as material from her correspondents in Australia, where so many Newgate women fetched up.

I have included only such elements of family life as were essential to inform Fry's career. I have not dwelt on her religious life, at least beyond the point where, as a young woman, she made a conscious decision to become a consistent 'plain' Quaker. Nor have I engaged with her reaction to the fact that so many of her siblings and children married out, or opted out, of the Religious Society of Friends. This is partly because her religious life has been documented admirably elsewhere; partly also because, with time, she became reconciled to that which was good in other denominations. But the main reason is this: Fry, like Florence Nightingale after her, always insisted that she was following a path chosen for her by God. There was, however, in her a personal drive – a compulsion almost – that owed at least as much to her temperament as it did to her Lord. Fry needed to feel that she was doing good.

I have called my subject Betsy up to the time of her marriage, after which I have called her Fry. The naming system within the Quaker community in the early nineteenth century is a potential minefield when it comes to identifying individual members, as a brief glance at the index of any Quaker biography will show. There was a limited pool of first names, which drew heavily on the

Bible. In the extended Gurney–Fry family, the names of the aunts and uncles were also given to the next generation. When Betsy married Joseph, she joined her mother-in-law and two sisters-in-law to become the fourth Elizabeth Fry in the immediate family. Sometimes she was known as Elizabeth Joseph Fry, to identify herself more clearly. Quakers do not distinguish between brothers, for example, and brothers-in-law, so 'brother Joseph' or 'sister Elizabeth' could be one of several relatives. Fry's Gurney sisters were Katherine, Rachel, Richenda, Hannah, Louisa and Priscilla. The Gurney boys were John, another John (the first having died infancy), Samuel and Joseph (later Joseph John), and Daniel; that meant that Fry's father, grandfather, two brothers and a son were all called John. Her brother Joseph added John (his father's name) to his own in order to distinguish himself from his uncle Joseph Gurney, a plain Quaker, who was the head of the family bank where the younger man also worked. The children of Elizabeth and Joseph Fry were Katherine, Rachel, John Gurney, William Storrs, Richenda, Joseph, Elizabeth, Hannah, Louisa, Samuel (known as 'Gurney') and Daniel ('Henry'). And so it continued with the grandchildren.

This book is the first to deal intensively with Fry's work on behalf of prisoners and transportees. No one except John Howard ever made such a personal contribution to the issue; no other private individuals apart from Howard and Fry ever accumulated such expertise in the field. And they did all this at their own expense. Howard invested his inheritance in the project; Fry had her dynamic Gurney brothers Joseph and Samuel, and other wealthy relatives, to thank for funding her extensive fact-finding tours and campaigns at home and abroad, as well as covering much of her own personal expenditure after bankruptcy hit her husband's family businesses.

With time, the efforts of these pioneering prison reform campaigners became enshrined in British law; although, for lack of state funding – then, as now – the implementation of those laws lagged far behind their enactment. With time, the 'establishment' took over what the philanthropists had begun, and the philanthropists moved on to other issues or, in Fry's case, to fresh fields in Continental Europe. This book charts that progress.

The history of Fry's involvement with the welfare of the women transported to Australia I have made into a self-contained chapter. I make no apology for this, despite the fact that it upsets the strict chronology of her life. The subject deserves its own narrative, and to fragment it by interspersing elements within the overall biographical narrative of her life, to my mind, dilutes its impact.

There is also the question of naming the various societies with which Fry was connected. The original umbrella organization was the 'British Society for Promoting the Reformation of Female Prisoners'. It spawned various committees at national and local level: ladies' visiting committees, ladies' associations, convict sub-committees, Bible sub-committees and so on. Most of the time, I have called these simply 'ladies' committees', and their members 'lady visitors', except when quoting a specific organization. The names varied; the spirit remained the same. These groups, or rather their male equivalents, became the Prison Boards of Visitors (originally exclusively Justices of the Peace), which gradually came to accept women and non-magistrates; in 2003, these, in turn, became the Independent Monitoring Boards of volunteers that are now attached to every British prison.

In 1910, the then Home Secretary Winston Churchill, who had himself been imprisoned during the Boer War, told the House of Commons that one of the tests of civilization in any society was the way it treated those whom it sent to prison: 'The mood and temper of the public in regard to the treatment of crime and criminals is one of the unfailing tests of the civilization of any country. A calm, dispassionate recognition of the rights of the accused, and even of the convicted criminal . . . measures the stored up strength of the nation.'

The debate about prison reform remains as alive today as ever; this is particularly true with regard to the treatment of women prisoners. A report by Baroness Corston in 2007 exposed the often dire conditions in which women and girls are still held in the British prison system, and drew the public's attention, as Fry did nearly two centuries earlier, to their particular vulnerability. At a time when society needs seriously to address the question of what it expects its prison service to achieve, there is much to be learned from the spirit of Fry's endeavours.

Introduction

It was a scene worthy of Dante's *Inferno*: a place that strong men feared to enter. Filth and depravity were on every side. The foulness of the air was almost unbearable. Into a single yard were packed four to five hundred women and children. The space was so tight that at night they slept in three layers – some on the floor, and the rest above in two tiers of hammocks. Only the slave ships were more cramped.

Lumped together were convicted prisoners and those not yet tried, murderesses, prostitutes, lunatics, political dissidents and newborn infants. The mad, the bad, the sad and the difficult all shared the same dreadful experience from which no one would emerge the better. Some women had too few clothes for decency. Others wore the clothes of recently hanged men. Many were too drunk to care. From behind the grille that separated them from polite society, the female underclass of Georgian life cursed, begged from and spat at those in the outside world.

Into this dark, dank hell above ground, there stepped one February morning in 1813 a tall, slim woman of 32. She wore the simple grey dress of a 'plain' Quaker. She had no previous experience of what she saw before her. She had been advised by some not to go in alone; others had advised her not to go there at all. But braver friends had encouraged her to rise to this challenge, saying none but a woman could do it.

It was the plight of the children that upset her most: the naked newborns, whose mothers fought over the clothes of a dead child; the filth-encrusted toddlers, whose first lisping words were curses. Fry was already the mother of eight children and would bear three more. She had brought with her flannel clothing for the babies and clean straw for the floor. That same night, she wrote to her children.

I have lately been to Newgate to see after the poor prisoners who had poor little infants without clothing, or with very little and I think if you saw how small a piece of bread they are each allowed a day you would be very sorry . . . how would you like to go all day with nothing but a piece of bread, and some water? We should feel it very sad and I could not help thinking, when there, what sorrow and trouble those have who do no wrong . . . I hope, if you should live to grow up, you will endeavour to be very useful and not spend all your time in pleasing yourselves. Farewell my darling children. Remember the way to be happy is to do good.

Personal misfortune meant that it would be three years before Fry could begin to devote herself seriously to the plight of the Newgate women. But the die was cast that winter's day. Elizabeth Fry had found her vocation.

PART ONE

An unlikely heroine

A Norfolk childhood

There was little in the early life of timid young Betsy Gurney that gave any hint of the formidable woman that Elizabeth Fry would become, since hers was, as she said, a childhood 'almost spoiled through fear'. It should, in fact, have been idyllic.

Betsy was born to John and Catherine Gurney on 21 May 1780 in a spacious, well-appointed house – Gurney Court – on Magdalen Street in the centre of the prosperous East Anglian market city of Norwich. She was their third daughter, and the fifth of twelve children. Norwich had been one of the leading commercial centres of England from the time of the Norman Conquest in 1066. Since the Middle Ages, the city had prospered through the wool trade and weaving. As such, it had attracted many dissident Flemish and Dutch weavers fleeing religious persecution. By the late sixteenth century, nearly a third of Norwich's population were immigrants, and the thriving city had developed a reputation for religious and cultural tolerance.

By the late eighteenth century, brewing, banking and insurance were the main emerging industries in Norwich. It had also become the home to a rapidly growing Quaker community. As early as 1676 – during the lifetime of the Society's founder, George Fox (1624–91), the Norwich Society of Friends had invested £80 in a piece of land at Upper Goat Lane, a place which still today forms part of the Meeting House site and is where the Gurney family worshipped.

The Gurneys were wealthy and well connected, and the marriage of Betsy's parents was a celebrated, if not universally approved, love match. The wedding took place in the face of the Gurneys' objections on the grounds that Catherine's family were of modest means, despite their illustrious antecedents.[1] In the event, the happy union went on to produce a total of twelve children — seven girls and five boys. At a time of high infant mortality, remarkably, all but one boy survived.

On both sides of the family, Betsy's Quaker credentials were impeccable. Her father John Gurney (1749–1809) was of Norman descent, of Crusader stock.

He was a banker and woollen manufacturer. His great-grandfather had been one of the earliest Quakers, joining the movement in 1655, during the lifetime of George Fox. His wife Catherine, née Bell, was a great granddaughter of the famous Quaker apologist Robert Barclay (1648–1690).

Yet while young John Gurney was educated as a Quaker, his liberal nature led him and his household into association with many of the new ideas circulating at the time. He was what then was described as a 'gay', or liberal, Quaker.

Traditional Quaker businesses were commerce, banking, manufacturing and engineering. As Dissenters, in the eighteenth century, they were denied access to universities, and therefore to the professions, or to positions within either Church or State. On conscientious grounds, they would not enter the armed forces, or undertake any activity that required them to swear an oath. Their considerable energies were therefore diverted elsewhere. Their egalitarian approach to life and their sense of social responsibility made them ideal employers – and many have survived to the present day. The names of Barclays, Hoare, Cadbury and Rowntree are but a few that echo down the centuries.

Betsy's childhood should, therefore, have been one of innocent and unselfconscious pleasure, as cheerful as it was comfortable. Since the Gurneys were 'gay' or modern, rather than 'plain' or traditional Quakers, they took an active part in a warm, extended family and even wider circle of acquaintances within and without the strict Quaker community. They wore normal (even extravagant) clothes, and expressed a keen interest in all new ideas, whether from literature or science: Paine, Voltaire, Rousseau and Wollstonecraft were all discussed at their dinner table. Though they expressed no aspects of Puritan self-denial, the Gurneys remained firmly wedded to the broad principles of their faith. Although they brought their children up in a manner that plain Quakers regarded as excessively liberal, mixing freely in society, they established a compromise by ensuring that their families attended weekly Meetings. What reinforced their credentials was the fact that they remained engaged with all the major social issues of the time, from the abolition of slavery to republicanism, from rights for women to prison reform.

Young Betsy's summers were spent at the family retreat at Bramerton, four miles outside Norwich in the Norfolk countryside. It was a magical place for children, set in beautiful, unspoilt countryside that more than compensated for the urban restrictions of Magdalen Street. In 1786, when she was six, the summer delights provided by Bramerton were acquired on a permanent basis when her father took the lease on Earlham Hall.[2] This was a substantial Norwich property belonging to a distant branch of the family, and one which combined the rural charm of Bramerton with the practical appeal of a property within easy distance of Norwich centre. It was here that Betsy's love of nature developed, encouraged by her mother. Her father bought some neighbouring land to extend the family grounds. Writing a century later, a Gurney descendant would describe Earlham Hall as a serene, 'space-encircled, isolated household'.[3]

But, despite all this, it was not a happy childhood. Betsy was always anxious. From an early age she kept a diary, expressing her deepest anxieties. And then, at the age of 38, a year of great trials on many fronts, she simply destroyed this record of the early years, replacing it with a summary of her life up to the age of 17.

'My spirits were not strong', she wrote of her early life. 'I frequently cried if looked at, and said that my eyes were weak.' Even as a child, she suffered episodes of real anxiety: 'I remember being so much afraid of a gun, that I gave up an expedition of pleasure with my father and mother, because there was a gun in the carriage.'

> I was also exceedingly afraid of the dark, and suffered so acutely from being left alone without a light after I went to bed, that I believe my nervous system was injured in consequence of it; also, I had so great a dread of bathing (to which I was at times obliged to submit) that the first sight of the sea, when we were as a family going to stay by it, would make me cry; indeed, fear was so strong a principle in my mind, as greatly to mar the natural pleasures of childhood.

Had she been able to express her fears, they might have been relieved. But she could not.

> I had, as well as a fearful, rather a reserved mind, for I never remember telling of my many painful fears, though I must often have shown them by weeping when left in the dark, and on other occasions: this reserve made me little understood, and thought very little of, except by my mother and one or two others. I was considered and called very stupid and obstinate. I certainly did not like learning, nor did I, I believe, attend to my lessons, partly from a delicate state of health, that produced languor of mind as well as body. But, I think, having the name of stupid really tended to make me so, and discouraged my efforts to learn. I remember having a poor, not to say low opinion of myself ... I believe I had not a name only for being obstinate, for my nature had then a strong tendency that way; and I was disposed to a spirit of contradiction, always ready to see things a little differently from others, and not willing to yield my sentiments to theirs.

Despite her natural anxiety, Betsy was very affectionate by nature.

> Such was the love for my mother, that the thought that she might die and leave me used
> to make me weep after I went to bed, and for the rest of the family . . . my childlike wish
> was, that two large walls might crush us all together, that we might die at once, and thus
> avoid the misery of each other's death. I seldom, if I could help it, left my mother's side.

But her abiding memory of her early years was of being haunted by a melancholy she could not articulate.

> I think I suffered much in my youth from the most tender nervous system; I certainly
> felt symptoms of ill health before my mother died, that I thought of speaking to her
> about, but never did, partly because I did not know how to explain them; but they ended
> afterwards in very severe attacks of illness.

Anxious, awkward, shy, sickly and painfully eager to please, Betsy was
also almost certainly dyslexic.[4] She described her young self – and her sisters
confirmed this – as being quick to grasp the essence of an idea, but very bad at
holding on to it. 'It soon vanishes', she admitted. As a result, she often gave the
impression of being wilfully slow and forgetful, of not really making an effort.
She was also an atrocious speller. And, as her diaries show, she remained a bad
and inconsistent speller all her life, even of the simplest words. In contrast to the
rest of her family, her handwriting was untidy, her style repetitive and rambling;
and her approach to punctuation and sentence structure unorthodox. Although
she was well loved within the family, these inadequacies – as Betsy saw them –
reinforced her low sense of self-esteem and her anxious personality, the whole
being compounded by a naturally fragile constitution with recurrent episodes
of ill health.[5]

Dyslexia was not identified as a condition until 1887, more than 40 years
after Fry's death, when a German ophthalmologist, Rudolf Berlin, coined the
word to describe a specific learning disability that manifests itself primarily as a
difficulty with written language, particularly with reading and spelling, despite
the patient's having typical intellectual and physical abilities in all other aspects.
Had such a diagnosis been available at the time, her parents might have taken
comfort from the fact that some people with dyslexia have exceptional oral
abilities. So it would prove to be with Betsy. While reading and writing would
never be her forte, her command of the spoken word would prove to be second

to none. In later years her spontaneous and heart-felt delivery, combined with an enchanting voice, would move prisoners and princes alike to tears.

And yet, with hindsight, this unpromising child already carried within her the qualities that would make Elizabeth Fry such a formidable woman, as her eldest sister Katherine (Kitty) observed many years later.

> Betsy had more genius than anyone, from her retiring disposition, gave her credit for in her early days . . . She was gentle in look and manner, and pleasing in person. Though she had not quite Rachel's glowing beauty, yet some thought her quite as attractive. She disliked learning languages, and was somewhat obstinate in temper, except towards her mother. After [mother's death], her aversion to learning was a serious disadvantage to her, and although she was quick in natural talent, her education was very imperfect and defective. Enterprise and benevolence were the predominant features of her character.

Kitty added that it was remarkable how the qualities in Betsy that were considered faults in a child became virtues in an adult, and essential attributes for the woman who would walk alone and unprotected into Newgate.

> Her natural timidity [became] the opposite virtue of courage . . . Her natural obstinacy became that firmness which enabled her to execute her projects for the good of others. What in childhood was something like cunning ripened into . . . long-sightedness and skill in influencing the minds of others. Her disinclination to the common methods of learning appeared to be connected with original thought, and mind acting on its own resource.[6]

In 1792, young Betsy's worst fears were realized. After an illness of just three weeks, Catherine Gurney died. Kitty was 16 years old; baby Daniel was just one; Betsy was 12. The painful memory stayed with Betsy. More than 30 years later, she wrote that 'the remembrance of her illness and death is sad, even to the present day'.

After her death, there were found amongst Catherine Gurney's papers some undated notes on the education of girls. They were addressed to 'my dear child' and were probably intended for Kitty, possibly in anticipation of her taking her mother's place, at some future date, in charge of the household and the upbringing of her younger sisters.

It would be certainly wise, in those engaged in the important office of instructing youth, to consider, what would render the objects of their care perfect, when men or women; rather than what will render them pleasing as children. These reflections have led me to decide upon what I most covet for my daughters, as the result of our daily pursuits. As piety is undoubtedly the shortest and securest route to all moral rectitude, young women should be virtuous and good, on the broad form basis of Christianity.

It is necessary and very agreeable, to be well informed of our own language, and the Latin as being the most permanent; and the French as being the most in general request. The simple beauties of mathematics appear to be so excellent an exercise to the understanding, that they ought on no account to be omitted, and are perhaps scarcely less essential, than a competent knowledge of ancient and modern history, geography and chronology. To which might be added, a knowledge of the most approved branches of natural history, and a capacity of drawing from nature, in order to promote that knowledge, and facilitate the pursuit of it.

However, the reality being that a great portion of a woman's life was spent in running a house and family, practical considerations were also covered.

She should work plain work neatly herself, understanding the cutting out of linen; also, she should not be ignorant of the common proprieties of a table, or deficient in the economy of any of the most minute affairs of a family. It should be here observed, that gentleness of manner is indispensably necessary in women, to say nothing of that polished behaviour, that adds a charm to every qualification; to both of which, it appears pretty certain, children may be led without vanity or affectation, by amiable and judicious instruction . . . Do not, my dear child, suffer thy thoughts to wander, or to dwell upon trifles.

In another note, Catherine laid down her daunting daily schedule, itemizing such details as when she saw the children together and individually, how she managed the kitchen, when she read the Bible, and what time she gave over to good works. But the overall scheme is clear. Her schedule was 'designed first to promote my duty to my Maker – secondly, my duty towards my husband and children, relations, servants and poor neighbours'.

Despite the fact that Catherine Gurney was assiduous in attending to her children's religious education, Betsy found no consolation in faith as a girl. 'My religious impressions, such as I had, were accompanied by gloom', she wrote in later years.

On this account, I think the utmost care is needed, in representing religious truth to children, that fearful views of it should be most carefully avoided, lest it should give a distaste for that which is most precious. First show them the love and mercy of God . . . and the sweetness and the blessedness of his service.

Perhaps it was Betsy's natural contrariness that made her reluctant to show any enthusiasm for religion – or indeed any subject – if she felt too much was being expected of her: 'Care is needful not to force children to learn too much, as it not only injures them, but gives a distaste for intellectual pursuits. Instruction should be adapted to their condition, and communicated in an easy and agreeable way.'

Despite being a kind and loving mother, who shared many interests with her daughter, especially a love of nature, Catherine Gurney failed to make religion come alive for Betsy, perhaps also because the daughter sensed that the mother's faith, though genuine, was not deeply examined.

My mother, as far as she knew, really trained us up in the fear and love of the Lord; my deep impression is, that she was a holy and devoted follower of the Lord Jesus; but that her understanding was not fully enlightened as to the fullness of gospel truth. She taught us as far as she knew, and I remember the solemn religious feelings I had whilst sitting in silence with her after reading the scriptures, or a psalm before we went to bed. I have no doubt that her prayers were not in vain.

With Catherine Gurney's death, life changed for ever. John Gurney never married again, but devoted himself as best he could to his children's welfare. Young Kitty, for whom life changed more than for anyone, took over her mother's domestic responsibilities and the day-to-day care of her younger siblings. She never married – nor would she expect to, under the circumstances; nor did the second daughter, Rachel. They would become the 'Norfolk aunts', on whom the extended family would depend over the years when practical help was needed.

'Here then we were left', Kitty wrote,

I not seventeen, at the head, wholly ignorant of common life and, from the retirement in which we had been educated, quite unprepared for filling an important station, and unaccustomed to act on independent principle. Still, my father placed me nominally at the head of the family – a continual weight and pain which wore my health and spirits. I never again had the joy and glee of youth.[7]

John Gurney soldiered on. But he wrote to a cousin:

> When I see my children delighting themselves in those pursuits in which my dear [wife] Catherine led them, and wherein she was chief companion, my feelings are truly mournful. But I feel the necessity of checking an indulgence of emotion, which may become injurious, and I am always so afraid of throwing a damp on my dear Kitty and the elder children, that I endeavour, as well as I can, to keep up the countenance of comfort.[8]

2

Awakenings

Betsy's bouts of depression continued into adolescence. She likened her periods of low spirits to being in a valley, and the expression entered the family vocabulary. The resulting volatility made her difficult to be with at times. Her sister Louisa, five years her junior, recording in her diary how she loved her various siblings, wrote that 'to Betsy I feel a particular sort of attachment: her ill-health and sweetness draw my heart to her entirely'.[1] Yet only ten days later, she was writing: 'I do not know what we shall do when Betsy comes home, for we are all afraid of her now, which is very shocking . . . Dearest Betsy! She seems to have no-one for her *friend*, for none of us are intimate with her.' During Kitty's occasional absences, Betsy would take over her job of teaching the younger girls. Louisa wrote: 'I hate Betsy's management of our lessons. Now that Kitty is away . . . Betsy does it, and is quite disagreeable, she is so soon worried.'[2]

Betsy's slightly superior, detached manner had a controlling element to it, even when she had the best of intentions. 'Betsy has talked to me, and quite convinced me that we do not treat my father with sufficient love', Louisa wrote; and again, 'Betsy had a talk with Kitty about me this evening; she opened my eyes as to how much Kitty does for us: so I love her more than ever, and intend to do everything to please her'. Louisa was at least prepared to see some fault in herself: 'One of my chief faults is speaking unkindly to Betsy: she does so provoke me. She behaves in some things so aristocratically . . . and nothing makes me so angry as that!'[3]

Meanwhile, Betsy was agonizing about what sort of a person she aspired to be, and what direction she wanted her life to take. With no mother to turn to for advice, she found comfort within the pages of her diary. She called the journal her 'little friend to my heart; it is next to communicating my feelings to another person'.

The Gurneys' active social life continued despite Catherine Gurney's death. Prince William Frederick, the future Duke of Gloucester, and his fellow officers from the garrison at Norwich were regular visitors at Earlham for fishing, shooting, dining, singing and dancing. At one New Year's party, when she was just 17, 'Betsy had an *offer* from an officer', Louisa wrote; 'I never knew anything so droll'. Harriet Martineau, who also lived in Norwich, described the Gurney girls as

> a set of dashing young people, dressing in gay riding-habits and scarlet boots, and riding about the country to balls and gaieties of all sorts. Accomplished and charming young ladies they were, and we children used to hear whispered gossip about the effects of their charms on heart-stricken young men.[4]

And yet there were aspects of the Gurneys' affluent, cultured, well-connected 'gay' lifestyle with which Betsy was beginning to feel uncomfortable, much as she enjoyed them at the time. In April 1797, she wrote:

> I feel by experience how much entering the world hurts me; worldly company, I think . . . excites a false stimulus, such as a love of pomp, pride, vanity, jealousy and ambition. It leads to think about dress, and such trifles; and, when out of it, we fly to novels and scandal, or something of that kind, for entertainment. I have lately been given up a good deal to worldly passions; by what I have felt, I can easily imagine how soon I should be quite led away.

Betsy craved excitement, but despised herself for resenting the anti-climaxes that inevitably followed. On first being introduced to Prince William, she wrote: 'I met the Prince, it showed me the folly of the world; my mind feels very flat after this storm of pleasure'. What she wanted above all was to feel emotion, any sort of emotion, whether it be exhilaration at dancing with a prince, or satisfaction at helping the local poor.

> There is a sort of luxury in giving way to the feelings. I love to feel for the sorrows of others, to pour wine and oil in the wounds of the afflicted; there is a luxury in feeling the heart glow, whether it be with joy or sorrow . . . I love to feel good.

She felt 'like a ship put out to sea without a pilot', she wrote shortly after her seventeenth birthday, 'my heart and mind so overburdened, I want someone to lean on'. In the meantime, she drew up a set of resolutions which she hoped would make her a better person: 'I must not flirt; I must never be out of temper with the children; I must not contradict without a cause; I must not mump when my sisters are liked and I am not'. She would not be angry, idle, or sarcastic, give way to luxury or exaggeration, or talk 'at random'. It was a tall order, particularly since the attraction of high society remained so strong. For several days, she confided to her diary that she was

> in a worldly state, dissipated, idle, relaxed, stupid, all outside and no inside. I feel I am a contemptible fine lady . . . I fear for myself, I feel in the course of a little time I shall be all outside frippery . . . I think I am by degrees losing many excellent qualities. I am more cross, more proud, more vain, more extravagant. I lay it to my great love of gaiety and the world . . . I am a bubble without reason, without mind or person . . . I am a fool.

Betsy longed for the comfort of religion and yet had 'the greatest fear' of it, since she said she had never met any religious person who was not fanatical. As the new year dawned, her adolescent *ennui* reached fever pitch. She longed for something, anything, to happen, and predicted that 'if some kind and great circumstance does not happen to me, I shall have my talents devoured by moth and rust'.

That kind and great circumstance was just weeks away. It took the form of the visiting American Quaker minister William Savery. Savery's major achievement would be to convince young Betsy Gurney that being good could also be exciting. Savery had not always been a serious Quaker – that was one of the things that endeared him to Betsy – but now he was a strict, consistent 'plain' Friend. His first visit to the Upper Goat Lane Meeting House in Norwich ('Goats' to Betsy and her sisters) was on 4 February 1798; and he was less than impressed with the appearance of the congregation that faced him.

> There were about two hundred . . . very few middle aged or young persons who had a consistent appearance in their dress; indeed, I thought it the gayest Meeting of Friends I ever sat in, and was grieved to see it. I expected to pass the Meeting in silent suffering.

However, Savery steeled himself to speak and was well received. A public meeting that evening proved more to his satisfaction, but Savery still observed that 'the marks of wealth and grandeur are too obvious in several families of Friends in this place, which made me sorrowful'. As to the younger members, 'it is uncertain whether, with all the alluring things of this world around them, they will choose the simple, safe path of self-denial'.

All seven Gurney sisters were at the morning Meeting. The middle sister, 15-year-old Richenda, commented in her diary that Betsy started off being her usual fidgety self. But then Savery began to speak. His voice and manner were 'arresting', Richenda wrote, 'and we all liked the sound'. Within seconds, Betsy's attention became fixed, and soon she began to weep.

Savery and his travelling companions were lodging in Norwich with Betsy's uncle, Joseph Gurney, another plain Quaker, at his home, The Grove. After the morning Meeting, Betsy asked if she might join them for their midday meal. 'After Meeting, I rode home to the Grove with Friend Savery. We had a sort of Meeting all the way. As soon as we got to the Grove, he had a regular one with me.' Later, all seven Gurney girls returned to Norwich for the afternoon Meeting. 'I have not the same remembrance of this Meeting', Richenda wrote,

> but the next scene that has fastened itself on my memory is our return home in the carriage. Betsy sat in the middle, and astonished us all by the great feeling she showed. She wept most of the way home.

The following morning, William Savery came to Earlham for breakfast. His impression of the Gurney family, as recorded in his journal, was warm-hearted and gentle but he was doubtful as to whether any of them would prove to be useful.

> J.G. is a widower. His children seem very kind and attentive to him and he is very indulgent to them; has provided them with an extensive library and every indulgence that Nature, within the bounds of mere morality, can desire. They were very respectful and kind to us, and very much regretted, I believe sincerely, our being like to leave them so soon. They are a family very capable of distinguishing, through grace, what the truth is and leads to; but, whether, with all the alluring things of this world about them, they will, any of them, choose to walk in it, time only must determine.[5]

Any of them, that is, except Betsy. Her sister Richenda noted in her diary that Savery spent most of his day at Earlham in preaching 'to our dear sister, prophesying of the high and important calling she would be led into. What she went through in her own mind, I cannot say, but the results were most powerful and most evident. From that day her love of pleasure and of the world seemed gone.' Louisa added that Savery seems 'a charming man and a most liberal-minded

Quaker. Betsy, who spent all day yesterday with him, not only admires, but quite loves him.'[6]

Betsy's recollection of her first meeting with Savery is profound. 'I have had a faint light spread over my mind', she wrote in her diary.

> It has caused me to feel religion. My imagination has been worked upon . . . at first I was frightened, that a plain Quaker should have made so deep an impression on me . . . but I hope I am now free of such fears. I wish the state of enthusiasm I am in may last, for today I have felt *that there is a God*. We had much serious conversation; in short, what he said and what I felt, was like a refreshing shower falling upon earth, that had been dried up for ages . . . I hope to be truly virtuous.

Betsy felt that her soul had been led from 'a state of great darkness', and that suddenly 'the light of Christianity burst upon my mind'. She sensed that Savery understood the religious uncertainty that she had been experiencing: 'He having been gay and unbelieving only a few years ago, made him better acquainted with one in the same situation'. Yet her resolution 'to be truly virtuous' was short lived. She confessed that she was still 'very prone to a love of bodily luxury' – a weakness that never left her throughout her life. And, just two days after meeting Savery, although she felt 'very serious' as she rode into Norwich, the fact of 'meeting, and being looked at, with apparent admiration, by some officers, brought on vanity; and I came home as full of the world, as I went out full of heaven'.

The turmoil through which Betsy was going was obvious to the family and, within a fortnight, John Gurney had decided to try to distract his daughter by sending her to London for a few weeks. She would stay with 'worldly' friends and experience all the delights that the capital had to offer. Betsy's mind was 'in a whirl' at the prospect. She was unsure what she anticipated with more delight: the balls, the theatre, the concerts, or the possibility of bumping into William Savery. She vowed 'not to get vain or silly, for I fear I shall . . . but if I see William Savery I shall not, I doubt, be over fond of gaieties'.

It was a wise move on John Gurney's part. If he had hoped that the trip would make Betsy's mind up one way or another, he was right. She spent one evening at Drury Lane, 'wishing the play was over'; the same happened the following night at Covent Garden. 'I enter into the gay world reluctantly', she wrote in her diary. 'I do not like plays . . . all seems so, so very far from pure virtue and nature'. She agreed to have her face 'painted' and her hair 'dressed' before she went out into society, 'but I felt like a monkey'.

She had spent about ten days in London – 'not the place for heartfelt pleasure, so I must not expect to find it' – when she went again to hear Savery speak. This time, his words 'sent at least a glimmering of light through him into my heart which I hope with care . . . will not be blown out'. She longed to be back in the quiet of Earlham, but was still not above being impressed by celebrity. She caught the eye of the Prince of Wales at a concert: 'I own, I do love grand company . . . I felt more pleasure, in looking at him, than in hearing the music'. In later life, Fry looked back on the London interlude as 'the casting die in my life'.

Two weeks after her return to Earlham, a letter arrived for Betsy from Savery, who was in Liverpool prior to his return to America. It was full of encouragement.

> Thou art favoured with amiable and benevolent dispositions which I hope thou hast wisely determined shall not be eclipsed by a conformity to the god of this world, nor enslaved by its . . . philosophy and vain deceit. Thou hast and will have many temptations to combat, thou will doubtless be frequently importuned to continue with thy gay acquaintance in pursuit of that unsubstantial and false glare of happiness which the world, in too bewitching and deceitful colours, holds out to the poor unwary young traveller.

He knew whereof he spoke, Savery added, having experienced what it was to be 'under the imperious and slavish dominion of my own uncontrolled passions . . . [but] I have been convinced there is an infinitely more happy state to be attained, even in this life!'

It was a long letter, full of exhortations to follow the Lord's will, to continue in the paths of obedience and virtue and avoid 'the gay, the giddy, the licentious and the proud'. It concluded:

> My dear child, my heart is full toward thee. I have wrote a great deal more than I expected – but I fain would take thee by the hand if I were qualified to do so and ascend as our heavenly father may enable us, together step by step up that ladder which reaches from earth to heaven. But alas . . . I can only recommend both myself and thee to that good hand that is able to do more abundantly for us that we can either think or ask – and bid thee for the present, in much Christian affection, farewell.

For an impressionable, unhappy girl of not yet 18, this was a powerful message. Back at Earlham, Betsy resumed her old routine of visiting the sick and dying, providing for the poor, and giving lessons to the local children. But things were not the same as before. Her spirit was calmer, 'my mind is not so fly-away'. Even more significant was the fact that her recurrent nightmare – one she had experienced every few days for as long as she could remember – had ceased. It was a dream with which the entire family had become well acquainted over the years. In it, she was 'nearly washed away by the sea, sometimes in one way, sometimes in another; and I felt all the terror of being drowned, or hope of being saved'. Once she felt she had achieved real faith, 'that night I dreamed the sea was coming as usual to wash me away, but I was beyond its reach'. She never had the nightmare again.

As her eighteenth birthday approached, Betsy drew up another set of good resolutions. They resembled, but were more positive than, the resolutions of the previous year. To them she had added: 'Always be in the habit of being employed'. And yet, still she was cautious about the question of religion, since 'many mistake mere meteors for that heavenly light that few receive'. Nevertheless, she was increasingly drawn to the idea of 'turning plain Friend'.

Meanwhile, as a way of being 'always employed', Betsy was tentatively drawing up a plan to introduce a modest programme of Bible reading classes for children of the local poor in the Earlham area, beginning with one boy she had already been instructing, and gradually taking on more. Such classes, she pronounced with all the wisdom of her 18 years, 'might increase morality among the lower classes . . . I believe I cannot exert myself too much; there is nothing that gives me such satisfaction as instructing the lower classes of people'.

In the event, nothing would come of the plan for the time being, as John Gurney had decided to take all seven daughters on an extended progress through Wales and the south of England. If her father had hoped that this would provide a counter-balance to the delights of London, he was not disappointed. The family were away for ten weeks, visiting castles, cathedrals and other historical sites, enjoying the scenery and staying, where possible, with other Quakers. And still Betsy remained susceptible to the frivolities she had been hoping to put behind her. At Landaly, 'a gentleman dined with us, to whom I did not attend, till I discovered he was a Lord. Oh pride, how it does creep in on me!' At Abergavenny, she went dancing and, although admitting that 'there are many dangers attending to it', could not help confessing that 'I think dancing and music the first pleasures in life'.

Towards the end of August, the party – now on its way homewards – arrived at Coalbrookdale in Staffordshire, where Betsy's cousin Priscilla Hannah Gurney lodged with the Reynolds, a powerful and influential family of industrialists and Quaker benefactors. Priscilla Gurney 'possessed singular beauty and elegance of manner, a figure small but perfect, her eyes of great brilliance and expression'. She was, in short, 'exactly the person to attract the young'. She was also a plain Quaker, having 'early renounced the world and its fashions', become a minister and settled into the local community of Friends. Betsy felt instantly at ease at Coalbrookdale, 'a place I have so much wished to be at', since her thoughts were turning increasingly to religion. 'It brings me into a sweet state, being with plain Friends like these, a sort of humility. I expect to be here some days, which I delight in. I feel . . . a calm and rather religious state of mind.'

The calm was about to be destroyed; but the religion was about to be reinforced. For young Betsy Gurney was about to make the acquaintance of Deborah Darby.

Deborah Darby (1754–1810) was an interesting role model for a young Quaker woman. She married into the Darby iron-making dynasty in 1776 when, at the age of 22, she wed Samuel, grandson of the first Abraham Darby. It appeared at the start to be a love-match, but Samuel was prone to mental breakdowns of an unspecified nature, and the marriage was not a happy one. As soon as she had produced two surviving sons, Deborah Darby embarked on a career as a travelling Quaker minister. She was regularly away from home, often for long periods of time, leaving Samuel and the children in the care of relatives – mainly, Samuel's unmarried sister, Sarah.

At the age of 39, Darby launched herself on her biggest adventure of all: a tour of America that was to last almost three years. The American War of Independence had been over for a decade when, in August 1793, Darby and fellow Quaker minister Rebecca Young set sail from Liverpool for the New World. These were resourceful women; as they boarded the *Thomas*, they took with them, alongside plum cakes and Madeira wine, their own side-saddles and saddle-bags, in anticipation of the long rides ahead.

Within a few weeks of their arrival in New York, Darby had made the acquaintance of William Savery at a Friends' Meeting in Philadelphia. Savery was already by then a seasoned and influential Quaker minister who, like Darby's father, was a tanner by profession. He had recently returned from an official mission, unsuccessful as it turned out, to try to negotiate a peace treaty with the Native American Iroquois tribes. During Darby's time in America, they met on several occasions. In Savery's company, she paid visits to the Philadelphia prison and the Pennsylvania hospital – both Quaker projects which were regarded as models for prisons and hospitals in Europe, and with which Savery had been involved. In fact, during Darby's stay, a major criminal justice reform was achieved when, in 1794, the Pennsylvania legislature voted to abolish capital punishment for all crimes except murder 'in the first degree'; it was also the first time that murder had been broken down into 'degrees'.

In September 1795, Darby met young French émigré Stephen Grellet. Grellet was born Étienne de Grellet de Mabillier at Limoges in 1773 into a wealthy Catholic family with close ties to the French aristocracy. Their business interests, like that of the Darbys, included iron-making. During the French Revolution, the Grellet estates were confiscated and, for two years, his parents were imprisoned. In the early 1790s, Grellet and his brother Joseph travelled, via Demerara, to New York, where they landed in 1795, when Stephen was 22. They had been living with a French-speaking family on Long Island, when they were taken to the Friends' Meeting at which they met Darby and Young.

Darby clearly made a bigger initial impression on Grellet than he did on her. She noticed him enough to record his presence at the meeting in her diary. For him, on the other hand, the meeting was a turning point. Though he understood little English, he found that her presence brought out 'solemn feelings' in him. Later, at dinner, Darby spoke to him personally. To this young man who had lost everything – home, family, country – she seemed 'like one reading the pages of my heart, with closeness describing how it had been, how it was with me . . . It was a memorable day. I was like one introduced to a new world. The creation and all things round me bore a different aspect – my heart glowed with love to all.'[7]

Grellet continued to meet Darby and Young during their American stay. The comfort and support the women offered, together with the guidance provided by William Savery, encouraged Grellet to join the Society of Friends. He was to become one of the most formidable international Quaker ministers and social reform campaigners of his age, and another major influence on Elizabeth Fry.

Meanwhile, Darby and Savery had become firm friends and when she and Rebecca Young set off back to England in May 1796, William Savery and three other American Quakers sailed with them on the *Sussex*. Stephen Grellet came to wave them goodbye. According to Quaker accounts, their six tickets cost a total of £210. The month-long voyage back across the Atlantic was particularly stormy, but at least it provided plenty of opportunity for Darby and Savery to talk.

The *Sussex* docked in Liverpool in mid-June and Darby headed home for Coalbrookdale. Samuel wasn't there. Whether he was already ill, or travelling, is not clear; but by August he was seriously unwell and on 1 September he died, 'released from all conflicts', as his wife wrote in her diary. Three weeks after being widowed, she resumed her travelling ministry.

Darby had been back from America for two years when she met 18-year-old Betsy Gurney in September 1798, a matter of weeks after the girl had fallen under the spell of William Savery.

After the afternoon Meeting on the third day of their stay at Coalbrookdale, the Gurney party went to have tea at Deborah Darby's house, Sunniside. Betsy was impressed. 'I felt much love towards her ... and [was] gratified when she said William Savery had mentioned me to her; and that Rebecca Young, who was out, was sorry she could not see me.' Betsy must have appeared unduly excited by the encounter, because 'when we came home, my father took me aside and gave me some good advice: to beware of passion and enthusiasm'.

Early the following day, Deborah Darby was again at the Reynolds' house, and again Betsy was overwhelmed.

> During breakfast, I felt my heart beat much; as soon as it was over, Deborah Darby preached in a deep, clear and striking manner. First, she said ... that God was a father to the fatherless and a mother to the motherless ... She then addressed me in particular. I do not remember her words, but she expressed first: I was (as I am) sick of the world; and looked higher (and I believe I do); and that I was to be dedicated to my God, and should have peace in this world ... I think I never felt such inward encouragement.

The promise of a mother substitute, and the possibility of a peaceful mind, must have seemed like the answer to a prayer.

Despite his reservations, John Gurney agreed to his daughter's staying on alone at Coalbrookdale a little longer and she saw much of the Darbys in the next couple of days. They were together the evening before she left, when Rebecca Young 'spoke most beautifully; she touched my heart'. Then Deborah Darby spoke directly to young Betsy.

> I only fear she says too much of what I am to be: a light to the blind, speech to the dumb, and feet to the lame; can it be? She seems as if she thought I was to be a minister of Christ. Can I ever be one? If I am obedient, I believe, I shall.

As she drove away from Coalbrookdale the following day, Betsy felt that there was 'a mountain for me to climb over'. She wrote later that the time she spent there was 'one of the happiest, if not *the* happiest time I ever spent in my life. I think my feelings at Deborah Darby's were the most exalted I ever remember.' She wanted to start making changes, but was concerned that people might think she was just jumping on a band-wagon, since 'it would appear so like conformity to the opinions of others, to alter so soon after being with these Friends'. But she felt that the time had come, 'for strength and courage have been given me'. As an outward sign of her inward commitment, she resolved from then on to use the traditional Quaker form of address: 'This day I have said thee instead of you.' It was a small first step up the mountain and at first she was embarrassed and inhibited about saying 'thee' to people in a formal situation, and yet 'I dare not draw back'. She hoped that it would show that her commitment was genuine, and would set a standard for her to live up to. 'It will, I think, make me lose all my dissipation of character, and be a guard upon my tongue.' Little by little, she found the courage to introduce the practice, and began to appreciate its advantages, for 'it makes me think before I speak, and avoid saying much, and also avoid the spirit of gaiety and flirting'.

Just as Darby and Savery had encouraged Stephen Grellet to a life of public service, they were now doing the same with Betsy Gurney. It is impossible not to believe that these two Quaker elders were actively seeking to identify and foster new young Quaker talent which, in the case of Grellet and Fry, would lead to even greater things than they themselves had been able to achieve.

Back at Earlham again, Betsy's inclination to become a plain Quaker was as strong as ever; but she was also as reluctant as ever to declare herself as such. As much as anything, her decision to move slowly was conditioned by the ambivalent attitude she sensed within the family, who were less than delighted by the direction in which she seemed to be moving, not least because it tacitly challenged their own, more worldly, position. Her sister Richenda, two years younger, commented:

I have felt extremely uncomfortable about Betsy's Quakerism which I saw to my sorrow increasing every day. She no longer joined in our dances, and singing she seemed to give up; she dressed as plain as she could, and spoke still more so. We all feel about it alike, and are truly sorry that one of us seven [sisters] should separate herself in principles, actions and appearance from the rest. But I think we ought to try to make the best of it, and reconcile it as much as possible to our own minds. Betsy's character is certainly, in many respects, extremely improved since she has adopted these principles. She is industrious, charitable to the poor, kind and attentive to all of us; in short, if it was not for that serious manner which Quakerism throws over a person, Betsy would indeed be a most improved character.[8]

In order to alarm her nearest and dearest as little as possible, Betsy took on the outward appearance of a plain Quaker by stealth. First, she stopped wearing jewellery; then she started favouring dresses in quiet colours and simple styles. Occasionally, the old Betsy shone through: one observer described her at this time wearing a plain slate-coloured silk dress, but accompanied by 'a black lace veil, twisted in the turban fashion of the day with her long blonde hair, the ends hanging on one side'.

Despite her measured approach, her eldest sister Kitty, who had taken over managing the household on their mother's death, told Betsy that she thought 'that my judgement is too young and inexperienced to be able to take up any particular opinions; she may be right. I am willing to give up the company of Friends and their books, if she request it.' Kitty seems not to have made that demand, fortunately for Betsy, who continued firmly to believe that unless she became a plain Quaker, 'my mind will never be easy or happy'.

Little by little, she became very uncomfortable with singing, then with dancing – not for itself, but for the flirtatious sentiments it brought forth. But she continued to keep her feelings secret, and to count her blessings. She had 'true friends, good health, a happy home, with all that riches can give – and yet, these are nothing without a satisfied conscience'. She decided to unburden herself, 'to tell the true state of the case' to her favourite sister, Rachel, whose kindness 'nothing I think could exceed'. For, although she had 'no one here to encourage me in Quakerism, I believe I must be one before I am content'.

Meanwhile, there was at last time to engage fully with her plan to establish a school for the children of the local poor. Such was the enthusiasm for the scheme in the neighbourhood that the school soon outgrew the premises provided at Earlham, and a nearby vacant laundry was acquired as a schoolroom. Here she would give lessons to over 70 young pupils, 'without assistance, without monitors, and without books or pictures'.

Running the school provided a solid and rewarding framework for her energy, since Betsy had decided that she needed to exercise more self-discipline. As 1799 drew to a close, she wrote in her diary: 'Regularity of thought and deed is what I much want; I appear to myself to have almost a confusion of ideas, which leads to a confusion of action; *I want order*'.

In this spirit, her first project of the new year was to overcome the fear of the dark that had plagued her since childhood. Her approach was simple.

My method has been to stay in the dark, and at night to go into those rooms not generally inhabited; there is a strange propensity in the human mind to fear in the dark, a sort of dread of something supernatural: I tried to overcome that, by considering that as far as I believed in ghosts, so far I must believe in a state after death, and it must confirm my belief in the Spirit of God.

John Gurney was not impressed by his daughter's goings-on, and Betsy was upset at this: 'My father not appearing to like all my present doings, has been rather a cloud over my mind'. She was generally anxious that her new direction might alienate old affections: 'I am inclined to think the time will come, when I shall not be quite so dear to my gay friends'. And yet she carried on with her quiet conversion. In April 1799, almost surreptitiously, and without warning, she changed the form in which she dated her diaries to the plain Quaker tradition. Gone were the January to December pagan month names. Her diary entry for 6 April 1799 is headed: '4th month, 6th'.

In the summer of 1798, John Gurney had taken his daughters on a tour of Wales and the south of England. This summer he took Betsy, Priscilla and Samuel to Scotland and the north of England. They visited the co-educational Quaker school at Ackworth, where Betsy spoke seriously for the first time in public, and the 'Friends' Retreat for crazy people at York, which my father thought extravagantly carried on'. From York they travelled via Darlington and Durham to John Gurney's estate at Sheepwash, near Newcastle, and thence to Edinburgh. They were back at Earlham at the end of August.

As the autumn progressed, Betsy's indecisiveness was annoying even to her.

I have felt lately quite in a hurry about what I have to do; and I do not think that is the way to do it well; it is better to go soberly and quietly about it, and not flurry and bluster.

By the end of the year, the transformation process was complete. Betsy's good works were increasing; she was no longer singing or dancing or going to the theatre; she was wearing a plain Quaker dress and cap; she was addressing people as 'thee'; and she had abolished pagan month names from her diary. However, no sooner was one source of mental turmoil laid to rest, than another raised its head. For now, quite unexpectedly, Betsy Gurney's hand was being sought in marriage. It wasn't the first time. Apart from the flirtatious proposal from one of the Prince's officers at an Earlham ball, there had been a genuine – if brief, and unsuccessful – engagement, when she was not yet 16, to a son of the founder of the Lloyds Bank. Its failure had left her wary: 'I believe in my life I have known *in a degree* what it is to love and not have it returned. It was when I was very young and *very silly*.' It had, however, taught her to respect the romantic feelings of others towards her.

Joseph Fry was a shy young man, a good plain Quaker from a respected London family whose situation, though well-to-do, bore no comparison with the immense affluence of the Gurneys. He was the youngest of three sons and three daughters born to William Storrs Fry and his wife Elizabeth. His father's family originated in Wiltshire, but he moved to London to establish a tea and banking business. Both Joseph and his brother William worked in the business with their father, although it was their mother who was credited with having the financial acumen in the family.[9] Why Joseph felt drawn to Betsy is unclear, since there seems to have been minimal, if any, previous connection. His only link with the family was through having been at school in Wandsworth with Betsy's brother, John. However, her family's wealth and influence made her a good 'catch'.

It was on the morning of 26 July 1799 that 'Joseph Fry made me an offer'. After a few days' thought, her mind 'in a state of agitation', Betsy declined. She had nothing against him as a person; on the contrary, she felt sorry for any pain she might be causing him. But the thought of taking on marital and domestic responsibilities was daunting to her. Her father was not opposed to the idea of a match. But, lacking the counsel of a wife and somewhat out of his depth in such matters as a result, John Gurney wrote a kind but firm letter to young Fry, suggesting that it might be better not to visit Earlham again for the foreseeable future, as it would do no good and might possibly compromise Betsy's reputation.

> It is no respect likely to further thy wishes . . . it must have a contrary effect, because it must call upon Betsy, if she cannot return thy affection for her, to take a line of absolute prohibition as to casual intercourse. She will have to consider that young women suffer a disadvantage in character when there shall be any appearance of allowing a young man to remain in the character of a suitor when there is no inclination, or intention to give a further encouragement.[10]

It was clumsy but wise advice. The young people continued to bump into each other casually elsewhere, and gradually built up their acquaintance. Betsy had been totally taken aback at Joseph's proposal, since the thought of marriage had not, until that point, crossed her mind. After many years of agonizing, she had just reached the point in her life where she believed her future lay in the Quaker ministry. Could this be compatible with marriage, she wondered? Suddenly, her hard-won courage failed her. Initially, she was reluctant even to engage with the subject. She was blessed with everything a person could want; she was accustomed to a cosseted existence where little was required of her in return. She lived as a plain Quaker, but within an affluent, liberal environment. What could marriage possibly have to offer her? On the other hand, the Frys were plain Quakers, while at the time the Gurneys remained resolutely 'gay'. Could the Frys perhaps provide her with the serious environment to which she thought she aspired? But what about the career she had planned? Might she dare to hope to have both?

The Gurneys were divided about whether Joseph was a good enough match for Betsy. Her father seemed to be in favour; but, then Betsy was a difficult girl, he had seven daughters in all, and seeing one settled was an attractive thought. Her sisters were less convinced. Joseph was well educated, well meaning, and sang beautifully. Handsome he was not. And his manners were regarded as 'uncaptivating' by the Earlham girls. In the future, these factors would prove less crucial than the fact that Joseph Fry failed to live up to the spirit of energy and dynamism to which Betsy was accustomed in her brothers; but then not many men could.

In October that year, one of Joseph's brothers became seriously ill and she openly expressed her sympathy with the whole family, and Joseph especially: 'What if Joe really loves me or loved me, which I believe he did. I think I must be hard-hearted not to feel for him.' Once she had overcome the shock of anticipating a life away from the cocoon of Earlham, a life of domestic and marital responsibilities, Betsy began to reconcile herself to the idea of marriage. In her diary she wrote shortly before Christmas 1799:

> I believe the true state of my mind is as follows: I have, almost ever since I have been a little under the influence of religion, thought marriage at this time was not a good thing for me; as it might lead my interests and affections from that Source in which they should be centred, and also, if I have any active duties to perform in the church . . . are they not rather incompatible with the duties of a wife and a mother? And is it not safest

to wait and see what is the probable course I shall take in this life, before I enter into any engagement that affects my future career? So I think, and so I have thought.

But to look on the other side: if Truth appears to tell me I may marry, I should leave the rest, and hope whatsoever my duties are, I shall be able to perform them; but it is now at this time the prayer of my heart, that if ever I should be a mother, I may rest with my children, and really find my duties lead to them and my husband; and if my duty ever leads me from my family, that it may be in single life. I must leave all to the wisdom of a superior Power, and in humble confidence pray for assistance.

Betsy decided to confide in her dear cousin, Joseph Bevan Gurney. Joseph was also a close friend of her father – he had confided to him his grief after his wife's death, and Betsy respected his opinion. In April 1800, she wrote to him from Clapham. 'My dearest cousin', she began, 'It is not pleasant to me, having a subject that is now of no small importance to me, unknown to thee, for I feel thee to be, and love thee as a kind friend'.

Some time ago, Joseph Fry, youngest son of William Storrs Fry of London, paid us a visit at Earlham and made me an offer of marriage. Since our stay in this neighbourhood, he has renewed his addresses. I have had many doubts, many risings and fallings about the affair. My most anxious wish is, that I may not hinder my spiritual welfare, which I have so much feared, as to make me often doubt if marriage were a desirable thing for me at this time, or even the thoughts of it; but as I wish (at least I think I wish), in this as in other things, beyond everything else to do the will of God, I hope that I shall be shown the path right for me to walk in.

I do not think I could have refused him with a proper authority, at this time. If I am to marry before very long, it overturns my theories, and may teach me that the ways of the Lord are unsearchable.

But could a woman marry and still carry out the vocation to which she felt that God had called her? Could she have a career as well as a husband and children, a public life as well as a private one? Years later, Florence Nightingale came to the conclusion that a woman of her time could not have it all, and it was marriage that she chose to forego.

Despite her emotional turmoil, Betsy continued to discharge her local responsibilities, including running the poor boys' school. It was gaining something of a reputation locally. One evening in September, her father appeared in the school room with some of his Quaker friends.

As I was reading to my children in the laundry, my father brought them all in; when I had finished reading in the Testament we were all silent, and soon [a visiting minister] knelt down in prayer and we all rose up; it was a very solemn time; my heart was not much moved, but I believe many of my dear children were much affected by it; he then preached to them, and it was surprising to me to see how much it seems the same spirit that works in all; and how solemn a thing it is to preach only from authority, and how very different an effect it has on the mind to other advice; however, it was an encouraging thing, and I hope it will not be passed over by me or the children.

After their visit, Betsy began to suspect that the good works one did carried more weight if one spoke with the authority of Quaker minister than if one were merely a lay person. Would that have to be the way forward?

Meanwhile, Joseph Fry continued to press his suit, and Betsy was beginning to be won over. The fact that his family were traditionally plain Quaker led Betsy to hope that they would provide the context within which her new identity could flourish. At a personal level, she found that 'my feelings towards Joseph are so calm and pleasant, and I look forward with so much cheerfulness to a connexion with him'. A week later, at the beginning of June 1800, she received from Joseph 'a letter I liked, and answered it this afternoon, I felt unwilling to represent my own faults to him, although I told him how faulty I was'.

The wedding date was fixed for 19 August 1800, at 'Goat's' Meeting House. The bride was just 20, the bridegroom 23. A few days beforehand, Betsy's 'imps' – the local lads who had attended her school – came to say goodbye.

It was rather a melancholy time to me. After having enjoyed themselves with playing about, I took them to the summerhouse and bade them farewell; there were about eighty-six of them, many of them wept; I felt rather coldly when with them. But when they went away, I shed my tears also; and then my desires took the turn of anxiously longing for the spiritual welfare of us all, as a family.

On the morning of her marriage, Betsy woke 'in a sort of terror at the prospect before me, but soon gained quietness and something of cheerfulness'.

After dressing, we set off for Meeting; I was altogether comfortable. The Meeting was crowded; I felt serious . . . It was to me a truly solemn time. I felt every word, and not only felt, but in my manner of speaking expressed how I felt; Joseph also spoke well. Most solemn it truly was . . . I believe words are inadequate to describe the feelings on such an occasion; I wept good part of the time, and my beloved father seemed as much overcome as I was. The day passed off well, and I think I was very comfortably supported under it, although cold hands and a beating heart were often my lot.

A Quaker marriage is a quiet affair. The Marriage Act of 1753, which abolished the concept of common law marriage in England and Wales, also gave Quakers permission to solemnize their own weddings. A committee of senior members of the local Meeting examines the marriage proposal, to establish that the couple are ready and that there are no obstacles. Beyond that, the bride and groom simply promise to be loving and faithful to each other. There is no priest to marry them. The father does not give his daughter away. And the woman makes no promise to obey, which in Betsy's case was just as well.

3

Marriage and ministry

In autumn 1800, after spending the first two months of marriage at Plashet, the Fry family mansion in then semi-rural East Ham, the young couple moved to the family's London home at St Mildred's Court in Cheapside, which also served as their business headquarters. Living with the in-laws over the shop in the commercial East End of London was not an ideal start to married life for a girl accustomed to the freedom, space and, above all, the fresh air of Earlham. St Mildred's Court was located in the part of Cheapside known as Poultry, named for the poulterers' stalls which once stood there. The Court itself was previously called Scalding Alley, the place where the birds were dipped in boiling water prior to sale. It was also the home of the Poultry Compter, a notoriously decrepit debtors' prison that at the time also held vagrants, prostitutes, homosexuals, religious Dissenters and released slaves. An official report in 1804 said that the prison was in such a state of decay that it was 'inadequate to the safe custody of the debtors and prisoners therein confined, and extremely dangerous'.[1] One commentator remarked that the Compter's 'mixture of scents that arose from the tobacco, foul feet, dirty shirts, stinking breaths and unclean carcasses, poisoned our nostrils far worse than a Southwark sewer'. The Poultry Compter remained in this parlous condition until it was closed in 1815; Fry would have been closely aware of it during her nine years at St Mildred's Court, as she would of Newgate itself, just a mile down the road.

In the early weeks of her marriage, Fry – accustomed since childhood to have only the best of everything – enjoyed buying things for her new household. 'My inclination is to have everything very handsome', she confessed, but was at the same time concerned lest she should become too 'chained down to the world and worldly things'. Life at St Mildred's Court was hectic and often chaotic: it was the London base for the entire extended family and their business colleagues and contacts, and there could be up to 60 for dinner. More attuned to the quiet of Earlham, she felt shy with the guests, anxious in dealing with the servants and frequently exhausted 'by the great deal I am required to talk'. Nor, amid all the bustle, did she feel she had enough time alone with her new husband. 'I value being alone with my husband; it is a quiet I have not lately enjoyed and it does seem to me, at this time, one of the great blessings of life.' But with so many blessings around, she pondered, was she not ungrateful to wish for more?

Having married into a traditional 'plain' Quaker family, Fry had ceased to be special in the way she had among the 'gay' Gurneys. But she failed to find in her new family the depth of religious feeling that she might have expected. Certainly, Joseph did not share her commitment or her social conscience, and was not above criticizing her fine Gurney ways. Within days of their being installed at Plashet, he remarked that her manners had 'too much of the courtier' in them, which gave her pause for thought. In her diary entry of 14 November that year, she admitted that perhaps self-love made her avoid being unkind to anyone, but defended a diplomatic approach to relationships.

> My disposition leads me to hurt no-one that I can avoid . . . It is among the things that produce the harmony of our society; for the truth must not be spoken out at all times, at least not the whole truth . . . It will not always do to tell our minds. This I have observed, and I am sorry for it, that I feel it hard when duty dictates to do what I think may hurt others.

One senses that Joseph had no such sensitive reservations. On one occasion, for example, he bought some drawings that were beyond their means. When Fry pointed this out, he reportedly threw them on the fire.

Just four months into her marriage, Fry was already experiencing feelings of emptiness which even attendances at Meeting could not dispel. In mid-December, she wrote:

> To attend our place of worship and there spend almost all the time in worldly thoughts is, I fear, too great a mark of how my time is mostly spent; indeed, my life appears at this time to be spent to little purpose other than eating, drinking, sleeping and clothing myself.

She was unfulfilled, yet unsure what to do about it. In January, she confided to a friend that although she was 'not yet quite forsaken as one dead to good works', she was, nevertheless, at a loss as to a remedy.

I am at times ready to feel, what shall I do? For if I were sure this state was out of my own power, I need only quietly rest, hoping for better times. But my fear is that . . . I am so continually devoted to the things of this world, as to blind my spiritual sight from observing things belonging to the other. There are times when my anxiety for good is great indeed . . . but alas, my good wishes and good endeavours are of short, very short duration.

As had happened when she first contemplated becoming a plain Quaker, Fry was daunted by the thought of the direction in which her need for useful activity might lead, and was 'tried by great fears about what duty might call me to'. By now three months pregnant, she felt herself like 'one who has in some measure lost his pilot, and is tossed about by the waves of the world'. She took consolation from the memory of her childhood nightmares in which she feared drowning, but was always saved. And still, despite her first pregnancy, she and Joseph were spending very little time together. In the summer she wrote:

It is quite a serious thing, our being so constantly liable to interruptions as we are. I do not think, since we married, we have had one fourth of our meals alone. I long for more retirement, but it appears out of our power to procure it; and therefore it is best to be as patient under interruptions as we can, but I think it a serious disadvantage to young people setting out in life . . . We are so much from home and in such constant bustles, that really when I am [at home] . . . I have just enough time for keeping things in order; engagement follows engagement so rapidly, day after day, week after week, owing principally to our number of near connexions, that we appear to live for others, rather than ourselves . . . to spend one's life in visiting and being visited seems sad.

In the September, her daughter Katherine was born. To her disappointment, Fry felt no immediate surge of maternal feelings. Initially, the baby was 'a quiet source of pleasure', but post-natal gloom was not far behind. 'She early became a subject for my weakness and low spirits to dwell upon, so that I almost wept when she cried . . . I hope, as bodily strength recovers, strength of mind will come with it.' But recovery was slow. She had no mother to support her, nor sisters with any experience yet of motherhood. There were also disagreements with her mother-in-law about childcare, with Fry being more robust in her approach, believing that 'being too tender and careful really makes them more subject to indisposition'. In October, she wrote in her diary that her anxiety over the baby was 'so acute as to render me at times unhappy'. When her husband and his friends went out to celebrate the temporary end of hostilities with France, she sat home listening to the 'great noise and bustle', with her month-old baby asleep beside her, and feeling miserable.

> This evening I am very tired, and the noise of the mob nearly makes my head ache. This is the way in which they show their joy! It does not seem to me the right manner of showing our gratitude, as it appears to lead to drunkenness and vice. I think true gratitude should lead us to endeavour to retain the blessing, or to make good use of it by more virtue in ourselves and encouraging others to the same.

A few days at Earlham in November to introduce baby Katherine to her Gurney relatives helped to raise Fry's spirits. But Fry returned to London with a serious cough, requiring a doctor to attend. While he was with her, they discussed the controversial question of smallpox inoculation for infants. The practice had been pioneered in Britain in the early eighteenth century by Lady Mary Wortley Montagu, whose brother had died as a child of this highly contagious and disfiguring disease. In 1716, Montagu's husband was appointed ambassador to Constantinople, then the capital of the Ottoman empire. Lady Montagu developed an interest in Turkish healthcare, including smallpox inoculation, or engrafting, as it was then called.[2] A common practice in local folk medicine, it was administered by specialist women practitioners, and said to be the reason the women of the area were known for their outstanding beauty.[3] With the support of a British Embassy physician, who later went on to establish the practice in London, Montagu had her own young children inoculated. The inherent dangers were fiercely debated in the media of the day and Montagu was accused of jeopardizing her children's health. But smallpox was a common cause of death in eighteenth-century England, and inoculations increased within her circle and beyond. The Princess of Wales showed an interest and persuaded George I to arrange for five condemned Newgate prisoners to be pardoned if they underwent voluntary inoculation. The experiment being a success, the Princess then had her own children inoculated. By 1724, the periodical *Plain Dealer* praised Montagu's 'courage for the introduction of this art, which gains such strength in its progress, that the memory of its illustrious foundress will be rendered sacred by it to future ages . . . many thousand British lives will be saved every year to the use and comfort of their country'.[4]

But the debate was not over. Although the French writer Voltaire estimated that one-fifth of all human beings were killed or permanently disfigured by smallpox, he wrote that it was 'whispered in Christian Europe that the English are mad and maniacs . . . because they cheerfully communicate to their children a certain and terrible illness with the object of preventing an uncertain one'. However, he conceded that 'if some French ambassador's wife had brought back this secret from Constantinople to Paris, she would have done the nation a lasting service'.[5] By 1762, official figures showed that in Britain, one in seven people were dying every year of smallpox in the natural way; and one in 312 from inoculation.[6]

The whole concept of inoculation continued to be dogged by controversy. In 1796, physician Edward Jenner – a student of the great surgeon John Hunter – made the connection with cowpox as a potential source of vaccine against smallpox. Despite the success of his trials, Jenner was still being discredited by much of the medical community at the time Fry was asking her family doctor about his views on inoculation; but by 1806, Parliament was voting him £2,000 in recognition of his services. One by one, governments throughout Europe began making vaccination against smallpox compulsory. In Britain, despite Montagu's pioneering efforts, it was 1853 before the inoculation of infants under the age of three years became compulsory, and the last recorded instance of smallpox was in 1979.

Fry's physician was wholeheartedly in favour of inoculation of even very young infants, and Fry thought highly of his judgement.

> I believe it to be our duty to avoid evil, both bodily and mentally. So trifling a complaint as the cow-pox, being likely to prevent so dreadful a disease as the small-pox, at least it appears justifiable to try it; although the idea is not pleasant it almost looks like taking too much on ourselves to give a child a disease. But I was altogether easy to do it. I felt a good deal about the operation, which was very little and easily performed. What a wonderful discovery it is, if it really prevents the small-pox.

Over the years, she had all her children inoculated. And, having been taught the technique herself, she carried out a vaccination programme for children throughout the villages around Plashet, where the disease became unknown.

Meanwhile, life at St Mildred's Court began to take on some sort of routine and, with a baby to focus on, there was less time for introspection. In August 1802, the Frys celebrated their second wedding anniversary and, in reviewing the 'trials and pleasures before unknown', she was able to remark that her family was 'to me in more comfortable order than it was, at least I feel more mistress of it'. In 1803, her younger brother Samuel Gurney came to live with them for several years. Sam was a boy of great common sense but, unlike his younger brother Joseph, had 'no literary taste or fondness for study', and was therefore sent to St Mildred's Court, aged 14, to work in the Fry family businesses, primarily in the book-keeping department. He took to business and clerical work immediately, and was a serious and steady worker. Fry was pleased – a little bit of Earlham had come to Cheapside. Samuel, who had been away at school from the age of seven, was able to reinforce their childhood closeness, with his sister on hand to keep him on the straight and narrow. As another sister, Hannah, observed:

> The serious and precious spirit of this sister no doubt had an invaluable effect on his mind, and he was uniformly steady and of good and wise conduct, most regular in every duty, and preserved from the temptations of youth . . . although he would, with great spirit, enter into pleasanter and lighter pursuits.[7]

In later years, Samuel and his brother Joseph were to become the staunchest supporters of Fry's prison reform work, as well as serious financial backers.

In March 1803 a second daughter, Rachel, was born, and this time the experience of childbirth proved much more positive, at least initially. 'My heart abounded with joy and gratitude . . . Words are not equal to express my feelings, for I was most mercifully dealt with'. But the euphoria was short-lived, and again she was overwhelmed by post-natal depression. 'It is difficult exactly to express what I have gone through', she wrote later of her 'serious indisposition'.

> It has been now and then a time of close trial; my feelings being such at times as to be doubtful whether life or death would be my portion. One night I was I believe very seriously ill; I never remember feeling so forcibly how hard a trial it was in prospect to part with life . . . I told those around me that I was so ill, I could almost forget my child . . . I have gone through so much since, in various ways from real bodily weakness, and also the trials of a nervous imagination: no one knows but those who have felt them, how hard they are to bear, for they lead the mind to look for trouble, and it requires much exertion not to be led away by them. Nothing I believe allays them so much as the quieting influence of religion . . . but they are a regular bodily disorder, that I believe no mental exertion can cure or overcome, but we must endeavour not to give way to them.

By the autumn of 1803, she was feeling better and engaged once more in the charitable works expected of a woman of her station, particularly among the destitute of inner London. She felt quite in her element in seeking out and serving the poor. Although she found it tiring, it gave her much pleasure: 'It is an occupation my nature is so fond of; I wish not to take merit unto myself beyond my desert, but it brings satisfaction with it more than most things'. Yet she was sometimes suspicious of her motives, because of the great satisfaction such work brought her.

> Attending the afflicted is one of those things that so remarkably brings its reward with it, that we may rest in a sort of self-satisfaction which is dangerous; but I often feel the blessing of being so situated as to be able to assist the afflicted, and sometimes a little to relieve their distress.

The year 1804 brought both life and death. Early in the year, Fry's mother-in-law died. She has been credited with being the brains behind the family businesses – brains which her sons may not have inherited – and it was perhaps from this time that the decline of the Fry banking, tea and spice interests began. But there was little immediate outward sign at the time, and life at St Mildred's Court carried on as usual. Fry continued to be plagued from time to time by illness, both physical and nervous, but she was beginning to learn to accommodate it. The birth in 1804 of her first son, John, their third child, was again followed by 'a trying and tedious illness, but not quite so bad'. Again, it was a few weeks after her confinement that prostration hit her.

> I have been very unwell, and passed through great suffering, owing to great sickness, faintness and nervous irritability: however, each trial has had its alleviation. I have not once quite sunk; I have experienced that, though at times it has been rather hard to bear, I do not think it has been too much for me.

In 1806, Fry, again heavily pregnant, was invited to become an official visitor to the Quaker school and workhouse in Islington. On her first visit, on 15 May, she took the children 'some things for tea' and a pamphlet to read to them. Despite her initial misgivings, it was a great success. After the reading, she offered them her own personal thoughts on the text, 'which appeared to affect the children and the governess, so that those who were on the point of tears really cried'. The outcome to this early attempt at public speaking, at an event which had required not inconsiderable courage on her part to attend, make her feel 'quite odd' in a positive sense, although she was anxious not to read too much into it.

> I have been desirous not to stamp such a thing too highly, for I am ready to believe, though the party appeared to feel what I said so much, it was principally owing to their great tenderness, as that which I said seemed rather to flow naturally from my heart and understanding, than anything really deep from the living fountain. I have desired that this little event may not encourage me too much, for hard things seemed made quite easy.

Two weeks later, she gave birth to her fourth child and second son, William. This time, she was much more serene. 'So far I have abundant cause for thankfulness; and though my poor mind has at times passed through a little of the depths; yet I have felt the delivering power near at hand.'

In December 1806, Fry's sister Louisa was married to Samuel Hoare. As Hoare was also a Quaker, all 11 Gurney siblings were able to attend, which was not the case when a Quaker married 'out'. Less than two weeks later, Fry's brother John married a cousin, Elizabeth Gurney. In May 1807, her sister Hannah married Thomas Fowell Buxton, an old family friend and distant cousin, who had spent much time with the Gurneys at Earlham. Buxton, an MP, was William Wilberforce's right-hand man in the campaign to abolish slavery, as well as a fervent prison reform campaigner. The extended family network that would support Fry's work was becoming very impressive.

The state of her own marriage remained an enigma. She rarely complained, and always referred to Joseph as 'my beloved husband', but he remains a shadowy figure throughout her diaries; he certainly never matched her brothers in stature, gravitas and social commitment, let alone wealth. In a letter to Hannah, shortly after her marriage to Buxton, Fry offered advice on how much one could expect from a husband. Hannah had clearly been feeling neglected while her husband went out shooting. As to their partners' faults, Fry suggested that women should

> do what we can to remove them by cheerfulness and tenderness, but not by worrying or too much pressing. A young wife must not be disappointed, or should carefully guard against it, to find her husband in some measure devoted to some things beside herself. I believe it is in the nature of *man* to be so; and if these objects do not lead into what is

really wrong, I think wisdom dictates not only bearing with them, but rather endeavouring to sympathise as far as one can.[8]

The family clearly thought that Fry was being neglected by her husband. Her brother Joseph wrote on one occasion: 'Tell Joseph to pay thee more attention than he generally does. Tell him though art in want of it, and that he owes it to thee!'[9]

In July 1807, Fry again suffered a period of nervous prostration, accompanied by an intermittent fever. Childbirth could not be blamed on this occasion, although perhaps the discovery that she was, yet again, pregnant may have been a contributing factor. But overall, it seemed that her inward dissatisfaction and self-doubt were getting the better of her. Her sister Priscilla visited her in London but saw little of her. She wrote to Hannah:

> I caught a little of dear Betsy's company at intervals. She was so interested about you, but she is never as warm about people as we are, which arises from her very superior principle – and yet it is perhaps a little damping.[10]

The first day of January 1808 Fry described as 'a new year, begun . . . to me with some weight to my heart'. Again it was a year of life and death. A third daughter, Richenda, was born in February, and in May her brother John was widowed. On 20 August, it was her eighth wedding anniversary. During her marriage she had borne five children and experienced 'various trials of faith and patience', not to say disappointment.

> My course has been very different to what I had expected, and instead of being, as I had hoped, a useful instrument in the Church Militant, here I am a care-worn wife and mother, outwardly nearly devoted to the things of this life. Though at times this difference in my destination has been trying to me, yet, I believe those trials (which have been very pinching) that I have had to go through have been very useful, and brought me to a feeling sense of what I am . . . I may also acknowledge that through all my trials, there does appear to have been a particular blessing attending me . . . The little efforts or small acts of duty I have ever performed, have often seemed remarkably blessed to me; and where others have been concerned, it has also I think been apparent in them, that the effort on my part has been blessed by both parties . . . Also, what shall I say when I look at my husband and my five lovely babes.

The same year, 1808, Fry's father-in-law, William Storrs Fry, died. He was an amiable man who had been kind to Fry, and she was fond of him. She had nursed him herself at St Mildred's Court during his final few weeks. But no sooner had Fry settled back into some sort of routine after his death than her nursing skills were called on again when, a month later, her sister Hannah contracted scarlet fever. This was a common, serious and highly contagious disease at the beginning of the nineteenth century, and one of the main causes of child mortality. Despite the danger of catching the fever and passing it on to any of her own children, Fry was the only sister free to nurse Hannah, but it was still a daunting prospect.

> This I consider a great privilege to be able to do; though I have felt it a very serious thing, with a young babe, and the mother of so many little lambs, to enter so catching a disorder. I have desired I might not enter it in my own will, or simply to gratify inclination, which leads me to enjoy nursing those I love so dearly . . . I have desired that what is really best for me may occur, even if it be to pass through trouble.

As always, she put her faith in a 'merciful Creator', and got on with the job.

On the death of his father, Joseph Fry inherited the estate at Plashet. During the winter of 1808–09, the family made plans to move house and thoughts of new domestic arrangements prompted Fry to review the question of servants.

> At this time there is no set of people I feel so much about as servants. I do not think they have generally justice done to them; they are too much considered as another race of beings, and we are apt to forget that the holy injunction holds good with them: do as thou wouldest be done unto. I believe, in striving to do so, we shall not take them out of their station in life, but endeavour to render them happy and contented in it, and be truly their friends – but not their familiars or equals, as to the things of this life, for we have reason to believe the difference in our stations is ordered by one wiser than ourselves, who directs us how to fill our different places. But we must never forget that, in the best sense, were are all one, and though our paths may be different, we have all souls equally valuable, and we have all the same work to do; which, if properly considered, should lead us to a great sympathy and love, and also to a constant care for their welfare, both here and hereafter.

In spring 1809, the Frys and their children, and another one on the way, exchanged the smoke and din of the city for the peace and fresh air of the country. It was the next best thing to being back at Earlham and, in Plashet's extensive grounds, Fry was able to indulge once more the love of gardening she had shared with her mother, and relax. In September she gave birth to her sixth child, Joseph, which proved a far more serene experience than previous births. But another cloud was hovering on the horizon. Young Joseph was just a month old when news arrived from Earlham that Fry's father was so ill that he was not expected to live. At the time another sister at Earlham, Priscilla, had contracted scarlet fever; their old Earlham nurse had recently died of it. Despite having 'a few nervous and painful moments' on this account, Fry set off immediately for Norfolk, arriving at her father's home towards midnight the next day. The following morning, on 28 October, with his children close by, John Gurney died.

> I was not with him, but on entering his room soon after it was over, my soul was so bowed within me, in love, not only for the deceased, but also for the living . . . that I could hardly help uttering my thanksgiving and praise . . . I cannot understand it; but the power was wonderful to myself, and the cross none – my heart was so full that I could hardly hinder utterance.

This feeling stayed with Fry in the days leading up to the funeral and 'under this solemn quiet calm, the fear of man appeared removed'. After her father's body was lowered into the grave, and her uncle Joseph had spoken some words, Fry fell to her knees and, 'not knowing how I should go on', began to pray aloud, giving thanks to God for her father's life. It was her first public expression of religious devotion, and a major step towards a life of public speaking. For the rest of the day, she remained in a 'quiet, calm and invigorated state . . . altogether a sweet day'; but during a 'very painful night', the shy Betsy of old came back to haunt her and she was racked with anxiety about what other people would think of her forwardness.

Back at Plashet, Fry immersed herself again in the domestic routine, determined not to neglect her family duties by spending too much time dwelling 'on the path that has appeared to be opening before me'. At a Meeting in November, she longed to speak her thoughts 'but my fright was extreme'. The conflict between wanting and not daring 'was so great as to shake my body as well as my mind'. She consulted her uncle Joseph Gurney who encouraged her to

> walk by faith and not by sight. He strongly advised a simple following of what arose, and expressed his experience of the benefit of giving up to it and the confusion of not doing so. How have I desired since, not to stand in the fear of man.

Day by day, her courage grew. She practised with the servants, by speaking a few words of explanation to the passages of Scripture she read to them each day; and after attending a Meeting in Plaistow in December, she was able to write in her diary with pride: 'Again I have dared to open my mouth in public'. For, after all, as she wrote a few months later,

> how very little it matters, when we look at the short time we remain here, what we appear to others; and how much too much we look at the things of this life. What does it signify, what we are thought of here, so long as we are not found wanting to our Heavenly Father? Why should we so much try to keep something back, and not be willing to offer ourselves up to Him, body, soul and spirit, to do with us what may seem best unto Him, and to make us what He would have us to be?

About this time, she wrote to a childhood friend, describing the breakthrough that had happened in her religious life since her father's death 'appeared to break the ice for me, and on my knees I publicly expressed my thankfulness'.

> This matter of publicly exposing myself, in this way, has for many years been struggling in my mind, long before I married, and once or twice with thee in London, I hardly knew how to refrain. The past I must leave; but I am ready to think extreme unwillingness to give up to this matter has kept me longer than I need in a lukewarm and sometimes wilderness state. However, since a way has been made for me, it appears as if I dare not stop the work. If it be a right one, may it go on and prosper; if not, the sooner stopped the better . . . I do not understand myself . . . At times I . . . feel power that I cannot but believe to be beyond myself; at others, brought very low, poor, weak and almost miserable.

One factor that contributed to her anxiety was how to find a balance between her personal life and her increased participation in Quaker activities, with a growing sense that a life of public duty was opening up to her. She had a large household to manage; and as her children became older, she often found them wilful and volatile, and stressful. In August 1810, Fry was again pregnant when she wrote:

> May my being led out of my own family, by what appear to me duties, never be permitted to hinder my doing my duty fully towards it; or so occupy my attention, as to make me in any degree forget or neglect home duties. I believe it matters not where we are, or

what we are about, so long as we keep our eye fixed on the great Master's work. When I feel as I do today, what a glorious service it is . . . and remember . . . how I have been helped and carried through, I fear for myself, lest even this great mercy should prove a temptation, and lead me to come before I am called, or enter service I am not prepared for.

In February 1811, Fry gave birth to a baby girl they called Elizabeth. It was their seventh child in ten years. The following month, Fry was 'acknowledged' as a minister by the Religious Society of Friends.

As well as her Quaker commitments, Fry had also become more involved with the welfare of the local poor since her move to Plashet two years earlier. She persuaded an elderly brother and sister pair, who lived opposite the gate of Plashet House, to let her convert part of their premises into a school for about 70 girls. She kept a ready supply of clothing, flannel and basic medicines for those in need. In very cold weather, she set up a soup kitchen in an out-house for hundreds of the local poor, and tried not to be hurt when some of them gave their soup and dumplings to their pigs. She ministered to visiting gypsies, and to a settlement of Irish paupers, providing practical and material help, persuading them to send their children to school, and encouraging them in more orderly habits, giving little presents as a reward. Most importantly, she carried out a rolling programme of smallpox inoculation throughout the villages of the parish. And, as usual, she took on too much. In September, she wrote in her diary:

I have lately been so much hurried by an almost constant change of company and employments, as to be at times a good deal tried, and I am fearful my temper will be made irritable by it . . . My desire is, to do my duty fully and faithfully to all connected with me, nearly and remotely, rich and poor; but I find I cannot satisfy all, and often feel to myself doing everything very imperfectly.

Now that she was a minister, Fry began travelling away from home to more distant Quaker Meetings, and widening the range of her contacts with representatives of other denominations. In Norwich, she attended a General Meeting of the Bible Society with her brother Joseph, who was closely involved with the organization, and at which a local branch was established; and afterwards she dined with many of the delegates at Earlham. In early 1812, she spent two weeks in London, attending Meetings with her sister Priscilla and American Quaker minister Henry Hull. In March, she returned to Norfolk to attend the

Monthly and Quarterly Meetings. This time, her sister-in-law Elizabeth Gurney went with her. Her husband Joseph almost always remained at Plashet with the children.

> It is a sacrifice of natural feeling to leave the comforts of home, and my beloved husband and children; and to my weak nervous habits, the going about, and alone (for so I feel it in one sense without my husband) is . . . a trial greater than I imagined; and my health suffers much. This consideration of its being a cross to my nature, I desire not to weigh in the scale; though no doubt for the sake of others, as well as myself, my health being so shaken is a serious thing. What I desire to consider most deeply is this: have I authority for leaving my home and evident duties? What leads me to believe I have! For I need not doubt but that when away, and at times greatly tried, this query is likely to arise. The prospect has come in that quiet, yet I think powerful way, that I have never been able to believe I should get rid of it . . . It seems to me as if in this journey I must be stripped of outward dependences.

In April, Fry was unwell again for several weeks, perhaps as a result of being again pregnant. Five of the children had whooping cough at the same time. She still managed to attend up to four Meetings a week. During the summer, the house was overrun with visitors: 18 guests in addition to the family stayed over one night in August. There was little time for the Frys to be alone. On the rare occasions that they were, she welcomed the opportunity to 'turn my attention to home duties', to 'stop and examine the state of my family and my house', and to remind herself 'how much I have to be thankful for'. In a quiet moment, she attempted to draw up a system of child management that would ensure she spent time with them all.

> Plan to try for the children: boys sent to tutor, after our reading. Little ones with me till nearly ten o'clock; again from two to three; from dinner till seven. See the elder girls at lessons twice during the morning, and have them with me from one till two; boys and girls from seven till eight together, besides their being at meals now and then.[11]

By this time, she had seven children: four girls and three boys, aged around eleven, nine, eight, six, four, three and one. In September she was safely delivered of an eighth – Hannah – to general relief, since she had approached this confinement 'with extreme fear'. But though her body recovered, her spirits were low. Towards the end of the year, she decided to transfer most of her family to St

Mildred's Court for the winter. Back in London, where there was more going on in the outside world to distract her, her mood lifted.

Resident in the capital at the time was the French-born American Quaker minister, Stephen Grellet, protégé of Fry's childhood mentor William Savery and admirer of Deborah Darby, whose example had also encouraged young Betsy Gurney to become a plain Quaker. Grellet was one of the most prominent international Quaker ministers of his age. His ministry lasted some 50 years. He was also probably the best travelled of contemporary Quaker ministers. His tours of duty included four extended trips to Europe, during which he pleaded for humanitarian reforms with the great and good – the highest, most influential people to whom he could negotiate an introduction, including royalty and, indeed, the Pope.

It was on the second of his visits to Europe, during which he spent two years in London, that Grellet first visited the women's wing at Newgate prison, in the company of another Quaker preacher, the philanthropist and abolitionist William Forster.[12] The day before his Newgate visit, Grellet had held a meeting at St Martin in the Fields, for thieves and prostitutes. Out of respect for their lifestyle, the meeting was held at seven in the evening, when most of them would be up, but not yet at work. The following day, having visited the men's section and the debtors' section of the Newgate prison, he asked that he and Forster be allowed to inspect the women's side as well, but his visit was 'very nearly frustrated'. The gaoler tried to prevent his going, saying that the women were 'so unruly and desperate that they would surely do me some mischief'. He had endeavoured in vain to reduce them to some sort of order, the gaoler said, but he would not be responsible for what they might do, adding that 'the very least I might expect was to have my clothes torn off'. But Grellet persisted.

When I came to the small yard, the only accommodation for about four or five hundred women . . . I found [that] owing to the darkness of the morning the prisoners had been unusually late in getting up, and many of them had not yet risen. They occupied two long rooms, where they slept in three tiers, some on the floor, and two tiers of hammocks over one another. They had the whole soon rolled up, and all the women came together in one room.

When I first entered, the foulness of the air was almost insupportable; and every thing that is base and depraved was so strongly depicted on the faces of the women who stood crowded before me, with looks of effrontery, boldness and wantonness of expression, that, for a while, my soul was greatly dismayed [but] . . . the more I beheld the awful consequences of sin, and the more deeply I felt the greatness of the depravity into which these poor objects had been plunged by the devices of Satan, the more I also felt the love of Christ who has come to save and has died for sinners. As I began to speak ... their countenances began to alter: soon they hung down their heads; their haughtiness and proud looks were brought low, and tears in abundance were seen to flow; great was the brokenness of heart manifested on this occasion.[13]

Grellet enquired as to whether there were any other women in the place, and was told that several sick ones were upstairs. On going up, he was

astonished beyond description at the mass of woe and misery I beheld. I found many very sick, lying on the bare floor or on some old straw, having very scanty covering over them, though it was quite cold; and there were several children born in the prison amongst them, almost naked.[14]

On leaving this 'abode of wretchedness and misery', Grellet went directly to St Mildred's Court to 'his much valued friend', Elizabeth Fry, 'to whom I described, out of the fullness of my heart, what I had just beheld, stating also that something must be done immediately for those poor suffering children'. The appeal 'to such a pious and sensible mind as Elizabeth possesses' was not in vain. She immediately sent for several lengths of green flannel, and rapidly contacted a number of other young women Friends. They must have stitched through the night to achieve their objective, for they 'went to work with such diligence, that on the very next day, Fry repaired to the prison with a bundle of hand-made garments for the naked children'.

What she then saw of the wretchedness of that prison induced her to devise some plan towards the amelioration of the condition of those poor women, and, if possible, the reform of their morals, and instilling into their minds the principles and love of Christian religion.[15]

Although Newgate was about to change her life for ever, Fry, in all modesty, was not aware of it. Her record of her early visits is scant. In a diary entry for 15 January 1813, she acknowledged that she was engaged 'in seeing after the prisoners in Newgate'. She was more concerned about being admired for this work: 'How very deeply I feel the temptation of ever being exalted or self-conceited'. But she conceded: 'I cannot preserve myself from this temptation, any more than being unduly cast down or crushed by others'. To her sons John and William, who had been staying at Earlham while she was in London, she wrote:

> I have lately been to Newgate prison to see after the poor prisoners, who had little infants almost without clothing. If you saw how small a piece of bread they are allowed every day, you would be very sorry, for they have nothing else to eat, unless their friends give them a trifle. I could not help thinking, when in the prison, what sorrow and trouble those have who do wrong; and they have not the comfort of feeling amidst their trials that they have endeavoured to do their duty. Good people are, no doubt, often much tried, but they have so much to comfort them when they remember that the Almighty is their friend, and will care for them. We may also hope if the poor wicked people are really sorry for their faults, God will pardon them, for His mercy is very great. If you were to grow up, I should like you to go to visit the poor sad people, to try and comfort them and do them good. I hope you will endeavour to be very useful, and not to spend all your time in pleasing yourselves, but try to serve others and prefer them before yourselves. How very much I love you. Let me have letters written by yourselves. Farewell my darling children. Remember the way to be happy is to do good.

On 16 February, she spent some hours at Newgate with her friend Anna Buxton, sister of Thomas Fowell Buxton, attending to the 'outward necessities of the poor female felons'. Before they left, Buxton spoke a few words of comfort and, emboldened, so did Fry. 'I heard weeping, and I thought they appeared much tendered. A very solemn quiet was observed. It was a striking scene, the poor people on their knees around us, and in their deplorable condition.'

In the cause of prison reform for women, Fry would find all the elements of social deprivation that most attracted her compassion: poverty, lack of education, lack of religion, lack of order, lack of healthy conditions both moral and physical. In the women of Newgate she had, quite literally, a captive audience for her philanthropy. But family circumstances and ill health would conspire to prevent her from embarking on the Newgate project for another three years.

The intervening period was a time of great trial and upheaval. The family banking and tea businesses were faring badly in the recession that followed the end of the Napoleonic Wars. The crisis was exacerbated by the fact that her brother-in-law William had lent a large amount of the bank's money to his wife's family, and insolvency threatened. It was averted only by the intervention of Fry's Gurney brothers Joseph and Samuel, who shored up the Frys' precarious financial position. Several children were sent to live with with their Gurney aunts and uncles, both to save money and to relieve the pressure on Fry herself. For money worries were not the only drain on her resources. In 1814, there was the birth of a daughter, Louise, and the death of Fry's brother John. All of this left her in a state of 'great bodily weakness, accompanied by nervous lowness of spirits, and much mental fear'. And worse was to come. In 1815, her daughter Elizabeth died, aged four. In 1816, she gave birth to Samuel, her tenth child in 16 years of marriage. Fry was overwhelmed by events, both physically and emotionally. She had a persistent cough, and often wished for a 'resting-place' beside her dear dead daughter.

In mid-August 1816, Fry was convalescing at Earlham when she confided to her diary that she was eating and drinking too much as a comfort, rather than just to keep her strength up. It was a weakness she continued to fight against all her life.

> I have a fear lest delicate health, and being wearied by the cares of life, and the kind care of others, should induce my indulging the flesh too much, in eating and drinking, and sleeping . . . When I remember how much, in the day of my first love, I watched over myself in these respects; but my constitution, for many years of my life, has had such a stress upon it, that I am fearful in my own will of giving up these indulgences, that appear so evidently to have contributed and yet contribute to its support. I desire to be watchful and careful in this respect . . . and yet I know not exactly how or in what to alter.

Fry pulled herself together, as she always did. Salvation was to come in the form of helping others. Early in 1817, Fry was back at Newgate, and a life's work was about to begin.

PART TWO

The Newgate experiment

4

Howard's inheritor

Early Quakers were no strangers to prison. In 1661, there were an estimated 4,200 imprisoned, mainly in London, Yorkshire, Lancashire and Warwickshire. Fry's own great-great-grandfather on her father's side spent three years confined for his belief. Nor was Fry the first English Quaker woman to expose the appalling conditions that prevailed in the country's gaols. That distinction goes to Elizabeth Hootten (1600–72).[1] Married, middle aged, middle class and a mother of six when she was 'convinced' by young George Fox, the founder of the Quaker movement, Hootten became the first female Quaker preacher. She may even have been Fox's first convert. Though 'pretty far advanced in years', Fox found her 'a very tender woman'. Despite the initial disapproval of her husband, which nearly led to their separation, the courage of this matronly figure made her a role model for future generations of Quaker women. Imprisoned repeatedly between 1651 and 1667, both in England and America, for protesting against the corruption of the clergy and the persecution of Quakers, Hootten was intimately acquainted with life 'inside'.

Her first recorded imprisonment was in 1651 in Derby at the age of 50, for criticizing the clergy. In 1653, she was imprisoned for a similar offence in York Castle, from where she wrote a long and vigorous letter to Oliver Cromwell, Lord Protector of England. In the letter, which was endorsed by Fox, she made no special plea for herself. But she fiercely attacked the maladministration of the legal system under the Commonwealth in general, and, in particular, the malpractices of judges, magistrates and gaolers. The issues that she raised foreshadowed many concerns that would be raised a hundred years later by John Howard, and afterwards reinforced by Elizabeth Fry. They include the practice of 'garnish' – a tax levied by existing inmates on new persons entering prison; payment for prison accommodation (which could far exceed the original sum for which a debtor had been gaoled); and the question of maintaining health, propriety and decency within the walls. 'Your judges', Hootten told Cromwell, 'judge for reward'.

> At York, many who committed murder escaped through friends and money, and poor people for lesser facts are put to death. Many lie in prison for fees [non-payment of prison accommodation] . . . The two great tyrants – the gaoler and the clerk of the Assize – keep many poor creatures in prison for fees. The gaoler must have twenty shillings four pence for his fee, the clerk of the Assize fifteen shillings eight pence. This they will have of the poor creatures, or else they must die in prison. They lie worse than dogs for want of straw . . . The judges and magistrates might as well have put them to death at the Assize as into the hands of these two tyrants who keep men for money, starving them in a hole till they be ruined or starved to death.[2]

She appealed to Cromwell's humanity: 'O, man, what dost thou there except thou stand for truth which is trampled under foot. Who knows but thou was called to deliver thy brethren out of bondage and slavery.'

In 1654, Hootten was imprisoned for the first time in Lincoln, and then again the following year, for allegedly 'exhorting the people to repentance'. Once more she wrote to Cromwell, pleading 'to him in authority to reform the abuses of the gaol', and 'redress the disorders in this rude place'.[3] She concluded with a striking description of the state of the gaols in the Commonwealth, and of the many abuses connected with their management. As Fry would do two centuries later, she appealed for a ban on strong drink in the prison, a separation of the sexes, the introduction of useful employment, reasonable accommodation fees and an enlightened management.

> O thou that art set in authority to do justice and judgment, and to let the oppressed go free, these things are required at thy hands. Look upon the poor prisoners: here [are those] that have not any allowance, although there be a great sum of money comes out of the country sufficient to help them all that is in want, both their due allowance and to set them to work that would labour. And those that are sent here for debts [let] their rates for beds . . . be taken down to reasonable rates.[4]

She called for fairer treatment for debtors imprisoned for small amounts, whose debts could spiral out of control when prison accommodation fees were added, reducing them to the misery of merely providing a source of income for their gaolers. She complained that Lincoln Castle was also a 'place of great disorder and of wickedness . . . for oppression and profanity, I never came in such a place'. The reason, she suggested, was the character of the 'malignant woman' who runs the gaol. As a result, there is oppression in meat and drink and in fees, and in that which they call 'garnishes', and in many other things. I myself am much abused [by] both her prisoners and her household, so that I cannot walk quietly abroad but be abused by those that belong to her . . . And, in drinking and profanity and wantonness, men and women [are] together many times part of the night, which grieves the spirit of God in me day and night.

This is required of thee, o man, to reform this place, as thy power and authority do allow. Either remove strong drink out of this place, or remove the gaoler. Secondly, [let] the rates for the beds be taken down. [Let] the 'garnishes' and the great fees be taken off, and [let] these oppressed prisoners come to some hearing, as are wrongfully imprisoned. And [let] there be some better order amongst the men and women prisoners to keep them asunder and set them to work . . . and take out the disorder in prisons.[5]

In 1661, Hootten travelled to America where, arriving in Boston, she was immediately imprisoned and then, as a punishment, driven out into the wilderness and left to starve. She and her companions survived, however, and made their way back to Boston to preach once more against persecution. Again they were arrested; and this time they were deported.

Back in England, Hootten petitioned King Charles for a royal licence to settle in the American colonies; this being granted, she returned to Boston. Despite the King's recommendation, the Boston authorities refused to accommodate her and she travelled east to where she was imprisoned first at Hampton, and then at Dover, for her anti-clerical teaching.

Her next move was to nearby Cambridge, where again she called on people to repent. In exchange, she spent two nights detained without food or water, before being whipped through the town and sent out into the wilderness to perish. And yet again she survived, returning to Cambridge, for further whipping before going back to Boston where she was imprisoned anew, whipped and cast out into the wilderness.

After further periods of imprisonment in Boston and Rhode Island, she was re-deported, in the early 1660s. She crossed the Atlantic one final time in 1671, with George Fox and other Friends, and died early the following year in Jamaica, where she is buried.

Elizabeth Hootten had been imprisoned 11 times for her faith, for periods ranging from two days to 16 months. She had been gaoled four times in England – in Derby (1651), York (1652) and Lincoln (1654 and 1655) – and seven times in America – at Boston (three times in the 1660s), Hampton, Dover, Cambridge and Rhode Island.

Hootten was the first female Quaker minister to draw attention to the appalling conditions in the nation's prisons. But it was John Howard, a non-Quaker, who first set about quantifying the problem in a systematic way that future generations could build on.

The commitment of John Howard (1726–90) to the welfare of prisoners was informed by first-hand experience. In 1756, aged 29 and recently widowed, he set sail on the *Hanover* for Portugal, to see for himself the devastating effects of the recent Great Lisbon Earthquake and subsequent tsunami. The Seven Years' War was just beginning. Britain and Portugal were on the same side; France was on the other. A few days out of Southampton, the *Hanover* was captured by a French privateer (a state-licensed private warship) and all the crew and passengers were taken to Brest in north-west France as prisoners-of-war. At Brest, Howard had nothing to eat and very little to drink for 40 hours and was kept for six days in the semi-darkness with only straw to lie on. From Brest he was transferred to a prison at Carpaix, where he spent another two months before he persuaded the authorities on both sides of the Channel to release him in exchange for the return of a French officer imprisoned in England. At Carpaix, he learned from letters exchanged with some of the others who had been on board the *Hanover*, and who were either still at Brest, or had been dispersed to other French prisons at Morlaix and Dinan, that they had been

> treated with such barbarity that many hundreds had perished, and that 36 were buried in one day at Dinan. When I came to England, still on parole, I made known to the Commissioners of Sick and Wounded Seamen, the sundry particulars . . . Remonstration was made to the French court: our sailors had redress, and those that were in the three prisons mentioned above were brought home in the first cartel ships[6] . . . Perhaps what I suffered on this occasion increased my sympathy for the unhappy people in prison.[7]

For the next 17 years, Howard concentrated on developing his model estate at Cardington in Shropshire, and promoting the material and moral welfare of his tenants. It was not until 1773, widowed for the second time and in his late forties, that he took on the expensive but prestigious post of High Sheriff of Bedfordshire. Not content with simply enjoying the kudos of his position, he determined to become actively involved with the management of Bedford prison, which came within his jurisdiction.

The distress of prisoners, of which there are few who have not some imperfect idea, came more immediately under my notice when I was Sheriff of the County of Bedford; and the circumstance which excited me to activity in their behalf was, the seeing some, who by the verdict of juries were declared *not guilty*; some, on whom the grand jury did not find such an appearance of guilt as subjected them to trial; and some whose prosecutors did not appear against them; after having been confined for months, dragged back to gaol, and locked up again till they should pay *sundry fees* to the gaoler, the clerk of assizes, etc.[8]

The equivalent situation today would be a remand prisoner, after being tried and found innocent, being required to pay a fee for his or her board and lodging while on remand to the prison governor in place of the governor's receiving a regular salary; and not being released until that fee had been paid. Howard was also appalled at the practice known as 'garnish', whereby incoming prisoners were required to pay a fee to the older prisoners or to the turnkey. If they did not, they might forfeit their clothes – 'garnish or strip'; the abuse continues today when fellow prisoners attempt to 'tax' an incoming prisoner for any unpaid debts incurred by the previous occupant of their cell.

In order to redress this hardship suffered by the financial demands made on remand prisoners who were subsequently acquitted, Howard applied to the justices of the county for the gaoler to be paid a salary in lieu of fees. There was no national superintendence of prisons at the time, and the Bedfordshire county authorities wanted to know if there was a precedent in other counties for the practice of charging the community with this expense.

I therefore rode into several counties in search of a precedent; but I soon learned that the same injustice was practised in them; and looking into the prisons, I beheld scenes of calamity which I grew daily more anxious to alleviate. In order therefore to gain a perfect knowledge of the particulars and extent of it, by various and accurate observation, I visited most of the county gaols in England.[9]

In two or three of these prisons, Howard came across 'some poor creatures whose aspect was singularly deplorable', and was told that they had recently been brought from the Bridewells.

This started a fresh subject of enquiry. I resolved to inspect the Bridewells: and for that purpose I travelled again into the counties where I had been; and, indeed, into all the rest; examining Houses of Correction, City and Town Gaols. I beheld in many of them, as well as in the County Gaols, a complication of distress. But my attention was principally fixed by the gaol-fever and the small-pox which I saw prevailing to the destruction of multitudes, not only of felons in their dungeons, but of debtors also.[10]

The effects of disease in prison were 'now so notorious, that what terrifies us most from looking into prisons, is the gaol-distemper so frequent in them'. Gaol-fever or gaol-distemper, a form of typhus, took hold when prisoners were cramped together in dark and filthy rooms. It was highly infectious and was frequently carried from the gaol to the outside community. Just as many prisoners died of gaol-fever as were executed.

John Howard first gave evidence to the House of Commons on the state of prisons in March 1774. Soon afterwards, the MP for Taunton, Alexander Popham, brought in a Bill 'for the relief of prisoners who should be acquitted, respecting their fees; and another Bill for preserving the health of prisoners, and preventing the gaol-distemper'. Both Bills were passed, and 'by these Acts, the fear was removed from many an eye; and the legislation has for them "the blessing of many that were ready to perish"'. Howard had copies of the Acts printed at his own expense, and circulated to the keepers of every gaol in England.

The introduction of these Acts to improve prison conditions encouraged Howard to go further still, because there were 'still many orders that ought to be rectified: prisoners suffer great hardships, from which I am desirous to set them free'.

Howard, as ever, looked to Parliament to enact the legislation that would reform prison management systems for ever. 'Much is yet to be done for the regulation of prisons; and I am not without hope, that the present Parliament will finish what was so laudably begun by the last.'

Howard may have begun his prison reform work because it was part of his job as a conscientious Sheriff of Bedfordshire; but he continued it out of compassion for his fellow citizens.

To the pursuit of it I was prompted by the sorrows of the sufferers, and love to my country. The work grew on me insensibly. I could not enjoy my ease and leisure in the neglect of an opportunity offered me by Providence of attempting the relief of the miserable. The attention of Parliament to the subject led me to conclude that some additional labour would not be lost; and I extended my plan.[11]

In 1775, Howard also began an inspection tour of Continental prisons. He covered up to 40 miles a day, mainly on horseback, having discovered early on that the stench of prison on his clothes made travelling in a closed carriage almost unbearable at the end of a working day. Suspecting that he had not been told the whole truth in many of the prisons he had previously inspected in England and Wales, Howard also decided

> to repeat my visits, and travel over the kingdom more than once; and after all, I suspect that many frauds have been concealed from me; and that sometimes the interest of my informants prevailed over their veracity.

In the space of two years, he paid 350 visits to 230 prison establishments. Since his first programme of visits, Howard had also gained considerably more first-hand experience of the negative effects of, for example, bad hygiene and the lack of fresh air, as a result of which he had 'in my latter visits these strong arguments to enforce by persuasions; and, in consequence, some gaolers grew at last more mindful and complying, for the sake not only of their prisoners, but of themselves and their own families'.

Howard made no attempt to play down the danger of entering prisons; not the danger from the inmates themselves, but the danger of disease.

> I was not, I own, without some apprehensions of danger, when I first visited the prisons; and I guarded myself by smelling vinegar when I was in those places, and changing my apparel afterwards. This I did constantly and carefully when I began; but by degrees I grew less cautious: not only because use abated the force of noxious impressions upon me, but also on account of the alteration made in some gaols by the Act for preserving the health of prisoners.[12]

Howard reportedly said that the best advice he could give about avoiding catching prison diseases was: have courage, trust in the Lord, and avoid breathing deeply. Sadly, it didn't always work for him and he was frequently ill as a result. However, many aspects of prison life had improved since his first visits. A person entering a prison in 1777 could have no idea of the even worse conditions that prevailed only a few years earlier, Howard observed, but there could be no cause for complacency or backsliding.

I wish the reformation to be not for the present only, but lasting. If the motive for amendment has any where been merely temporary, there is no doubt but that the effect will cease with the cause . . . and prisons that have been amended will lapse into their former state.[13]

By 1777, Howard was ready to publish his findings as *The State of Prisons in England and Wales with Preliminary Observations, and an Account of Some Foreign Prisons*. He dedicated the survey to the House of Commons 'in gratitude for the encouragement they have given [to this book] . . . and the honour they have conferred on the author'. It consists of a detailed catalogue of all the places he visited, documenting the massive scale of prison mismanagement that he uncovered. While the recommendations for improvement that he put forward were not necessarily new, this was the first time that tangible evidence had been brought together and presented in such a straightforward way. Howard's audit provided an overview of a chaotic and disparate prison system, and high-lighted the scale and range of inhumane treatment and abuses, many of which, even then, were strictly illegal. He provided a blueprint for future generations of prison reformers, and benchmarks for individual prisons against which improvements – or backsliding – could be measured. And he insisted that he had not overstated his case.

As to what is still wrong, I set down matters of fact without amplification; which would in the end impede rather than promote the object of my wishes; that is, the correction of what is really amiss. These journals were not undertaken for the traveller's amusement; and the collections are not published for general entertainment; but for the perusal of those who have it in their power to give redress to the sufferers.

The book provides an overview of the level of distress in prisons, instances of good (rare) and bad (frequent) practice, proposed improvements for the structure and management of prisons, and an account of some prisons in France, Switzerland, Germany, Holland and Flanders.

There then follows a 300-page survey of individual prisons in England and Wales, with specific details such as the type of prison, governor's salary, provision of food, straw and water, medical and pastoral care. The London and Southwark prisons he audited included Newgate, the Fleet, New Ludgate, the Poultry Compter, the Wood Street Compter, the Blackfriars Bridewell (where he had some warm words for elements of the women's wing), the New prison at Clerkenwell, the Clerkenwell Bridewell, the Tower Hamlets gaol, the Savoy, the Tothill Fields Bridewell, the Westminster Gatehouse, the King's Bench, the Marshalsea and the Borough Compter. Some prisons were owned by the local authorities, some by the Crown; some were private, some ecclesiastical. There were special prisons or wings for soldiers, clergymen, Jewish prisoners, debtors, lawyers; and even, at the Marshalsea, for pirates and smugglers, prostitutes and homosexuals. Of Newgate he wrote that the builders of 'old Newgate prison seem to have regarded in their plan nothing but the single article of keeping prisoners in safe custody. The rooms and cells were so close as to be almost the constant seats of disease and sources of infection: to the destruction of multitudes', not only inside the prison but outside as well. Newgate had been rebuilt since his first visit and he noted that 'many inconveniences of the old gaol are avoided in this new one: but it has some manifest errors. It is now too late to point out particulars. All I will say is, that without more than ordinary care, the prisoners in it will be in great danger of the gaol fever.'

On the specific conditions under which women were kept in prison, Howard had little to say, except to recommend providing a fire in winter where women had infants with them. He was, however, adamant that men and women should be kept apart all the time, a practice that was followed in few prisons in the day-time, and whose absence Howard saw as dangerously 'pernicious to their morals'.[14]

In 1778, Howard was again called as an expert witness to give evidence to a parliamentary committee investigating the use of prison hulks to hold convicts who would previously have been transported to America, before it gained independence. He also co-drafted a Bill to provide for the construction of two new prisons in London – one for men, one for women – a plan which never materialized. Soon after, he returned to the Continent to continue and revisit his surveys. He estimated that he had travelled over 42,000 miles, at his own expense, carrying out his audits. He was still pursuing his project when he died of a fever in southern Russia, where he is buried.

5

'Hell above ground'

Newgate prison was not the oldest in London. There is a record of repairs being made to the Fleet prison in 1155, while the first reference to Newgate is dated 1188, the penultimate year of the reign of Henry II, an important legal reformer. But Newgate was always the most notorious, not just in London but throughout the kingdom. John Howard believed that half the crimes committed in and around London were planned in the prison itself, which he called 'the greatest nursery of crime'. Charles Dickens prefaced the trial of Charles Darnay in *A Tale of Two Cities* with an attack on the criminal law and penal system of the 1770s in which he called Newgate (to which he also committed Fagin, the villain of *Oliver Twist*) 'a vile place, in which most kinds of debauchery and villainy were practised and where dire diseases were bred'.[1] Even the establishment's view was that 'no-one can enter the walls of Newgate without going out from there more depraved and corrupted than when first committed thereto'.[2]

The prison that Fry knew was the fifth on the site of the medieval city gate-house. The first was part of a network of gaols established by Henry II throughout the kingdom, where suspected felons would be held until the King's Justices visited to administer what became known as common law. The second Newgate was an early fifteenth-century reconstruction carried out with funds bequeathed by London's four-times mayor, the famous Richard ('Dick') Whittington. This, in turn, was destroyed in the Great Fire of London in 1666. It was rebuilt but fell into disrepair in the course of the next hundred years. A project to rebuild the establishment as the fourth Newgate was almost complete when it was burned down in the Gordon Riots of 1780. The final prison – the one associated with Elizabeth Fry – opened in 1785 and survived until 1902, when it was demolished. The prison site is now incorporated into the Central Criminal Courts at the Old Bailey where, on the first floor landing, stands a statue of Fry.

It was just days after Fry's birth in May 1780 that the Gordon Riots broke out.[3] They were the most serious anti-Catholic riots that the country had ever witnessed. The eccentric Lord George Gordon (1751–93) was an MP who had recently formed the Protestant Association with the specific aim of lobbying Parliament for the repeal of the 1778 Catholic Relief Act; this Act had restored to British Roman Catholics some restricted privileges which had been curtailed during the reign of William III. The Protestant Association allegedly collected 120,000 signatures to a petition calling for an end to even modest rights for 'papists', and, on 2 June 1778, Gordon and tens of thousands of disaffected anti-Catholics set off from St George's Field south of the river Thames to march to Westminster. By the time it reached Parliament, the initial crowd of 50,000 or 60,000 had swelled to perhaps twice that and had taken on the nature of a mob.

At this point, many genuine petitioners went home in dismay. What remained was the nastiest, most violent element. For the next few hours they brayed and thundered at the gates, smashing carriages, jostling and attacking people as they went in and out of Parliament; inside, Gordon tried to persuade his colleagues to pay attention to his petition, while at the same time exhorting his followers to remain calm and civilized. The Commons took a vote on Gordon's motion, with only eight of 198 members in favour. At first, the defeat seemed only further to inflame the demonstrators. But then, after a modest display of force by the Horse Guards, the mob began to disperse. And that appeared to be the end of the matter. But it was a false truce. Towards midnight, the ugly mood revived; and groups of drunken 'demonstrators' began a week-long orgy of destruction and mayhem throughout the capital, with the loss of 300 lives.

Chapels were destroyed, their treasures looted. Irish communities were terrorized as 'dens of popery'. Law-abiding Catholics were spat on and insulted in the street, while their homes were being torched, their belongings ransacked and their pantries plundered to feed the mob. And then, since some of their number had been arrested over the past few days, the mob turned their attention to the capital's prisons. They began with torching Newgate. Within an hour, 300 prisoners were out on the streets while those who remained trapped in the warren of corridors within screamed in horror as the flames engulfed them. Other prisons followed. At the height of the trouble, there were an estimated 2,000 convicts at large in London. Some were seriously dangerous; but many vulnerable prisoners were observed hanging about near Newgate in particular, hoping to be taken back into a prison which, however dreadful, was the only home they knew.[4]

Gordon was held in the Tower of London and tried for high treason. But since he had genuinely tried to contain the worst of the rioting, he was acquitted and resumed his bizarre, high-risk political career. Meanwhile, architects, builders and planners pressed on with work to create yet another Newgate prison. It was completed in 1785 – in good time to receive Lord George as an inmate. For in 1787 he was convicted of libelling French Queen Marie Antoinette. He spent the rest of his life in Newgate where, after a brief flirtation with the Quaker movement, he converted to Judaism and died of gaol fever – a form of typhus – in 1793, having taken the name Israel bar Abraham Gordon.[5]

George Gordon was not Newgate's only celebrity inmate. Others included William Penn, Titus Oates, Daniel Defoe, Jonathan Wild, Giovanni Giacomo Casanova and Edward Gibbon Wakefield, Fry's cousin. Penn (1644–1718), Quaker leader and founder of Pennsylvania – one of the 13 original American states – was convicted of championing the rights of Dissenters, and sent to Newgate where he found the place 'full of fellow Quakers'. Oates (1649–1705), informer, conspirator and agitator, was convicted of perjury and sent to Newgate in 1681 (and again in 1685). His speciality was to concoct stories of popish plots so plausible that the authorities paid him for his trouble. Journalist, novelist and pamphleteer Defoe (1660–1731) was confined to Newgate in 1702 for publishing a work that ridiculed the established Church's attitude to Dissenters. He was also sentenced to be pilloried but supporters draped the stocks with garlands of flowers instead. He incorporated his Newgate prison experience into his novel, *Moll Flanders*. Wild (1683?–1725), police informant, thief-taker and the greatest criminal mastermind of the eighteenth century, was immortalized first in John Gay's *The Beggars' Opera* (1728) and then, two hundred years later, in Bertolt Brecht's *The Threepenny Opera* (*Die Dreigroschenoper*) which turned the tale into a Marxist critique. Casanova (1725–98), the famous Venetian adventurer and libertine, was imprisoned briefly on remand in Newgate on a charge of reneging on a promise of marriage to a young woman he had seduced. After even just a short spell in Newgate, he described it as 'a hell such as Dante might have conceived'.

The case of colonialist Edward Gibbon Wakefield (1796–1862) is interesting, in that he was a cousin of Fry.[6] He came from a well-established Westmorland Quaker family, but it was not for his Dissenting views that he was imprisoned. His predicament had more in common with Casanova's. His crime was to abduct a young heiress.[7] And she wasn't the only one. He had done the same with his first, late, rich wife – and on that occasion got away with it.

The subject of the 'Shrigley Abduction', as it came to be known, was the 15-year-old daughter of a wealthy Cheshire manufacturer. Wakefield did not even know her. However, in 1826, with the help of his brother and stepmother, Edward (then a handsome, charming man of the world, aged 30 but in need of funds to further his career) snatched Ellen Turner from her boarding school in Liverpool on the pretence that her mother was ill. He drove her to Gretna Green, having convinced her *en route* that her father's fortune depended on her marrying him, to which she – by then also charmed by the handsome stranger – agreed. They were intercepted at Calais by two of her uncles, a policeman and a solicitor, and forced to return to England, where he was exposed. Edward and his brother William were each sentenced to three years' imprisonment, William at Lancaster Castle and Edward at Newgate. The marriage, which had not been consummated, was annulled a year later by an Act of Parliament.[8]

Edward Wakefield made the most of being at Newgate. He behaved impeccably, made friends with the management, and lodged his children and their governess nearby. During his time inside (1826–29), he developed a keen interest in the campaign to abolish capital punishment, of which cousin Fry also disapproved; and, on his release, published his thoughts on the subject.[9] The press welcomed the book. The *Athenaeum* wrote:

> Out of evil comes good, for to Mr Wakefield's three years' imprisonment in Newgate we are indebted for this judicious, sensible and serviceable publication. Mr Wakefield has laboured wisely and diligently to atone for the wrongs he committed, and every good man will be content to forget that he ever erred.[10]

Wakefield's other interest in prison was the question of colonization. After he left Newgate, he spent two decades master-minding programmes of colonization for Canada, Australia and New Zealand – imaginative programmes which earned him a reputation as the 'builder of the Commonwealth'.[11] When Wakefield was in Newgate, Fry visited him just once – in February 1828. He mentioned it in a letter to a relative. She didn't mention it at all. But their interests overlapped on the issue of transportation. Fry's concerns were focused on mitigating its effects; Wakefield, from 1831 onwards, was adamant that the existing system of transportation should be ended. There should be no convicts, just immigrants; land should be paid for, not given; and self-government should be guaranteed once a community reached the 50,000 mark.

Towards the end of 1816, Fry felt that the moment had come seriously to address the welfare of Newgate's female prisoners. She was 36 years old. With the birth of a son earlier in the year, there were now four sons (John, William,

Joseph and Samuel) and five surviving daughters (Katherine, Rachel, Richenda, Hannah and Louisa). Her family was just one child short of being complete. Her three eldest sons were away at school; and members of the extended family – particularly her unmarried sisters Katherine and Rachel – and, to a lesser extent Priscilla, who became a Quaker minister and was often away 'travelling in the ministry' herself – were more than willing to help her husband Joseph to take care of the girls and the baby when required. Fry at last had time and energy to devote to substantial humanitarian work outside the domestic sphere. She was also encouraged by the current prison reform work of two of her brothers-in-law, Samuel Hoare (husband of Louisa), and Thomas Fowell Buxton (husband of Hannah). Together with a group of like-minded acquaintants, the men had recently formed the Society for the Reformation of Prison Discipline. Fry and Buxton together had also formed an organization to work for the reformation of juvenile delinquents. That winter, following the example of her brothers-in-law, Fry and 11 other volunteers from among her friends, most of them Quakers, embarked on a regular programme of visits to the women of Newgate.

Some small improvements had been introduced at Newgate in 1815, following an inspection of various prisons by the Gaol Committee of the City of London. Double gratings had been installed to provide a buffer between the women's wing and the outside world, and sleeping mats had been provided. Unlike many of the 500 or so prisons operating in Britain at the time, Newgate did at least attempt to segregate men and women.

> Notwithstanding these improvements, [the women] remained 'in an unchecked condition of idleness, riot and vice of every description . . . filthy in their persons, disgusting in their habits, and ignorant not only of religious truth but of the most familiar duties of family life.[12]

On her first return visit to the prison since 1813, Fry asked to be left alone with the women, much against the advice of the authorities. As the gate was locked behind her, she realized that little had changed in the intervening years. There was still 'begging, swearing, gaming, fighting, singing, dancing, dressing up in [dead] men's clothes – scenes too bad to be described'; so bad, in fact, that the married lady visitors decided it was not suitable to take younger women into the prison with them.

As curiosity overtook the crowd, and the jostling grew quieter, Fry began to read to them stories from the Bible. When she had finished, she spoke to them of the hope of salvation. Some asked who this Christ was. Others expressed the view that hope had passed them by long ago.

As on her first experience of Newgate, Fry was moved almost to tears by the state of the children present: half naked, half starved, filthy and foul mouthed. She asked their mothers if they would like a little school to be set up for them. Support was strong, and a young woman, recently imprisoned for stealing a watch, was chosen there and then to be the teacher. It was with this school in a cell that the Newgate experiment began.

In the course of their daily visits to the school, the confidence of Fry's lady visitors grew, and they began to look beyond saving the children to a scheme for saving their mothers as well. Many had been clamouring from the start to be allowed to join the school, which had already expanded to take in all young women up to the age of 25, but did not have the capacity to accept more.

The prison authorities were opposed to any idea of reclaiming women prisoners as an unworkable, fanciful notion. Fry remained convinced that the idea had potential but was unsure about her personal ability to see such a project through. In March 1817, she recorded in her diary:

> My mind is tossed by a variety of interests and duties – husband, children, household accounts, Meetings, the Church, near relations, friends and Newgate. I hope I am not undertaking too much. It is a little like being in the whirlwind and the storm; may I not be hurt in it, but enabled quietly to perform that which ought to be done.[13]

Despite her misgivings at the scope of the personal commitment required, things moved on surprisingly well. April 1817 saw the establishment of an Association for the Improvement of the Female Prisoners at Newgate. Its mission was

> To provide for the clothing, the instruction, and the employment of the women; to introduce them to a knowledge of Holy Scriptures; and to form in them, as much as possible, those habits of order, sobriety and industry which may render them docile and peaceable while in prison, and respectable when they leave it.

Only a month later, she was writing that

> I have found in my late attention to Newgate a peace and prosperity in the undertaking, that I seldom, if ever, remember to have done before. A way has remarkably been opened for us, beyond all expectations, to bring into order the poor prisoners; those

who are in power are so very willing to help us, in short the time appears come to work amongst them. Already, from being like wild beasts, they appear harmless and kind.

The sheriffs of Newgate prison, and the magistrates of the City of London, had given their tentative permission for a Newgate women's 'improvement' initiative to proceed; but they remained doubtful as to whether the prisoners themselves would submit to the necessary restraints on their behaviour. To establish the point, the sheriffs, the lady visitors and the women prisoners assembled one afternoon in the presence of the governor. The women were asked by Fry if they were willing to abide by the rules that would need to be established if a new order was to be achieved. Their promise was unanimous. The sheriffs gave their support. And the Ladies' Newgate Association was formed.

The first challenge was to find some work for idle hands, some activity that would focus the women's energies and give them something in which they could take pride. One of the lady visitors – unnamed but obviously with influence – came up with the idea that the prisoners could be usefully employed making stockings and other items of clothing for export to – where else? – Botany Bay.[14] She approached the firm Richard Dixon and Co. of Fenchurch Street, London, who currently held the contract and told them: first, that she would like to deprive them of this business; and, second, that she would like their advice on how to conduct the said business. According to Fowell Buxton, who reported the case, 'they said at once that they should not in any way obstruct such laudable designs, and that no further trouble need be taken to provide work, for they would engage to do it'.[15]

All that remained was to prepare suitable accommodation at Newgate. Within a few days, a former laundry had been cleaned and whitewashed, and the refurbishments necessary to convert it to a suitable workshop had been carried out by carpenters provided by the sheriffs. Fry assembled all the convicted women in the new premises; and she spoke to them of the advantages to be derived from hard work and sobriety, and the satisfaction of doing the right thing. She explained why she and her friends had stepped outside the safety of their comfortable homes 'to mingle amongst those from whom all others fled'. They came, she said, 'animated by an ardent and affectionate desire to rescue their fellow-creatures from evil', because they wanted to impart to them 'the knowledge which they, from their education and circumstances, had been so happy as to receive'. They did not come intending to give orders, she continued. All were 'to act in concert . . . not a rule should be made, or a monitor appointed, without [the women's] full and unanimous concurrence'. At this point she read out to them, item by item, the proposed Newgate Rules; and, item by item, she asked the women to raise their hands if they accepted them. The rules, she said, would be posted on the wall of the women's wing, and, for the benefit of prisoners who could not read, they would be read out once a week as a reminder. The rules stipulated that:

I　　The Matron, on behalf of 'The Association for the Improvement of the Female Prisoners in Newgate', has the general superintendence of them, both with respect to their conduct and the various kinds of work procured for them, of which she is required to keep an exact account.

II　　The women, being divided into classes, a monitor, chosen from among the most orderly, is instructed with the particular oversight of each class; and each woman is required to wear constantly a ticket, denoting the class to which she belongs, and her place therein.

III　　One of the most suitable for the office is appointed as keeper of the Women's Yard, to prevent any disorder there, to inform her fellow-prisoners, in a proper manner, when their friends come to visit them, and to take care that they do not spend any time at the grating (the place where their friends meet them), except whilst with their friends.

IV　　No begging is allowed. If money should be offered to the women by any of those who regularly visit the prison, they are to decline accepting it; but they may, in a respectful manner, direct [would-be donors] to the box placed between the gates for receiving donations, which, at a suitable time, are divided amongst them.

V　　They are enjoined carefully to guard against every thing that is likely to occasion quarrelling or disagreement; not upbraiding one another on account of any previous conduct or circumstances; but rather, by a peaceable and orderly demeanour, endeavouring to promote each other's comfort and improvement.

VI　　Swearing, or in any manner taking the Sacred Name 'in vain' – all bad words, immoral conversation, and indecent behaviour – [is] to be especially avoided.

VII　　Card-playing, and all other gaming, as also plays, novels, and other pernicious books, with all immoral songs, are strictly prohibited.

VIII　　The women are required to attend in the work-room every forenoon (except when the chapel is open for them), and occasionally in the evening, to hear a portion of the Holy Scriptures: for which purpose, on the first ringing of the bell, ten minutes before the reading commences, the monitors are to collect them in their respective wards, that all may be ready at the second ringing, when they are to proceed in regular order (each monitor conducting her class) to take their seats, in silence; retiring afterwards with the same quietness and regularity.

IX   Cleanliness, both in their persons and apartments, is particularly required of all the women; also that they be careful to avoid increasing each other's difficulties in this respect. And the pledging of any article of apparel is strictly forbidden.

X   The monitors are expected not only to take charge of their own particular classes, but also, as they have opportunity, to extend a watchful care over all their fellow-prisoners. And they are required (besides applying to the matron whenever her interference may appear necessary) to make a regular and faithful report to the visitors in attendance, whether or not these rules have been duly observed.

XI   If a monitor transgress any of the rules, she is to be dismissed from her office, and one more orderly selected to take her place.

XII   Any woman who may consider herself ill-treated by a monitor has full liberty, in a civil, quiet manner, to represent her case to a visitor, or the matron; but any refractory or unbecoming behaviour towards a monitor, who is properly exercising her office, must be accounted a serious offence.

The overwhelming acceptance of the Newgate model by the convicted (tried and sentenced) women prisoners, whose fate was probably either death or transportation, was a defining moment. With the success of the model's implementation, remand (untried) prisoners were, within months, begging the authorities that they be given the same treatment, in exchange for which they would promise the same obedience to the rules. Their petition was granted but the experiment was not so great a success, as prisoners who hoped for release were less inclined to work.

About this time an apparently important but unidentified male visitor to the women's wing at Newgate recorded his impressions inside the prison.

I obtained permission to see Mrs Fry, and was taken to the entrance of the women's wards. On my approach, no loud or angry voices indicated that I was about to enter a place which had long been known as 'hell above ground'. The courtyard into which I was admitted, instead of being peopled with beings scarcely human, blaspheming, fighting, tearing each others' hair, or gaming with a filthy pack of cards for the very clothes they wore (which often did not suffice even for decency), presented a scene where stillness and propriety reigned. I was conducted by a decently-dressed person, the newly appointed yards-woman, to the door of a ward, where, at the head of a long table, sat a lady belonging to the Society of Friends. She was reading aloud to about sixteen women, who were engaged in needlework around it. Each wore a clean-looking blue apron and bib, with a ticket having a number on it suspended from her neck by a red tape. They all rose on my entrance, curtsied respectfully, and then at a given signal resumed their seats and employments. Instead of a scowl or an ill-suppressed laugh, their countenances wore an air of self-respect and gravity, a sort of consciousness of their improved character, and the altered position in which they were placed.[16]

Another visitor, the clergyman C. B. Thomas, was both shocked and impressed on the two occasions on which he accompanied Fry to Newgate to attend her regular Bible readings.

Tier above tier rose the seats at the end of the room, a gallery of wooden steps many feet high, and extending from wall to wall. On that gallery the female prisoners, many of them the very refuse of society, were seated. And as the eye passed from face to face, different as the features were, the expression of almost every countenance was, in one sense, alike, for they wore the unmistakable stamp of boldness, degradation, and vice; on some the bleared flatness of face, from whence all trace of womanly feeling had disappeared; on others the vulgar snivel, seeming from time to time to twist the lips and nose together. It was indeed a shocking and most distressing spectacle, that range of about a hundred women's faces, with the various types of vice and crime written on the lines of almost every one.

But there they sat in respectful silence, every eye fixed on the grave sweet countenance of the gentle lady who was about to address them.[17]

After a few minutes' silent prayer, Thomas wrote, Fry opened her Bible and began to read from the fifty-third chapter of the book of the prophet Isaiah, the passage said to predict the coming and suffering of Christ and immortalized in Handel's *Messiah*: 'he was despised and rejected of men, a man of sorrows and acquainted with grief'.

Never till then, and never since then, have I heard any one read as Elizabeth Fry read that chapter – the solemn reverence of her manner, the articulation, so exquisitely modulated, so distinct, that not a word of that sweet and touching voice could fail to be heard. While she read, her mind seemed to be intensely absorbed in the passage of Scripture and nothing else. She seemed to take into her own soul the words which she read, and to apply them to herself; and then she raised her head, and, after another period of silence, she spoke to the wretched women before her.[18]

Her address was short and the words simple, to ensure that her audience understood, 'and it was soon evident that it had come home to the hearts of many by the subdued expression of their countenances, and by the tears that flowed freely from eyes which perhaps had never shed such tears till then'. Nor was the effect of her presence confined to the assembly, Thomas added.

> As I passed with her through the various rooms of the prison, where the women were occupied with the various works she had seen the means of procuring for them, the looks of tender reverence they cast on her as she moved among them, and the way in which some whispered a blessing after her, testified to the influence she has obtained amongst them.[19]

Before long, a matron was appointed to the women's wing, as recommended in the Newgate Rules; she was funded partly by the Corporation of the City of London, and partly by the ladies' committee, whose members continued to spend most of every day with the women. As news of the Newgate experiment spread, Fry began to receive letters from women all over the country, eager for advice on how to set up their own local visiting committees. Enquiries also came from interested parties on the Continent. Despite her Newgate commitments, Fry endeavoured to do justice to all her correspondents and thus began to build up a formidable network of international contacts.

On 27 February 1818, less than a year after the Newgate experiment began, Elizabeth Fry became probably the first woman ever to be invited to give evidence to a British parliamentary Select Committee. It was a heaven-sent opportunity (and she believed it was *exactly* that). It enabled her to put across her general ideas on the practical and moral management of the women prisoners – based on her unique experience at Newgate – to the male establishment of the day. At the same time, it helped to clarify in her own mind the most important individual elements of her prison management philosophy that would later crystallize into a universal manifesto for the superintendence of women prisoners anywhere. The publicity that followed such a high-profile public appearance would also seriously propel her into the limelight as a formidable social reformer of early nineteenth-century Britain.

The committee was chaired by Alderman Sir Matthew Wood, a former Lord Mayor of the City of London. Its remit was to report on the state of prisons in the City of London (which included Newgate), the Borough of Southwark, and Dartmoor prison.

Thirty-four witnesses were called. They included a second woman – Mary Bolland, the matron of the Bridewell house of correction – as well as Fry's brother-in-law, Thomas Fowell Buxton. The Buxtons had not long returned from a trip with the Joseph John Gurneys to the Continent where, in addition to establishing a branch of the Bible Society in Paris, they had also inspected prisons in Antwerp and Ghent. Buxton, who is perhaps best known for being the inheritor of William Wilberforce in the anti-slavery movement, had been invited to give evidence in his capacity as a representative of both The Society for the Improvement of Prison Discipline and The Society for the Reformation of Juvenile Offenders. He was there to report on his impression of the conditions that prevailed at the Borough Compter, a debtors' prison in Bermondsey. The other witnesses represented a wide range of professions including medicine, the law, the Church, and the armed forces, as well as the prison establishment itself and the City of London authority.

Fry was the fourth witness to be called to give evidence; Buxton was the eighth. How long she was interviewed is not clear, but her contribution covered 12 pages of the 200-plus pages of evidence listed in the minutes – or around 10,000 words. She did not squander this opportunity to be heard.

It was an unusual examination, with questions ranging from the deeply serious to the profoundly trivial, perhaps reflecting the calibre of the members of the panel. What is remarkable is the way in which, with consummate diplomacy, Fry deflected all requests for information into areas where she could convert them for her own advantage.

Under examination, Fry explained that it was the plight of the children of Newgate that had first attracted her attention. During her occasional visits to Newgate in the early years – this would have been between 1813 and 1817 – she had been upset to see so many infants exposed to adult vice, to the extent that the first words they learned to say were oaths and curses. When she became a regular visitor in 1817, she decided to do something about this. She asked the women whether they would agree to having the children be separated from the convicts during the day, in rooms of their own and under the care of a school mistress. The mothers consented 'with tears in their eyes . . . for they knew so much of the miseries of vice, that they hoped their children would never be trained up in it'.

She told the committee that, thinking it of utmost importance to find a governess from among the women themselves, she asked if there was anyone they thought they could recommend for the post, someone who could be trusted with the care of children. There was, so that was another hurdle overcome. She then asked the prison authorities for permission to seek out, within the prison, some premises that would be suitable for a school for the children. They agreed, and an apartment was located. No sooner had the children been installed than the younger girl convicts came forward to ask if they, too, could be admitted to the school, adding that 'if they could be reformed also, what comfort it would give them'. As a result, several young women were also allowed to join the school,

> which prospered beyond all expectation; the order and regularity that was preserved, and the progress that the young people and children made in learning to read, and in other branches in which we had them instructed, such as working and knitting, was highly satisfactory.[20]

Unfortunately, much of the good work that was achieved during the day was undone at night when the children and girls had to return to their communal sleeping arrangements on the main prison wards, with all that implied in terms of bad association. Many of Fry's lady visitor colleagues attended the school at Newgate almost every day, and witnessed the dreadful things that happened on the women's side of the prison: 'the begging, swearing, gaming, fighting, singing, dancing, dressing up in men's clothes: the scenes are too bad to be described', she told the Select Committee.

They had not observed much drunkenness, she replied under questioning, but that was probably because the prisoners knew when she and her colleagues would be visiting, and abstained for the duration. There was certainly ample evidence that alcohol was being brought in from so-called 'friends' outside. What disturbed the ladies' committee more, she explained, was what went on at the iron grating that separated the women from the outside world, by a distance of about three feet. 'The women would be on one side, begging or conversing improperly, and the other side used to be continually filled by men; and I am confident that what was extremely improper took place.' One can only assume she meant some sort of sexual exchange. The experience affected Fry deeply.

> At this time it struck me what a very lamentable thing it was, that a prison should be thus, what I would call as school for every vice that could be committed there. I thought it could be remedied.[21]

The women prisoners seemed delighted at the prospect of a regime change. So many were keen to be taught at the prison school that Fry began to devise a set of rules – to be agreed by all, of course – which would provide a system that ensured that they could all receive some instruction. It would depend on a system of monitors. The prison management, however, had been less than enthusiastic, Fry explained. It would never work, they said. If the ladies brought in work for the prisoners to do, it would be stolen. Rules might be obeyed for a week but, once the novelty had worn off, they would be broken daily. Most insulting of all for Fry was management's view that 'for a number of ladies to think of ruling women whom they themselves [as men] could not govern, was out of the question'.

Fry was as doggedly determined as she was well connected. So she had asked the prison management to indulge her a little, she explained to the panel. Might she not at least be allowed to meet all the convicted prisoners as a group, to see if her plan for a better way forward met with their approval, she asked, 'for I said I would never undertake it, unless they entirely concurred'. Here Fry had known she was on safe ground. She knew how the prisoners were thinking; she had already consulted with them. So it came as no great surprise to her, but 'I believe to the great surprise of the gentlemen who accompanied us [that] there was not one dissenting voice'. The female prisoners agreed to submit to any rules whatsoever, if only they could be given employment and instruction. Suddenly, there was accommodation available in the prison, and permission was given to appoint a matron, whose salary would soon be paid jointly by the prison authorities and the ladies' committee. Project Newgate was under way.

Fry decided that it would be sensible to wait a month or so before approaching the city council to apply for financial support. That way, the ladies' committee would have time to get the project up and running, with some results to show.

> We therefore assembled our women, read over our rules, brought them work, knitting and other things, and our instruction commenced . . . Our rules have occasionally been broken but very seldom; order has been generally observed. I think I may say we have full power amongst them, for one of them said it was more terrible to be brought before me than before the judge.[22]

The Newgate experiment had been running for ten months by the time Fry was called to address the Select Committee. In that time, the women had made 20,000 articles of clothing. They were knitting between 60 and 100 pairs of

stockings a month. Their earnings were about eighteen pence a week in old currency, or about seven and a half pence in a decimal equivalent.[23] The women's
earnings were generally spent on helping them to live and clothe themselves
decently. Together they contributed a total of about £4 a month to a central
fund, to which the ladies' committee added another £8.

Fry told the committee that, for her personally, one of the most gratifying
aspects of the Newgate experiment was 'the excellent effect we have found to
result from religious education'. Scriptures were read to the prisoners twice a
day, and some had even learned how to read a little themselves.

> It has had an astonishing effect. I never saw the Scriptures received in the same way, and
> to many of [the women] they have been entirely new, both the great system of religion
> and the morality contained in them. And it has been very satisfactory to observe the
> effect upon their minds. When I have sometimes gone [to Newgate] and said it was my
> intention to read, they would flock upstairs after me, as if it was a great pleasure I had
> to afford them.[24]

Apart from anything else, the prisoners were clearly starving for some sort of
diversion. The Select Committee was anxious for reassurance that nothing but
the morals of the Scriptures were being taught, and not 'any peculiar doctrine'
which one must take to mean 'Quaker'. Fry agreed diplomatically, if not a little
haughtily, that it would be 'highly improper to press any peculiar doctrine of any
kind, anything beyond the fundamental doctrines of Scripture'. Then, smoothly
changing the subject back to her own agenda, she mentioned with some satisfaction what a dramatic improvement there had been in the behaviour of
the Newgate women under her care. This had also been commented upon by
the governor and clergymen at the new Millbank penitentiary, to which many
Newgate women had been transferred prior to their transportation.

Previously, she said, when women were about to be transported to Australia
and leave their loved ones, they created an understandable fuss. However, now
when women left Newgate for Botany Bay,

> such a thing was never known in the prison before, as the quietness and order with
> which they left it. Instead of tearing everything down, it was impossible to leave [the
> prison] more peaceably than they did, proof that their moral and religious instruction
> had had some effect upon their minds.[25]

The Newgate experience had also increased the prisoners' sense of sisterly solidarity, she added. When the Newgate women were about to set off for Australia, they were allowed to take with them the small amount of savings they had accumulated through their work in prison. But they asked that it be shared between all women prisoners who were being transported – including those from prisons other than Newgate – while those who remained behind requested that their little share of the profit be given to the others who were leaving.

By this point, Fry had covered most of what she had been hoping to say in support of the Newgate project. The Select Committee now turned its questions to matters of detail. Could she report on the accommodation for prisoners? She could, and she thought that 'a very great deal more might be achieved . . . if we could separate [the women] in the night'.

Did those convicted for all offences pass the day together, the committee wondered? They were very much intermixed, she replied: 'old and young, hardened offenders with those who have committed only a minor offence, or the first crimes; the very lowest of women with respectable married women and maid servants. It is more injurious than can be described in its effects and its consequences.' Nor could it be remedied until there was more prison space made available to enable the classification of prisoners into separate groups.

Were the women punished, or threatened with punishment, the panel wanted to know? With the permission of the prison authorities, the ladies' committee had available to them the sanction of committing women to solitary confinement for two or three days, Fry replied, adding that she thought this may have been done perhaps four times during the last ten months.

Asked about the reward system that operated in the female prison at Newgate, Fry explained that, in addition to their earnings from their own work, there was also an incentive scheme in operation for good behaviour. Women could earn points which went towards 'good marks' for which they might gain privileges such as small articles of clothing or religious tracts. The hope of pardon was never implied, she insisted, although Home Secretary Lord Sidmouth had kindly indicated that he would at least be prepared 'to listen to our wishes, respecting the mitigation of punishment'.

The Select Committee then moved on to questions relating to the health and diet of prisoners. For example, was the basic prison allowance – a pound of brown bread a day (or 14 ounces of white) plus a pound of meat twice a week – sufficient to keep prisoners healthy? It was not, she replied. Some women received considerable assistance from 'friends' outside the prison, often their former associates in crime. Some received 'too much . . . even luxuries, even poultry sometimes, that we think very improper for prisons. For prisons should not be made palaces, but they ought to have sufficient.' On the other hand, four women and four children who had come into Newgate malnourished in the previous ten months had died, she said, because they had no 'friends' outside the wall to offer them assistance, and had been unable to work in prison to support themselves. Did she mean that these prisoners were in a state of famine, the Select Committee wanted to know?

> Famine would be too strong, but they would be in a very poor state. They get very thin, they look very pale, and very frequently become dropsical, which is a sign of poverty of the blood; three have died dropsical out of the four women I have mentioned . . . I think, if they had been in good health when they first went in [to prison], they hardly would have lost their lives [from the deficiency of food]. But I think, if they had sufficient nourishment during their residence in prison, their lives might have been saved.[26]

Starvation in prison had killed them – and they might even only have been on remand. On the diet front, however, things looked set to improve. There were plans to stew the weekly meat allowance, in order to provide broth on alternate days; gruel (thin porridge) was to be provided every morning; and Fry recommended the introduction into prisoners' diets of plenty of potatoes, which were 'very nutritious, very cheap, and, I think, intend greatly to health'.[27]

At this point, the interview descended to a surreal level of questioning. It may have reflected issues that were important at the time, or it may simply have reflected the specific interests of the panel members. Either way, the examination continued with a debate on the relative merits of different cuts of meat and a discussion on the digestibility of brown bread versus white, with the committee's being informed that 'in London it is not the habit to eat brown bread – one of the poor women who was executed lately complained that it disagreed with her digestion'. If an upset stomach was all that troubled her as she prepared to meet her Maker, she was indeed blessed.

A more serious issue was the question of alcohol, banned in prison but being sent in to inmates from 'friends' on the outside, either for the prisoners' own consumption or for sale to others at a profit. From the point of view of public decency, however, most important for Fry was the question of adequate clothing for the women in her care. She confirmed to the Select Committee that no regular clothing allowance was provided for the women by the City authorities, a service that was left almost exclusively to the good offices of the ladies' committee. She recalled the case of one particular woman brought in to Newgate on remand ('untried', and therefore technically innocent) who was about to give birth.

> I could describe such scenes as I should hardly think it delicate to mention. We had a woman the other day on the point of lying-in, brought to bed not many hours after she came in. She had hardly a covering, no stockings and only a thin gown. Whilst we are there, we can never see a woman in that state, without applying to our fund.[28]

When they are brought in, are they almost naked, a horrified committee member asked? Often they are, Fry replied, adding that when the woman she mentioned (who was found not guilty) came in,

> we had to send her up almost every article of clothing, and to clothe the baby. She could not be tried the next session, but after she had been tried, and when she was discharged, she went out comfortably discharged. There are many such instances.

The panel wanted to know whether it was true 'that when gentlemen have come to see the prison, you have been obliged to stand before the women who were in prison in a condition not fit to be seen?' There was one such instance, she confirmed, but she had not been in Newgate long, 'for we do not, since we have been there, suffer them to be a day without being clothed'.

Is there no fund to which you can apply for money to buy clothing for these women except your own pockets, the committee asked? There are the pockets of our friends who have subscribed to our fund, she replied, and some of them had done so 'very handsomely'. There was the occasional goodwill donation from the prison authorities but it was an unreliable source of funding. Quite simply, 'we cannot suffer them to remain unclothed and therefore do it from our own fund'.

Moving on to questions of personal hygiene and sanitation in prisons, Fry bemoaned the fact that there was no regular, reliable soap allowance for prisoners, which was very demoralizing. There was supposed to be an allowance of two ounces of soap a week; but sometimes they received it, sometimes they did not. Cleanliness being next to godliness, 'it is so very important, that it seems an essential in prison, and therefore ought not to depend on uncertainty'.

As to the general state of hygiene and sanitation in the women's quarters at Newgate, Fry commented that considering how very crowded we almost are, it is as clean as we can expect; but where a ward is washed out, and [there are] perhaps thirty women cooking and washing, and everything going forward in the same room, it is what I should call dirty in about an hour afterwards.[29]

What 'everything going forward' meant in practical terms is not clear, but if it referred to normal bodily functions, the situation must indeed have been dire. There were indeed some 'little passages' where women could wash themselves and their clothes, but there were no basins and no towels, except as the ladies' committee provided out of their own pockets.

'So in what manner were the women washed?', the Select Committee wanted to know. 'Hardly at all', came Fry's reply.

As regards their bedding, Fry explained that, when she first visited Newgate, the women had to sleep directly on the floor, with two rugs to cover them; now at least they had a sort of rope mat to lie on, and three rugs to keep them warm. A separate bed and bedstead would be ideal, she admitted under questioning, but at the present time the space available in the female prison at Newgate was far too cramped. 'It is much too crowded', she explained. 'Thirty women lie in a room; it is almost like a slave-ship, I have sometimes thought', she commented, adding yet another emotionally laden comparison to her deposition. In fact, Newgate women at the time had a personal sleeping space of about 18 inches by 6 feet. They were almost literally sleeping on top of each other, with all that that implied in a deeply emotionally deprived environment. Fry understood the dangers.

> I believe the moral discipline of a prison can never be complete, while [female prisoners] are allowed to sleep together in one room. If I may be allowed to state it, I should prefer a prison where women were allowed to work together in companies; to have their meals together, under proper superintendence, and their recreation also. But I would always have them separated in the night; I believe it would conduce to the health, both of body and mind. Their being in companies during the day, tends, under proper regulations, to the advancement of principle and industry; for it affords a stimulus.[30]

So far, Fry had expertly pursued her reform agenda. She had engaged with questions that she must have thought stupid, diplomatically skimmed over problem areas, and gently deflected awkward topics towards issues that *she* wanted to discuss. As the interview was clearly reaching its conclusion, she had one final trump card to play in the discussion of the practical and moral management of women at Newgate prison.

> There is one very important thing which ought to be stated on the subject of women taking care of women. It has been said, that there were three things which were requisite in forming a prison that would really tend to the reformation of women; but there is a fourth, namely that women should be taken care of entirely by women, and have no male attendants, unless it be a medical man, or any minister of religion. For I am convinced that much harm arises from the communication not only to the women themselves, but those who have care of them.
>
> If I had a prison completely such as I would like it to be, it would be a prison quite separate from the men's prison, and into which no turnkeys or any body else should enter but female attendants, and the Inspecting Committee of Ladies, except indeed such gentlemen as come to look after their welfare . . .
>
> In what does the turnkey interfere now with that prison? Very little. And yet there is a certain intercourse which it is impossible for us to prevent, and it must be where there is a prison for women and men, and there are various officers who are men in the prison . . . We must have turnkeys, and a governor to refer to; but I should like to have a [women's] prison which had nothing to do with men, except those who attend to them medically or spiritually.

Did this mean that she wanted men to be excluded from all communication with the women as far as possible, in the present state of Newgate, the Select Committee asked tentatively. Yes, she said, she did.

In their report, the members of the Select Committee, who had personally visited all those 'receptacles of wretchedness and crime, scenes so painful and repulsive to the feelings', had clearly been shocked by the experience. And, 'while bound to recollect that certain hardships are necessary and unavoidable' in prison, they had no intention of turning a blind eye to any evidence of 'neglect, or abuse, or undue severity'.

> The whole system of enlightened criminal jurisprudence is devised for the *prevention* of crime, not of abstract punishment . . . While the hardships of a prison . . . may be wisely and justly inflicted, it is our duty to take care that no more is done or suffered than is conducive to the real object; and still more, that the means we employ to check may not contribute to the increase in crime.

The trouble with Newgate, they added, was that it was basically no longer fit for purpose. They warned that 'the public interest requires a speedy attention to its condition'. Some individual aspects they found acceptable – food had improved, and the premises seemed reasonably clean, for example; others they found less acceptable, such as the inadequacy of clothing and bedding, and inadequate personal hygiene. What concerned them most, however, was the problem of overcrowding. The prison was holding up to twice the number of inmates for which it was designed, with no classification of those prisoners, resulting in 'a promiscuous assemblage of persons of all descriptions, ages and characters of crime'. Newgate handled newly convicted convicts straight from the courts, prisoners on remand, prisoners serving custodial sentences and prisoners awaiting transportation. Its original design was 'defective and the accommodation inadequate for the purpose to which it is now applied'.

The trouble was: there was no money available to fix it. The cost to the City of London of maintaining Newgate was already great, and it could not be expected that the present gaol should be pulled down and 'a better constructed, more commodious, and more extended prison erected in its place, which could only be effected at a most enormous expense'.

The only practical recommendations the committee were able to make, therefore, were organizational ones, with a view to reducing overcrowding which might, in turn, provide the opportunity to introduce some effective form of classification and improved management of inmates. Newgate could be used exclusively for prisoners on remand who were due to be tried at the Old Bailey next door; convicts could be passed on to other prisons immediately after sentencing; and cases of larceny could be tried at the county and borough Quarter Sessions. This would not, of course, do anything directly to improving the treatment of prisoners overall. It just shifted the problem out of the City of London, by redistributing the prison population elsewhere.

The sole suggestion that would benefit the prisoners personally was that the men should be found useful employment. This had already been achieved on the women's side of the prison, thanks to Fry's 'unremitting personal attention and influence', they reported. On the male side, however, 'attempts to give employment have been baffled by the dishonest practices of those on whom the experiment has been made'. The committee said that it could not conclude its report

without expressing in an especial manner the peculiar gratification they experience in observing the important service rendered by Mrs Fry and her friends, and the habits of religion, order, industry and cleanliness which her humane, benevolent and praise-worthy exertions have introduced among the female prisoners; and that if the principles which govern her regulations were adopted towards the males, as well as the females, it would be the means of converting a prison into a school of reform; and, instead of sending criminals back into the world hardened in vice and depravity, they would be restored to it repentant, and probably become useful members of society.

Similar sentiments were expressed in a personal letter from the Select Committee to Fry, which also included a donation to the Newgate cause.

6

Exiles to a distant land

Exile or execution was the fate facing most of the convicted women at Newgate, and it was inevitable that Fry would become involved with both issues. Some of her earliest memories of the prison were of visiting condemned women before they were hanged. On the first occasion, in February 1817, she sat with a woman who had murdered her baby, and thought 'how inexpressibly awful now to have *her* life taken away'. It was an experience that left her with 'distressingly nervous sensations in the night' and a sense of 'deep humiliation to me, thus witnessing the effect and consequences of sin'.

Fry was implacably opposed to the death penalty, believing that all life was sacred. She also believed that the death penalty was counter-productive and an ineffective deterrent to crime. 'Persons who have carefully attended to the subject, and who have *personally watched* the effect ... both on offenders themselves and on the multitude by whom they are surrounded, generally and strongly unite in the sentiment – especially as it is applied to crimes against property only – that it [the death penalty] is very injurious to the best interests of society.' When punishment was unduly severe, she added, it ceased to have the desired effect.

> If we would ensure the cordial cooperation of the public – especially of prosecutors, witnesses and jurymen – in the punishment of crime, the provisions of our criminal code must be made *mild enough* to coincide with those unalterable principles of justice and humanity which God has implanted in the breast of man, and which will ever be supported by the feelings of a free and enlightened community.[1]

It was a dreadful thing, she wrote, to dispatch the soul of a fellow man from here to eternity. While some condemned prisoners may indeed repent as the dreaded end approached, their execution deprived them of the chance to prove their redemption, in that it 'cuts off the possibility of that amendment of life which can alone prove the reality [of redemption]'. Others failed to repent in time because they clung, to the very end, in the hope of a reprieve. Others remained defiant and brazen – 'evidence of a heart unconverted and estranged from God' – while pacifying their consciences 'with the dangerous and most fallacious notion, that the violent death which awaits them will serve as a full atonement for all their sins'. Also, Fry contended, capital punishment served only to brutalize society at large.

> The frequent public destruction of life has a fearfully hardening effect on those whom it is intended to intimidate. While it excites them in the spirit of revenge, it seldom fails to lower their estimate of the life of man, and renders them less afraid of taking it away, in their turn, by acts of personal violence.[2]

In short, the death sentence – particularly for trivial offences against property – sent out the message that human life was cheap; and Fry was convinced that it contributed to increasing rates of both murder and suicide. Punishments 'of a milder and less injurious nature' were far more effective, she argued.

> Let our prison discipline be severe in proportion to the enormity of the crimes of those on whom it is exercised; and let its strictness be such as to deter others from a similar course of iniquity; but let it be accompanied by a religious care, and a Christian kindness, and let us ever aim at the diminution of crime, through the just and happy medium of the reformation of criminals.[3]

Fry's views on capital punishment were highly regarded by legal reformer Sir Samuel Romilly, who campaigned tirelessly to reduce the severity of the English legal system.[4] Romilly praised Fry's humanitarian works in the House of Commons; and in his journal for February 1818, when Fry was giving evidence to the Select Committee on London prisons, he explained what he had understood from their discussions.

> I learned from her some curious facts respecting the effects produced by capital punishments. Her observations are the more valuable, as she has such opportunities of seeing and conversing with the prisoners. She told me that there prevails among them a very strong and general sense of the great injustice of punishing mere thefts and forgery in the same manner as murders: that it is frequently said by them, that the crimes of which they have been guilty are nothing when compared with the crimes of Government

towards themselves: that they have only been thieves, but that their governors are murderers. There is an opinion, too, very prevalent among them, that those who suffer under such unjust and cruel sentences are sure of their salvation.[5]

Not everyone was so kindly disposed to Fry's views. She succeeded in alienating Home Secretary Lord Sidmouth by seeking mitigation for a Newgate woman condemned to hang because, with Fry's encouragement, she had pleaded innocent to a charge of passing forged bank notes, when a guilty plea would have secured transportation. On this occasion, Fry's intervention made a bad situation worse and only rarely in future did she become involved in this way. Her mission was not to change the sentencing system, but to improve conditions for those on the wrong side of it.

At the time, long-term imprisonment was still mainly the fate of debtors like the father of Dickens' heroine Little Dorrit (and, indeed, Dickens' own father who was also confined in the Marshalsea prison) until they, their families or friends, had discharged their financial obligations.[6] In previous centuries, punishment for other crimes – and they were primarily crimes against property – had taken the form of physical chastisement: whipping, branding, amputation, a period in the stocks and other more imaginative punishments. In the first half of the nineteenth century, imprisonment was rarely used to punish criminals except for short sentences for a limited number of minor misdemeanours. It was only with the 1853 Penal Servitude Act that custodial sentences for convicted criminals became a regular procedure.[7] It was therefore a logical extension of Fry's concern for her Newgate protégées that she should be concerned about the conditions surrounding their transportation, and their welfare when they arrived on the distant shores of Australia. For those condemned to hang, she could do little but try to ease their final hours. For those condemned to be transported to Australia, there was much more that she could do.

The history of the banishment of individual criminals from England to distant parts goes back as far as the late sixteenth century. It was in the early seventeenth century that Parliament specifically named America and the East Indies as appropriate destinations for convicts. In fact, few transportations took place in those early years. Transportation only really became a regular activity when a massive increase in the number of capital offences introduced during the Georgian period in Britain seriously criminalized vast numbers of the population. Whereas in the late seventeenth century there were some 50 crimes punishable by death, this figure had risen to around 300 by 1830. Virtually all were crimes against property – many as trivial as poaching, shoplifting, cutting down a tree or minor forms of counterfeiting or forgery, a particular Hanoverian obsession. People who might previously have received some form of corporal punishment now found themselves sentenced to death or exile. There was little regard to the individual circumstances of the criminal: extreme youth or extreme poverty could not be factored into the judicial process. As a result, more humane judges might conjure up a technical reason to set aside a case completely rather than condemn a defendant. Enlisting in the armed forces was also sometimes offered as an option, particularly during the Napoleonic Wars.

The hidden agenda of this draconian punishment regime was that the process of hanging or transporting large numbers of criminals, however minor their crimes, was a very efficient method of social cleansing. Permanently (or at least semi-permanently, since transportation was usually for seven or 14 years), and at a stroke, it removed many undesirable elements from the streets of the country's towns and cities. This underclass of society included the poor, the destitute, the sick in body and spirit – many of them victims of the social and economic upheaval of the Industrial Revolution; but they also included religious Dissenters and political opponents of the establishment. Among them were many Quakers, although in the early years of transportation they were sent to the Caribbean rather than to America, where there was a risk that their anti-authoritarian views might have been sympathetically received.

By the 1770s, some 50,000 convicts had been sent to America. After the American War of Independence, the former colony immediately refused to take any more. The British government was faced with a sudden and urgent need to house hundreds of criminals who would normally have been transported across the Atlantic. Lacking adequate prison places, temporary accommodation was provided for them on redundant, decommissioned – and frequently rotting – ex-naval ships. These 'prison hulks', as they were known, were anchored mainly on the Thames and the Medway rivers, and were disease-ridden, rat-infested places often worse than the most desperate prison.[8]

The use of prison hulks could only ever be a temporary solution, although it lasted 80 years; and the government began looking at other possible destinations to which criminals could be transported. Various locations were considered and rejected, including several in West Africa; the East India Company refused categorically to have anything to do with the transportation scheme in the areas under its jurisdiction.

Eventually, in 1786, a decision was made to send convicts to Australia – specifically, in the first instance, to Botany Bay. The area, in what would become known as New South Wales, had been 'discovered' by Captain James Cook, who first sailed his expedition ship *Endeavour* into the bay in 1770. Favourable reports had been sent back to Britain, indicating that the region offered a temperate climate, good farming land, lots of fish and wildlife, plenty of timber with which to construct ships and buildings, and hemp, essential for sails and ropes. In the event, conditions at Botany Bay turned out not to be as ideal as originally portrayed, but the neighbouring area offered more potential. The other obvious advantage was that colonizing Australia offered the British government the opportunity to establish a presence in the region.

And so, one Sunday morning in May 1787, the first British convict fleet set sail from Portsmouth for Australia. It comprised 11 ships, of which six carried convicts: 550 men, 192 women and a dozen or so of their children. Contractor William Richard was paid £54,000 to take them. Calling at Tenerife, Rio de Janeiro and Cape Town *en route*, the fleet covered 15,000 miles, arriving in Botany Bay some eight months later.[9] It was a remarkable moment when the first European settlers set foot on the continent. 'The decision to transport convicted felons to Australia remains the only occasion in history when convicts were forced to be instruments in creating the society in which they underwent their punishment.'

The history of transportation and the early colonization of Australia is widely documented.[10] Between 1787 and 1868, when the practice finally ended, over 160,000 convicts were transported on over 800 ships to New South Wales, Van Diemen's Land (now Tasmania) and Western Australia. No women convicts were sent to Western Australia, since the region's main concern was for a free labour force.

When Fry first became involved with the issue, in 1818, transportation was on the increase, peaking in the early 1830s. The popular view was that crime was spiralling even further out of control at home, as some 300,000 soldiers returned from the Napoleonic Wars to swell the ranks of the disaffected unemployed, and to exacerbate an already depressed economic climate.

Opinions remained divided as to whether transportation was the answer. Prison reform pioneer John Howard had been in favour of it as a means of permanently removing felons from the negative influence of their associates. But in 1813, the *Edinburgh Review* expressed itself appalled at the practice.

The reality is that the miserable wretch, after rotting in hulks for a year or two, is crammed with some hundred of his fellows into a floating prison, or maybe a pest-house, in which, if he survives the risk of famine, pestilence, mutiny, fire, shipwreck and explosion, he is conveyed . . . to a life of alternating slavery and rebellion . . . [with] exquisite suffering [and] uniform rebellion . . . All this happens at the opposite extremity of the earth, from whence it operates no more upon the inhabitants of England than if it were passing on the moon.[11]

Many years later, in 1828, the *Quarterly Review* endorsed Howard's view.

The entire removal of the individual to a new scene of life affords at once the one security to society against his future crimes and the contagion of his habits, and the only chance left to himself for regaining decency and respectability.

Others, including clergyman and liberal publisher Sydney Smith, saw transportation as a soft option and therefore an inadequate deterrent to crime. Despite the harsh conditions that prevailed on the transport ships; despite the havoc that transportation caused to distraught families; despite the years of forced labour on arrival – many thought that to reward criminals with a fresh start in a land of promise and adventure was fundamentally wrong. There were also those in the abolitionist lobby who denounced the practice of 'assigning' convicts to employers on arrival as tantamount to slavery. Those who had first-hand experience of the convict ships were wont to change camps. Surgeon-superintendent Thomas Reid, for example, served on two convict ships, in 1818 and 1820.[12] He wrote of his experiences in *Two Voyages to New South Wales and Van Diemen's Land*, which he dedicated to Elizabeth Fry. He became a strong opponent of transportation and refused to take any further part in the programme after 1820. Fry herself did not debate the rights or wrongs of transportation; her role, as she saw it, was to work within the existing system to ensure that transportees were treated with kindness and dignity.

These qualities were significantly absent from the procedures in place for handling the transfer of women from Newgate prison to the convict ships bound for Australia and Tasmania. The usual scenario was that, the night before a convict ship was due to load, the women – in a final act of defiance and rage against a system which was about to tear them from their families – would get drunk and riot. The next day, they would appear in public chained together and would be driven in an open cart to the docks through abusive and jeering crowds. When Fry became aware of this procedure, she persuaded the Newgate governor to drive 'her' women to the dock in closed carriages. In exchange, she promised to persuade the women to go quietly. Her promise was fulfilled.

Encouraged by this significant breakthrough, Fry's ladies' committee set about drawing up a programme that would convert even the unfortunate experience of transportation into an opportunity; and every convict ship into 'a place for industry, conviction and reform'.[13] The committee duly issued a series of recommendations. They advised that female convicts with small babies should be allowed to remain in England until the infant was weaned, and that they should be allowed to take with them on the ships any children under seven years of age. The women should also not be kept in irons for the removal from prison to convict ship – some had been chained so closely that they could scarcely walk without falling over each other. For its part, the lady volunteers would undertake to provide a suitable library of books for the voyage, plus, for each woman, a variety of articles 'intended to afford them during their voyage some little accommodations and the means of useful and profitable occupation'.

Finding something useful for the women to do on the voyage had been a major challenge. Hearing that there was a market for patchwork goods in New South Wales – and even at ports of call *en route* – the ladies' committee put out an appeal to the Manchester cotton manufacturers and, within days, had received enough off-cuts for the 128 women on board the first ship with which they became involved. The next challenge was to find some way of occupying the 14 accompanying children. During the five weeks before the ship set sail, the children were taught to read, knit and sew, under the supervision of a convict who had volunteered to act as schoolmistress, in a small space set aside specially for them. How far these arrangements remained in place on any ship on the open seas was, of course, very much dependent on the commitment of the ship's management.

Fry visited as many of the female convict ships as she could before they sailed – 106 in all. She would conduct an impromptu farewell service of Bible readings, prayers, and a blessing for the welfare of the women in their uncertain future. Thanks to the endeavours of the ladies' committee, each woman took with her a parcel of donated items, funded initially by the committee members. These articles included: one hessian apron, and one black apron; one large hessian bag (to keep her clothes in), plus one small bag, containing one piece of tape, one ounce of pins, one hundred needles, four balls of white sewing cotton, one each of black, blue and red, two balls of black worsted (weighing half an ounce each),

24 balls of coloured thread, one of cloth, with eight darning needles, one small bodkin fastened on to it, two stay laces, one thimble, one pair of scissors, two pounds of patchwork pieces, two combs and a ball of string. There should be a knife and fork for each mess; spectacles would be provided for those who needed them. And each woman was to be provided with a Bible, even if she could not yet read it.

If the women behaved in an orderly manner on the voyage out, they would be given a certificate by the surgeon of the vessel and, on arriving at their destination, had a chance of being hired immediately as servants 'by the most respectable families in the colony'. But the fear of being 'assigned' into prostitution was a real and justified one; even Parliament had warned that new arrivals in Australia ran that risk, rather than being taken into domestic service, as they expected. On the other hand, there were many who thought all female convicts were nothing more than drunken whores anyway, although contemporary statistics indicate that only one-fifth had previously worked as prostitutes. However, it was true that many of that minority continued to ply their trade with the crew. Typically most convicts were low-grade domestic servants in their early twenties, with no previous convictions. About 2 per cent were political prisoners. And all were worried about what awaited them on the other side of the world.

To help to alleviate their anxiety, and to try to ensure some continuity of order from Newgate to Australia, members of the ladies' committee would go on board each ship while it was preparing for the voyage and address the women in groups of about 12. They explained the routine, rules and procedures that they were recommending, the division of women into classes based on the tried and tested Newgate model, the appointment of schoolmistresses and monitors from their own number, and the arrangements for sick-bed facilities, religious services and the library. The change from the seclusion of their cells to the bustle and tumult of the convict ship could be very trying for the women prisoners and had a distressing effect on all concerned, convicts and helpers alike.

Over the years of Fry's involvement, 106 ships carried 12,000 female convicts to Australia. The involvement of the ladies' committee – with their books, tracts, clothes, quilt-making packages, and exhortations to good behaviour on the voyage – were appreciated by the more enlightened ships' management. William Evans, surgeon-superintendent of the *Lady of the Lake*, commended Fry's colleagues Elizabeth Pryor and Lydia Irving in particular for their practical and spiritual support; they were 'indefatigable in endeavouring to impress upon the prisoners the necessity of abandoning their evil ways and becoming useful members of society'.[14]

Fry and her colleagues did all that they could to provide for the welfare of the women on their voyage. But what would happen to them on their arrival at their destination? And how, at such a distance, could she influence what happened? One of the ways that occurred to her was to encourage missionaries of her acquaintance, who were going out to Australia, to travel on the female convict ships. Passengers on these ships were rarely just convicts and crew; there were often ordinary citizens travelling as well. For example, when the *George Hibbert* left London for Sydney in 1834, it was carrying nine free women and 23 of their children, as well as 150 convicts and 41 of their children. Also on board, thanks to Fry's intervention, were Baptist missionary John Saunders and his wife. Fry had negotiated a free passage for the Saunders couple on the basis that their presence would help to promote the convicts' spiritual welfare, and ensure a regular programme of religious services, Bible readings and lectures. On the ship's arrival in Sydney, the master, Captain Livesay, wrote back to England that Saunders had proved 'a very great acquisition', particularly in his 'kind affection to the unfortunate criminals'. Even better, the missionary and his wife had taught many of the women to read and write.

Fry also prevailed on other clergymen travelling on the female convict ships to offer their professional services on board, and to report back to her on how they found the experience. One unnamed minister wrote to the ladies' committee describing a Sunday afternoon religious service in the tropics.

> It was, as you will imagine from our latitude, excessively hot. But an awning was fixed up, and gave the deck much the appearance of a court. Seats were temporarily made of planks and tubs, so that all the women were accommodated in an orderly manner; while apart, but in equal order, were ranged all the sailors.
>
> The women, for the first time, put on the cool white jackets and checked aprons provided for them; and I cannot tell you how really picturesque and neat they looked from the uniformity of their dress: it was equalled only by their breathless attention during the service. The congregation so interesting, the circumstances of more than 200 persons assembled . . . on the deck of a ship, to worship God – alone on the ocean, or at least not within many miles of other human beings – all provided such feelings as, I believe, none of us ever before experienced. We only wished that you could have been present to witness the fruit of your exertions.[15]

The usual procedure was that, on arrival, convict women were inspected by local officials who verified the surgeon-superintendent's reports (any subsequent complaints about them might affect his fee), and were then registered, documented and sent to a holding depot before being assigned to various employers who would provide food, shelter and clothing. The luckiest could find themselves enjoying better conditions than they had known back in Britain. While that was the hoped-for outcome, the reality was that, all too often, they were whisked away by predatory men – officers and convicts alike – the minute they landed, and ended up as prostitutes or beggars.

However, it was a source of some gratification to Fry to hear reports from New South Wales that women from prisons like Newgate, where ladies' committees had become involved, were much better behaved than those from prisons not under such benevolent supervision. Clearly, obtaining any sort of overview at such a distance was difficult. However, Fry's supporters felt that enough individual cases 'of a highly satisfactory nature' were received 'such as to induce us reasonably to hope that there are many others equally encouraging that we may never hear of'.[16]

If women were not assigned to an employer, there might be various reasons. They might be difficult characters, violent, pregnant, have small children, or simply be unsuited to domestic service. In Fry's day, women who were not 'assigned' on arrival at Sydney were taken by boat to Parramatta where there was a rope-making factory with prisoner accommodation provided locally. Built in 1804, Parramatta was Australia's first female 'factory' and became notorious for its riots and the general lawlessness of its women. Others were built later at Launceston and at Cascades in Van Diemen's Land and were equally unruly. On one occasion, it is reported that one hundred Parramatta inmates marched into the local town to seize provisions when their prison rations were cut; on another, they seized a wardress and shaved her head in protest against being ordered to have their own heads shaved.[17]

Almost since it was built, the Parramatta chaplain, Samuel Marsden, had been campaigning to have a secure barracks-type hostel added to accommodate the women who worked at the 'factory'. For years he wrote to MPs, leading churchmen and government officials, but all to no avail. Hearing of Fry's work at Newgate, he wrote to her in desperation in February 1819.

Having learned from the public papers, as well as from my friends in England, the lively interest you have taken in promoting the temporal and eternal welfare of those unhappy females who fall under the sentence of law, I am induced to address a few lines to you respecting such as visit our distant shores. It may be gratifying to you, madam, to hear that I meet with those wretched exiles who have shared your attentions, and who mention your maternal care with gratitude and affection.

Marsden explained that he had been striving for more than 20 years to improve the female convicts' lot but to no avail. 'It has not been in my power to move those in authority to pay much attention to their wants and miseries.' As far back as 1807 he had been given assurances that a hostel would be built at Parramatta to accommodate female convicts who were driven to prostitution by the need to fund accommodation.

All the female convicts have not run the same lengths in vice. All are not equally hardened in crime. And it is most dreadful that all should alike, on their arrival here, be liable and exposed to the same dangerous temptations, without any remedy.

Marsden begged Fry to give support to his cause. She did so immediately, and began a relentless charm offensive with high-level colonial and Admiralty officials. There was no point in teaching her Newgate women orderly behaviour, and sustaining them in this on the passage out, only to have the more vulnerable pitched back into chaos once they arrived. A year after Fry began her assault on the establishment, construction work began on a female barracks at Parramatta. Government officials maintained that the project was already in the pipeline before Fry raised the matter.

However, New South Wales was not the only destination for female convicts from Britain. About half of the 25,000 transported over the years went to Van Diemen's Land, now known as Tasmania; indeed, in the later years of transportation, this was the only place they were sent. In 1823, Fry began lobbying the British government to build a separate prison for women there as well. Three years later, the Cascades factory was established and operated until 1856.

In 1835, Fry made the acquaintance of Charlotte Anley, who was about to go out to Australia to visit her cousin Frances Dumaresq, whose husband Edward was a former surveyor-general, magistrate, land-owner and brother-in-law of the former governor of New South Wales, Sir Ralph Darling. Such connections were not to be wasted. Fry secured a promise from Anley who 'entered warmly into Mrs Fry's views', to visit Parramatta which, thanks to Fry's earlier efforts, was now a house of correction comprising both factory and hostel, or 'barracks'. She asked Anley to report back on the conditions she found there, particularly the state of the Newgate women. She also asked her to try to set up a ladies' visiting committee.

Anley was in some doubt as to whether enough respectable women could be found to form a committee of visitors, since she had heard a

> general report [that] gave me small encouragement to hope for success in such a proposal, or to go forth myself into scenes which others had found fraught with insult and disappointment; and I was even told by some, not friendly to my mission, that they were scenes such as no female of education or delicacy could, with propriety encounter.[18]

She was also daunted at the prospect of inspecting the 'factory', but took heart from Fry's own example.

> One, whose name will ever be recorded as doing honour both to her country and to her sex, has proved, in her own experience, that where woman will plead with woman, upon the broad ground of Christian charity – not to condemn, but to persuade; to soothe and not to irritate – the most iniquitous will scarcely fail to respect such sympathy, should it win nothing beyond it. I therefore resolved . . . to execute my commission . . . being pledged to report a faithful statement to those who had requested it . . . bound by that promise, personally to investigate the object of Mrs Fry's solicitude.[19]

In the event, she found at Parramatta a large, clean, airy building providing accommodation for 700 prisoners, who were divided into three classes, as provided by the Fry Newgate model. The first group comprised women still waiting to be assigned, together with those who had returned after a period in domestic service. The second, larger group, consisted of women convicted of more serious offences; they included the mothers of illegitimate children, 'all of whom were women of the lowest description', and infants too young to separate from their mothers. After this, the prospect of meeting a third, even worse, group caused Fry's envoy 'some feelings of nervous timidity' and, indeed, on entering their quarters, she found 300 female convicts 'of desperate and most degraded characters'. They all looked 'fearfully depraved'. Some were lying on the ground, 'apparently in a state of intoxication; some sleeping, others quarrelling or swearing'. Almost immediately, a throng of women gathered round Anley, some with an air of defiance, as if expecting some unwelcome reproach but this soon passed away, as I called those especially to come forward who had been in Newgate prison previously to their transportation – as to such I was the bearer of a message. I then explained to them that I was a stranger just arrived from England and stood there as their friend, deeply concerned to see so many fellow-creatures of my own sex thus abandoned and punished.[20]

She spoke of Mrs Fry's 'unremitting zeal on behalf of prisoners; her anxious prayers, her unwearied exertions to benefit and reform them', and

> I appealed to them all, whether she deserved to be forgotten, or her counsels so disregarded, as to have one of those for whom she had laboured, in that class of infamy and disgrace.

At first there was dead silence, broken only by some 'heart-drawn sighs', until slowly some of the women gathered closer and

> entreated me to listen while they told of wrongs which no-one heeded or seemed to care for; that in service they were treated 'like dogs', and seldom spoken to without an oath, or 'as devils' rather than human beings.
>
> I heard these complaints without contradiction as, of course, I had no means of judging as to their truth; but I endeavoured to soften their feelings . . . [asking them] to examine their own souls, and seek for pardon and repentance, leaving it to God to visit others for injustice, cruelty and unkindness, rather than add to their own guilt by revenge and imitation.[21]

The women asked that Anley visit them the next day to read the Bible to them for an hour and, to her great surprise, several of them curtsied to her as she left, 'a mark of respect which I found very rare in the colony'.

The next day, she read them the parable of the prodigal son and promised them that, if they repented, God would not turn them away unpardoned. Again, 'no sound was heard but that of sobbing'. Anxious to make the most of their softened feelings, she spoke to them of their early days of childhood innocence and asked 'whether any one of those sins, which had brought them to exile and sorrow, had ever made them really happy, even for one moment?'[22]

As she prepared to leave, Anley assured the women of her continued interest and prayers and promised she would never visit the area without coming to see them if at all possible, 'although I cordially hoped to find few present in that class again'.

> I cannot describe the touching scene which followed this farewell exhortation. Some took hold of my cloak and kissed it; many were sobbing bitterly; others had fallen on their knees, and were rocking themselves as if in an agony of sorrow. I could not but deeply pity them . . . and feel that they deserved encouragement.[23]

Anley returned home, 'but my heart was too full of sorrow for those whom I had just left, immediately to regain cheerful feelings'. She went to bed, 'chastened by the scenes of human misery I had witnessed . . . and humbled'. She recalled that, although confined for two hours with 300 'women of the most abandoned characters', she had heard not one word which could offend 'the most refined or delicate mind', although she stood alone 'with no defence against insult but that which the Bible afforded me.' As for the women being allegedly so bad that nothing could be done for them, that fact alone 'should be the strongest appeal to every Christian mind to [find an] immediate remedy . . . with all the force and energy which human efforts can command', and called for the establishment of a ladies' visiting society at Parramatta.

On her return to Britain, Anley recorded her experiences in *Prisoners of Australia*, which was published in 1841. That same year, another group of 180 female prisoners was setting off to Van Diemen's Land on the *Rajah*, with another Fry protégée on board as the matron. Mastered by a young Scot, Captain Charles Ferguson, the ship left Woolwich dock on 5 April and landed on 19 July at Hobart, from where the women were sent on to the female factory at Cascades. The matron on the ship was Kezia Hayter, cousin of the famous miniaturist, Sir George Hayter. Hayter, aged just 23, had been a prison officer at the Millbank Penitentiary when she was seconded, at Fry's request, to travel out to Australia to help the wife of the Lieutenant-Governor of Van Diemen's Land, Sir John Franklin, to establish the island colony's own Ladies' Society for the Reformation of Female Prisoners; she would also be reporting back to Fry on the conditions at the female factory at Cascades, as Charlotte Anley had done for Parramatta.[24]

During the voyage out, Hayter supervised the creation of a quilt, using the materials that Fry and her associates donated to every woman convict. The completed quilt was presented to Lady Franklin 'as tangible evidence of the cooperative work that could be achieved under such circumstances'.[25] It is the quilt that makes the *Rajah* voyage special, because it has survived and can be attributed. Similar convict quilts may also have withstood the ravages of time but are lost. On the *Rajah* quilt, however, the women embroidered a dedication to Fry's endeavours:

> To the ladies of the convict ship committee, this quilt worked by the convicts of the ship Rajah during their voyage to van Dieman's [sic] Land, is presented as a testimony of the gratitude with which they remember their exertions for their welfare while in England and during their passage and also as a proof that they have not neglected the ladies kind admonitions of being industrious.

The patchwork quilt measures over ten feet square and is made up of 2,815 pieces, using the pieced-medallion style of the time. A central panel of embroidered and appliquéd birds and flowers in chintz is surrounded by borders of printed cloth, appliquéd flowers and flower shapes. The cross-stitch dedication is finely worked in silk thread. It is not known how many women worked on the quilt. Fifteen women on the ship gave their occupations as tailoring or needlework but there was a considerable variation in the skills of the participants, and about twice as many probably participated. There are small blood stains on the quilt, 'probably from the pierced fingers of the less skilled workers'.[26]

Although Lady Franklin expressed admiration for Fry's work, she opposed from the start the foundation of a local ladies' committee for prisoner reform, believing it would do more harm than good in the colony. An authoritarian, overbearing character in comparison with her liberal and enlightened husband, she may have resented the thought of any women except herself having public influence.[27] A Tasmanian Ladies' Society was formed anyway, with Hayter as secretary, but it was short lived and collapsed under the weight of public animosity and press hostility, by which time Hayter had already resigned. Sir John, who despite enjoying public popularity was unequal to the task of managing the divisive politics of a convict settlement as it evolved into a colony, was removed from office in 1843 and recalled to London. He resumed his earlier Arctic expeditionary activities, embarking on his last voyage in 1843, during which he and all his crew were lost.

Hayter stayed on to enjoy her own adventure. Managing the quilt project had not been her only success on the *Rajah*. Within months of arriving in Hobart, she had become engaged to young Captain Ferguson. Resigning from prison work, she became a teacher while he fulfilled his sailing commitments and they married in July 1843. She spent several years sailing around the world with him – and a son and a daughter – before they made their permanent home in Australia, where Ferguson would become the first chief harbour master of the Port of Melbourne.

By this time, conditions on the convict ships had changed out of all recognition since the early years. Eliza Grindrod, who sailed out to Van Diemen's Land on the *Garland Grove*, wrote to Fry from Hobart Town in March 1843 with a description of the voyage out, during which all the children 'old enough to be taught their letters were able to read very nicely' by the end of the journey. Ten of the 15 totally illiterate women on board were taught to read and write, and others had their literacy skills improved. Grindrod found 'a rich reward in thus blessing our feeble and imperfect efforts'. Listening to the women sing an evening hymn from their berths, she was deeply affected, asking herself:

> Who hath made thee to differ from these? My resolution to benefit them has been strengthened; a lesson of humility and a spirit of thankfulness have been imparted [to me] in a manner I never before felt . . . Numbers of these poor exiles are endeared to me; their affectionate gratitude I shall ever remember . . . When [we] landed in Hobart Town, the separation was a trial to my feelings which I had little anticipated. The four months spent with those poor outcasts, endeavouring to benefit them, will ever be numbered amongst the happiest of my life.[28]

In 1845, the year of Fry's death, the convict ship *Sir George Seymour* set sail for Australia. It was a model of its kind. The ship had its own weekly newspaper and the more intelligent convicts were encouraged to give talks on subjects that interested them; these included music, history, astronomy, poetry, architecture, and the circulation of the blood. Regular classes in reading, writing and arithmetic left transportees with new or improved skills to prepare them for a new life. All possible means were used 'to excite and keep up a healthy, vigorous tone of mind amongst the convicts, and with the most pleasing results'. The ship's surgeon-superintendent John Hampton, who had been involved with transportation for many years, and who went on to be the governor of Western Australia, declared that he had 'never met with anything to equal the uniform orderly conduct of the prisoners on board'.[29]

When transportation from Britain finally came to an end, which it did in various colonies of the Australian continent at different times up to 1868, it was because of a number of factors. The cost was becoming prohibitive, particularly once the government realized it could make good use of forced convict labour at home. There was the extensive new prison-building programme which began with the construction of London's Pentonville in 1842, and saw over 50 more gaols built in the next six years alone; there were therefore many more cells to accommodate criminals, given the custodial sentences that replaced transportation with the introduction of the Penal Servitude Act of 1853. There was also the resistance of respectable second- and third-generation citizens in Australia to having the colony seen, and used, as a dumping-ground for undesirables from Britain. And not least, there was a growing supply of voluntary settlers, particularly after the discovery of gold in New South Wales in 1853 – a fact which caused considerable unrest in some prisons when convicts realized they would not, after all, be transported free of charge to the land of promise.

7

Celebrity and crash

With the publication in 1818 of the Select Committee report on London prisons, news of Fry's pioneering work with the Newgate women spread beyond the capital, into the country and overseas. Almost overnight she became a celebrity. During a debate on theft in the House of Commons, William Wilberforce followed Samuel Romilly when he stated:

> The Honourable Member here has alluded to the very great success which a benevolent and truly humane lady, Mrs Fry, had exerted herself in reforming the numerous class of female prisoners, who have been from time to time in Newgate. Such an example shown by a lady ought to be a stimulus to all in whose power it [is] to exert themselves in so benevolent and public an object as that of improving the morals of the lower classes, and of reclaiming those who were but partially acquainted with crime. What [has] been done by a single individual [is] an indication of what their united efforts might achieve.[1]

Fry began to build up an impressive network of international contacts with like-minded prison reform campaigners, and a visit to her Friday Bible reading sessions at Newgate became an important – almost fashionable – item on the social agenda of the great, the good and the merely curious. Fry was deeply ambivalent about this; but while the prison reform issue was still in its infancy, public interest had to be encouraged, by whatever means. She wrote in her diary on 28 October:

> Entering my public life again is a very serious thing to me, more particularly my readings at Newgate. They are, to my feelings, too much like making a show of a good thing.

However, so many hearts had already been won over to the cause, 'that I believe I must not be hasty in preventing them, or hindering people coming to them'.

One of those who attended a Friday reading was Melesina Trench, grand-daughter of the Bishop of Waterford, who described the experience in a letter to her son.

I went yesterday to Newgate, to see Mrs Fry's performance. I by no means wish to underrate her merits by the phrase . . . [A maidservant] led us up two narrow and steep flights of stairs to a small, homely room, in the middle of which . . . Mrs Fry sat at a table with books and papers before her. The female convicts, I suppose about sixty in number, faced her on rows of benches, raised as in the gallery of a theatre. Opposite to these were two or three rows for the visitors, and a single row on each side, all as full as possible.

The smell was oppressive, and the heat unpleasant, but this was instantly forgotten in the interest of the scene. The convicts first drew my attention. They were of decent appearance and deportment, habited like the lowest class of servants. They were singularly plain . . . Among the visitors I saw a few of my acquaintances, and some persons of note.

Mrs Fry read a lesson, adding some simple explanations of the Scripture. There were prayers and a psalm, after which the convicts left. There was a collection, and then Mrs Fry offered to show us the jail. I went part of the way; but as we seemed to walk through narrow, dark and winding passages cut out of the cold rock, my courage failed. Thought dwelt intensively on those that went in that way, never to return but to death and banishment, and I felt that I was exposing myself perhaps to illness, when uncalled on by any duty. I prevailed on a good, kind Quaker friend to be my Orpheus [out of the underworld], and was very glad to see the light of day once more.

It was a fine lesson in humility and gratitude. The doubt whether in similar circumstances one might not have been more guilty than the worst of these women; the reflection how deeply they might have been assailed by the temptations of want, added to every other infirmity of our nature; and how bitterly they might expiate in this world the offences of which they had repented, all pressed on the mind at once.[2]

'A fine lesson in humility and gratitude' was probably exactly what Fry hoped to achieve with her audience. Visitors might come, for whatever motive, to observe her protégées in the sanitized environment of morning worship; but invite them behind the scenes to see the real horror of life in Newgate, and their spirits failed them.

Liberal writer and clergyman Sydney Smith recalled his own impression of a visit to see Fry in action at Newgate.

There is a spectacle which this town exhibits, that I will venture to call the most solemn, the most Christian, the most affecting which any human being ever witnessed. To see that holy woman in the midst of the wretched prisoners, to see them all calling earnestly upon God, soothed by her voice, animated by her look, clinging to the hem of her garment, and worshipping her as the only being who has ever loved them, or taught them, or noticed them, or spoken to them of God! This is the sight which breaks down the pageant of the world, which tells us that the short hour of life is passing away, and that we must prepare by some good deeds to meet God; that it is time to give, to pray, to comfort, to go – like this blessed woman – and do the work of our heavenly Saviour, Jesus, among the guilty, among the broken-hearted and the sick, and to labour in the deepest and darkest wretchedness of life.[3]

Yet while applauding her compassion, not everyone approved of Fry's methods of reform, including Smith himself. Despite his radical leanings – he was anti-slavery, in favour of the education of women and supported Catholic emancipation – Smith was opposed to the idea of introducing meaningful activity and productive work in prisons, as an inadequate deterrent to crime.

We would banish all the looms . . . and substitute nothing but the tread-wheel or the capstan, or some species of labour where the prisoner could not see the result of his toil – where it was as monotonous, irksome and dull as possible – pulling and pushing, instead of reading and writing – no share of the profits – not a single shilling. There should be no tea and sugar – no assemblage of female felons round the washtub – nothing but beating hemp and pulling oakum, and pounding bricks – no work but what was tedious, unusual and unfeminine . . . Mrs Fry is an amiable excellent woman . . . but hers is not the method to stop crimes. In prisons . . . there must be a great deal of solitude; coarse food; a dress of shame; hard, incessant, irksome, eternal labour; a planned and regulated and unrelenting exclusion of happiness and comfort.[4]

Hannah More, the writer, philanthropist, abolitionist and renowned 'bluestocking', remarked in a letter to friends that Fry could not have dared to embark on her prison reform work, had she not had the advantage of being a Quaker minister, which had taken away her 'fear of men'.

Her exertions have struck me forcibly as proof of how the Almighty chooses his instruments – such, perhaps, as our short-sighted wisdom would not have selected. None but a woman, and none but a Quaker woman *could* have ventured, or if venturing could have succeeded. Their habits of public speaking have taken away that fear of men which would have intimidated one of *us*, even if we had more zeal and piety than are commonly found amongst us; besides which, they are aided by their practical conviction that the spirit instantaneously suggests what they shall say. Again, had you or I, or any churchwoman, possessed the heroic piety of Mrs Fry, what a cry would have been raised against us; 'enthusiastic and fanatic' would have been the human award of our endeavours. Not all the sobriety of mind and judgment which this good woman has shown, would have been of any avail in *our* case. So you see how God fits the instrument to the work![5]

Charles Dickens glimpsed Fry one day in Newgate and declared in *Sketches by Boz* that he had 'a great respect for her'; but his friend George Chesterton, the governor of Cold Bath Fields prison (the Middlesex house of correction), refused to allow her access to his prisoners because his board of directors objected to her on religious grounds. Fry and her work even had a walk-on part in Lord Byron's epic satire, *Don Juan*, where he wrote that the country's corrupt leaders were more in need of reform than her prisoners.

Oh Mrs Fry! Why go to Newgate? Why
Preach to poor rogues? And wherefore not begin
With Carlton, or with other houses? Try
Your hand at hardened and imperial sin.
To mend the People's an absurdity,
A jargon, a mere philanthropic din,
Unless you make their betters better: Fie!
I thought you had more religion, Mrs Fry.[6]

In May 1818, Fry was invited to be presented to Queen Charlotte at a Mansion House event. It was a memorable meeting: the diminutive queen 'covered with diamonds but her countenance lighted up with an expression of the kindest benevolence'; and Fry, her simple Quaker dress adding to her height, looking slightly flushed but wearing her 'wonted calmness of look and manner'. Several bishops stood nearby, the platform was 'crowded with waving feathers, jewels and orders', the hall lined with spectators. And then a remarkable thing happened.

A murmur of applause ran through the assembly, followed by a simultaneous clap, and a shout, which was taken up by the multitude without, and died away in the distance.

They hailed the scene before them; they saw in it not so much the Queen and the
Philanthropist, as royalty offering its approval at the shrine of mercy and good works.

It had been the best and worst of days for Fry. Earlier she had called on
Home Secretary Lord Sidmouth in a final attempt to win a reprieve for Newgate
prisoner Harriet Skelton, convicted of forgery. Fry had persuaded Skelton to
plead innocent; as a result of which, being found guilty, she was condemned
to death rather than transportation. Fry had tried all avenues, even persuading
the Duke of Gloucester – her old dancing-partner prince from the Earlham
days – to making representations to the bank involved. After a heated argument
with Lord Sidmouth, she had failed to secure Skelton's life. The law took its
course, and Skelton was hanged. These two significant events on the day she met
the Queen could not have been more different. The one, an abject failure, her
interference having unwittingly cost a woman's life; the other, the highest social
accolade she could have hoped for.

Gratifying though her Newgate success was, it also brought home to Fry that,
in the absence of a central prisons inspectorate, little information had been
gathered about the conditions in prisons outside London since John Howard's
tours of inspection decades earlier. An amateur like herself was becoming the
expert. She became increasingly aware that what she had achieved for women
in the London prison was only a small part of a bigger picture. In August
1818, determined to cast the net wider, she set off for Scotland and the north
of England with her brother Joseph Gurney, his second wife Mary, and Fry's
second daughter Rachel, aged 15. Both Fry and Gurney had been granted
certificates by the Society of Friends to 'travel in the ministry'. There would be
Quaker meetings, and public Meetings with a religious theme. There would also
be the opportunity to visit and report on prisons and other institutions; to set
up ladies' visiting committees for women prisoners; and to build on what was
already becoming an impressive network of useful contacts for the benefit of
prison reform.

Departing for Scotland, Fry left behind eight other children aged between
two and 17 years. Her eldest daughter Katherine and the three youngest children were lodged at Earlham, now the residence of her brother Joseph after
John's death. Katherine was being obliged to take on that same role of *mater-
familias* that, a generation earlier, fell to Fry's sister Katherine on the death of
their mother. Two more young children were staying with other relatives; two
boys were away at boarding school.

Within the week Fry was suffering from homesickness. In Aberdeen, she wrote in her diary: 'I have felt low upon arriving here, five hundred miles from my beloved husband and children'. She questioned what she was doing there, 'but as my coming is not my own choice or my own ordering, I desire . . . to commit myself . . . and all that is dear to me, absent and present, to Christ my redeemer'.

At first their activities were mainly related to Quaker business, and met with varied success. Fry found that she was lacking the necessary spirit at Meeting, and relied much on Joseph to retrieve the situation at the Aberdeen and Kilmuck sessions. By the middle of September, the party had reached Edinburgh, where Fry, exhausted, was relieved to find that they were well through their travel programme.

> Our journey through life is a little like a common journey. We may, after a day's travel-
> ling, lie down and rest, but we have at the morrow to set off again upon our travels. So
> I find my journey in life. I am not infrequently permitted to come for a short time to a
> sweet, quiet resting place; but I find that I soon have to set forth again.

In Edinburgh, there was the first opportunity to visit some prisons. There was also a public meeting which caused Fry a great deal of alarm. 'People flocked much after us. Our being there was mentioned in the newspapers, which accounted for this; but it was to my own feelings a low time.' The following day they left for Glasgow, where there was a Bridewell and a prison to inspect. There were also two meetings – one for Friends, and one for the public which, while successful, left Fry feeling 'awful'. Although she wrote little of her personal experience of the Glasgow prison visits, a detailed account of her effect on prospective volunteers and female prisoners was recorded by a relative, Anna Gurney.

Of Fry's appearance at the Glasgow Bridewell, Anna Gurney declared she had 'never felt anything before so like enchantment or inspiration'. Fry cast a 'charm above the fairy's spell or poet's dream'. With her in the prison, 'difficulties seemed to melt away like the dew before the sun'.

> She is about forty, tall, sedate with a physiognomy gentle yet very observing, at first
> not giving or calling for much sympathy . . . Mrs Fry's manner and voice are delightful
> and her communication free and unembarrassed. She met by appointment several
> of the Magistrates . . . and a number of Ladies at the Bridewell. She told them, with

much simplicity, what had been done at Newgate, and proposed something similar, if it should be found practicable, at Glasgow. She entered into very pleasant conversation with everyone; all were delighted when she offered 'to speak a little to the poor women'.[7]

The keeper of the Bridewell objected on the grounds that he feared it was a dangerous experiment; for the women never, but by compulsion, listened to reading, and were generally disposed to laugh and turn everything to ridicule. Fry replied that, although she agreed this might happen, she thought a reading might give pleasure to some, and would serve to show the ladies what she meant. So about a hundred women were assembled in one large room, and Fry's party entered with some hesitation. Once inside, Fry:

> took off her bonnet and sat down on a large seat fronting the women; and looking round with a kind of conciliating aspect, but with an eye that met every eye there, she said: 'I had better tell you what we are come about'.

She told them that she had worked with a great many poor women, sadly wicked, more wicked than any there present, and that now they had recovered from evil. She asked them if they would like the opportunity to do the same, with the help of lady visitors.

> Would you like to turn from that which is wrong? Would you like it if Ladies would visit you and speak comfort to you, and help you to be better? You would tell them your grief, for they who have done wrong have many sorrows.

As she read the women prisoners the rules that had been introduced at Newgate, she asked them at each stage to put their hands up if they approved. At first the hands stayed down, but after a while, as Anna Gurney recalls, as she spoke, 'tears began to flow'.

> One very beautiful girl near me had her eyes swimming with tears. The hands were now almost all ready to rise at every pause, and these callous and obstinate offenders were with one consent bowed before her.

At this moment, Fry took the Bible and began to read the parables of the lost sheep, and of the prodigal son.

It is not in my power to describe to you the effect of her saintly voice in speaking such blessed words. She often paused and looked at the poor women (as she named them) with such sweetness as won all their confidence.

After the reading, Fry knelt down before the women and her prayer was 'soothing and elevating, and her musical voice in the recitative style of the Quakers, felt like a mother's song to a suffering child'.

The Scottish journey was coming to an end. By October, Fry was back home at Plashet, nursing a seriously ill daughter and a convalescent husband. But her prison work continued to flourish. 'Surely in that a blessing appears to attend me', she wrote, 'more, apparently, than in some of my home duties'.

Among the gaols they had visited in Scotland and the north of England, Durham Old Gaol and House of Correction, and the gaols at Haddington, Aberdeen and Glasgow were 'of the worst possible description . . . a misery'. The Aberdeen Bridewell and the House of Correction at Preston, by comparison, were approaching what was then considered a standard of excellence. The following year, 1819, Joseph Gurney compiled the notes of their visit, with an individual report on each establishment, outlining the best and worst practices they had encountered. It was published as *Notes on a Visit Made to Some of the Prisons in Scotland and the North of England, in Company with Elizabeth Fry*.

The two of them had visited almost 40 gaols in as many days, and sometimes three in a day. Practices in the worst, which predominated, included: the confinement of lunatics in prisons, filthy conditions, the use of 'black hole' cells, prisoners being kept in irons, gaolers living off the premises, and an almost total absence of care. The report, not surprisingly, received a mixed reception, particularly from those who felt themselves criticized. Gurney remained unperturbed.

I think it right to communicate to the public the information which we collected, in the hope that it may afford some fresh stimulus, to the zeal already prevalent for improving our system of prison discipline.

It appears the more desirable to take this step, because incorrect statements respecting some of these prisons have found their way, in connexion with our visit, into the provincial newspapers; and it is evidently a matter of importance that the public should be made acquainted with the *real* condition of these places of confinement.

The better the actual state of our prisons is known and understood, the more clearly will all men see the necessity of those arrangements, by which they may be rendered schools of industry and virtue, instead of the very nurseries of crime. Prisons . . . in which the prisoners are classified, inspected, instructed and employed, have a powerful tendency to that by which crime and misery will certainly be lessened, viz. the reformation of criminals.[8]

In 1819, Fry suffered one of her periodic bouts of nervous exhaustion and a family party went to Brighton so that she could recuperate. While she was there, she received a letter from some Newgate women apologizing for a disturbance they had caused at the prison during her absence. She wrote back a letter full of forgiveness, but reminding them what damage such behaviour could inflict on the cause of prison reform. She begged them,

> whatever trying or even provoking things may happen, to do so no more, for you sadly hurt the cause of poor prisoners by doing so . . . as you thus enable your enemies to say, that our plans of kindness do not answer, and therefore they will not let others be treated kindly.[9]

She hoped to be back among them before long, she added; and she asked them in the meantime to guard against the two temptations that had brought most of them to prison: 'The one is giving way to drink too much, the other is freedom with men. I find I can most frequently trace the fall of women to these two things.'

Back in London, the cycle of life and death and celebrity rolled on. In 1821, Fry's sister Priscilla died; in early 1822, Fry was pregnant again at nearly 42. In May that year, the Prince and Princess Royal of Denmark were visiting England, inspecting public institutions and charities established for the 'moral and religious welfare of the people'. Fry was introduced to the royal couple by the Duchess of Gloucester. A few days later, the Princess invited herself to Plashet for breakfast, stayed several hours, and began a friendship that lasted the rest of their lives.

In November, Fry's family was complete when her son Daniel, her eleventh child, was born on the same day that her eldest child Rachel produced the first Fry grandchild. Six weeks later, Fry was back at Newgate. There had also been a political disappointment that year, when a motion to reduce the number of offences punishable by death, proposed by Sir James Mackintosh and supported by Sir Samuel Romilly, was defeated by a small majority in the House of Commons. But the fight to minimize the application of the death penalty continued.

During the early 1820s, Fry was 'a good deal occupied by temporal things'. There was charitable work within the parishes around Plashet, the ongoing Newgate project, and the establishment of more District Visiting Societies – a project that began with the one at Brighton – through which the deserving poor were encouraged in habits of thrift, faith and sobriety. Fry's work left her little time to record her thoughts. Her fame at home and abroad continued unabated; but, in a diary entry for 5 November 1820, she wrote that she did not feel 'exalted by the approbation of men, though being greatly cast down by their disapprobation leads me to think I still like it!' Several of her children continued to live with aunts and uncles, or were away at school, and she confessed that, although she loved them all, 'I do not have that patience and forbearance that I ought to have, and I think I am too easily provoked – not sufficiently long-suffering with their faults'. She was finding the Newgate readings particularly taxing: 'so many attend, and often such a variety; and some of such high rank, I should think so little accustomed to hearing the truth spoken'.

In August 1822, she had been married for 22 years.

I have known much of good health and real sickness; great bodily suffering, particularly during my confinements, and deep depression of spirits. I have known the ease of abundance of riches, and the sorrow and perplexity of relative deprivations. I have known to the full, I think, the enjoyment of domestic life . . . and also some of its most sorrowful and most painful reverses.

There were more reverses on the way as the country slipped back into recession. In 1825, a second crisis hit the Fry family, which was again averted by the intervention of the Gurney brothers. But this time even they were worried about the panic in the financial and commercial markets and the sudden run on the banks in London and the country. Joseph Gurney wrote in his diary on 10 July 1826:

Business has been productive of trial to me, and has led me to reflect on the equity of God, who measures out his salutary chastisements, even in this world, to the rich as well as to the poor. I can certainly testify that some of the greatest pains and most burdensome cares which I have had to endure, have arisen out of being what is usually called 'a monied man'.[10]

Of Samuel Gurney, it was said at this time that his 'clear, sound judgment . . . can scarcely be too highly commended or gratefully estimated'. His continuing to lend money to other banks during the crisis 'saved hundreds from utter ruin, and promoted, in no common degree, the safety and interests of the banking and commercial world'. And yet there were times – 'when the money market was disturbed and failures impended' – when even the usually calm Sam Gurney experienced 'intense anxiety, knowing intimately as he did the sufferings which awaited those who could no longer command credit or obtain supplies from other quarters'.[11]

That same summer of 1826, Fry paid a visit to the influential philanthropist, educationalist and religious writer, Hannah More at her home at Barley Wood. The two had met briefly in 1823, when Fry visited Somerset to attend Quaker Meetings and visit a prison in Bristol; and Fry was keen to renew their acquaintance. More, nearly 80 years age by then, was equally excited at the prospect of meeting 'Mrs Newgate Fry' properly at last.

The women were delighted with each other. 'We were ready to eat one another up', More wrote. 'She is indeed delightful. At parting, she knelt down and put up a feeling prayer for unworthy me.' Joseph Gurney was equally impressed, calling More an 'extraordinary and excellent person . . . most vivacious and productive . . . very like Wilberforce'.[12] As they left, More gave Fry a copy of her book, *Practical Piety*, in which she wrote:

> Presented to Elizabeth Fry by Hannah More, as a token of veneration of her heroic zeal, Christian charity, and persevering kindness, to the most forlorn of human beings. They were naked and she clothed them; in prison and she visited them; ignorant and she taught them; for *His* sake, in *His* name, and by *His* word, who went about doing good.

Meanwhile, financial problems with the Fry family businesses were refusing to go away. Fry's response to such a situation was, as ever, to throw herself into even more good works; and in February 1827, she and Joseph embarked on a three-month trip to Ireland. Gurney described their programme as

> paying a general visit to Friends, holding many public meetings, inspecting prisons, communicating with persons in authority as required, and mingling with members of various denominations in the pursuit of works of benevolence, Roman Catholics at times as well as Protestants. When not engaged in ministerial labours, it was very much my office to help my beloved sister in her comprehensive design for the benefit of her fellow men.[13]

In Dublin they paid a courtesy call on the Viceroy, and visited an institution for the deaf and dumb, and a mental asylum, both run by Quakers. They inspected four prisons, 'two of them very bad, particularly the Dublin Newgate: an awful scene of multitudinous wickedness and misery', Gurney wrote. He was appalled by the 'vast crowds of criminals without occupation, without instruction, without any provided clothing, and therefore half-naked, herded together in great dens'. He found the Irish capital a place of great contrasts.

> There is prevalent in Dublin great zeal, and a great love of truth; but there is wanted more of the garment of universal charity, and more of the ornament of a meek and quiet spirit. Yet there is a blessed work going on, which is far more conspicuous in the upper classes of society there, than in any part of England with which I am acquainted.

Quaker Meetings they attended were 'flocked ... and our dear sister's ministry was, as usual, very touching. I think it has produced a very considerable impression, her way having been remarkably made to the hearts of the people.' Their programme of prison inspections included Kilmainham – a county gaol, several debtors' prisons, and then the imposing Richmond Bridewell. This was

> a great prison, where we were met by several gentlemen, including the Inspectors General of the prisons of Ireland, and I suppose nearly one hundred ladies, many of them of consideration and station. The object of the meeting was to organise a Ladies' Association for visiting prisons; our dear sister was, of course, in the chair, and I sat by as her secretary; the Inspectors General on the other side. She managed the whole affair with great ability. The association was formed, with large Visiting Committees appointed for the four principal prisons. We had afterwards to examine the prison itself. We returned home, dear Elizabeth much fagged.

There followed tours of the 'wonderful ... finely managed' Dublin House of Industry, 'a vast receptacle of aged, infirm, lunatic, and idiot paupers', the Richmond Lunatic Asylum and the Richmond General Penitentiary. Alongside the religious Meetings, and the relentless networking with people of influence, it was a punishing schedule. When the time came to leave, both brother and sister were quietly relieved. Gurney wrote that he felt 'it would have been unsafe to have continued longer in that city; for our dear sister's strength would probably have failed under the impetuous attentions of the throng multitude'. They had faced meetings of up to 1,500 people, with hundreds more turned away;

there were crowds following them everywhere they went. There was frequent overt hostility from some parts of the Roman Catholic Church; there was often, in short, a sense of menace.

From Dublin, their progress through Ireland took in 'wretched' Christiantown, Edenderry, and Trim in County Meath, where they found the prison one of the worst in Ireland and noted with dismay the 'wretched earthen huts on the sides of the road, the inhabitants of which appeared to be but little elevated above the conditions of the heathen world . . . nothing can well exceed the filth in the midst of which they live'.[14] From Trim they travelled to Kells, and thence to Ballborough, Cootehill, Lisburn, Armagh, Lurgan and Belfast. In Belfast, 'the Liverpool of Ireland', they arrived for an overcrowded public meeting on the top floor of a school house, from which people were being turned away in hundreds. 'We were put to difficulty to get into the room', Gurney wrote. 'The crowd was very overpowering to our dear sister, and I was afraid she would have fainted.' The audience was estimated at about a thousand, which paled into insignificance at their next major meeting, at Londonderry, where the crowd was believed to be around double that of Belfast.

Despite the enthusiasm of the Irish population at large, they repeatedly came up against considerable resistance from the Roman Catholic Church. The tracts that Fry and Gurney distributed were eagerly and gratefully taken by local people, but deplored by 'papist' priests, as Gurney reported.

Sometimes [the people] were afraid to receive them. I happened to give a poor man [one] just as a priest was riding towards him. The man immediately delivered his treasure to the priest who, with an expression of peculiar bitterness, tore it in half and threw it into a ditch. A sly little boy, however, ran off with the fragments.

The thirst for information which prevails in the parts of Ireland where we have lately been is most remarkable. I believe that the system of the papal priesthood begins to be shaken to its centre; and we have seen enough to convince us that the sooner it falls, the better; for it is an iron yoke.[15]

The Roman Catholic priesthood also hindered Fry and Gurney's prison work. At Carlow, Bible readings in prison were only permitted after lengthy negotiation with the local bishop, and then only under severe restrictions, with the local Roman Catholic priest both choosing and reading the passages. This was much to the annoyance of Gurney who wrote that it was unquestionable 'that Popery presents an effective bar to free and fair religious instruction. There is a perpetual fight going on between the tyranny of their system, and the desire for knowledge which is everywhere arising.'

From Coleraine, a centre of Quakerism in Ireland, the journey took them onwards to Sligo, Boyle and Roscommon, where they visited the infirmary, gaol and lunatic asylum, 'the last a horrid place indeed', as Gurney observed.

> Some of the scenes we have late witnessed in public institutions have been most dis-tressing; vice and misery in abundance. Nobody can tell what this country is, without visiting it; but long must be our visit, were it required of us to obtain a full knowledge of the Irish character.

Next came Mountmellick, Roscrea, Birr and Ballnasloe. Wherever they went, Fry was mobbed; and, as they reached Waterford, and the refuge of friends, her health began to break down 'under the effects of over-exertion and fatigue'. It was to become a familiar pattern during the next 15 years of her British and Continental campaigns. Gurney wrote: 'We spent a very anxious week at Waterford, our invalid requiring the closest watching and attention. The attacks of fever were certainly violent, and we could not tell what might become of it, as a dangerous fever was very prevalent in the place.'[16] Fry felt herself 'completely sinking, hardly able to hold up my head'. By degrees, she became seriously ill.

> Fever came on and ran very high, and I found myself in one of my distressing, faint states, indeed a few hours were most conflicting, I never remember to have known a more painful time; tried without, tested within, feeling such fears lest it should try the faith of others my being thus stopped by illness, and lest my own faith should fail. My pain too in being from home was great.

Fry, as ever, rallied after a few days' rest; and although she was still weak, she was well enough to set off for Clonmel. On the way, they remarked that 'the contrast between the extreme fertility of the land, and the wretchedness of the inhabitants, which we never observed more striking at Carrick on Suir, is melancholy and almost unaccountable'. Gurney (who some years later would publish a temperance leaflet entitled 'Water is best') attributed this to the 'whiskey shops, which abound on every side. Alas! What a work the Prince of darkness has wrought in this land.'

From Carlow, where the Roman Catholic priesthood caused difficulty for Fry and Gurney as they went about their prison work, it was onwards to Ballitore,

Elizabeth Fry and friend Mary Sanderson entering Newgate women's prison (after a painting by Henrietta Ward).

Female prisoners at Newgate, from Knapp and Baldwin's *Newgate Calendar*.

Elizabeth Fry, an engraving by Cochrane from an 1823 painting by C. R. Leslie, when Fry was 43.

Joseph Fry, Elizabeth's husband, by C. R. Leslie.

Samuel Gurney, Elizabeth's brother (artist unknown).

Joseph John Gurney, Elizabeth's brother, from a watercolour by George Richmond.

The *Rajah* quilt, sewn by Newgate women convicts travelling on the ship of that name from England to Van Diemen's Land (Tasmania) in 1841. The women embroidered on the quilt a dedication of thanks to Fry's convict committee who provided the materials.

Statue of Fry in the Grand Hall of the Central Criminal Court at the Old Bailey in London, the original site of Newgate prison.

another centre of Quakerism in Ireland and home to a Quaker international school. Arriving in the evening they found a completely unexpected crowd awaiting them, which made Gurney worry for his sister's fragile health: 'I was frightened for our weary invalid; but there was no alternative, and she was wonderfully carried over the difficulty, being enabled to minister . . . with great effect.'

The Irish tour was drawing to a close. Back in Dublin, they paid a final call on the Viceroy, in whom they found a kindred spirit regarding the need to reduce the use of capital punishment. Wellesley requested that Fry and Gurney compile a personal account for him 'on every subject which we may deem worthy of notice in connexion with the state of Ireland'. The last stopping-point before sailing home was a public meeting at Wexford, as Gurney wrote home,

> and truly it was an evening of overpowering exertion. Crowds were waiting for us at the jail, at the entry of the town. It was in vain to attempt to pass by it, though a public meeting was appointed for seven o'clock. We visited [the prison], and my sister formed her committee. When we went to the appointed place of meeting in the evening – a large assembly room on an upper floor – we found it fearfully crowded and almost insufferably close. Dear Elizabeth seemed much overcome, and what with this, and with the ticklish state of the people, the noise of a hooting boy-mob under the windows, and the idea that the floor might possibly or probably give way, it was a time of some real conflict of mind to us.
>
> You can hardly imagine how really appalling some of our public meetings have been in this land . . . this place is one of the strongholds of popery, and it was in vain that we proposed to the Romish priesthood, our conciliatory plans for the reading of scriptures in jail. They set their faces against it, under every modification. How long will such a bondage be maintained?[17]

Two days later, the party took the boat home from Dunmore. It was early May. By the autumn, Gurney had completed, on behalf of Fry and himself, an account of the state of Ireland for the Viceroy. It covered prisons, lunatic asylums, houses of industry, charitable associations, infirmaries, and the general condition of the people. Unsurprisingly, it was not popular with the management of those institutions he criticized, but Gurney, as ever, was unconcerned, since the end proved to have justified the means. In many cases the result of their report was a pronounced change for the better, even when prison managers claimed they had been about to make such changes in any case.

An Association for the Improvement of Prisons and Prison Discipline had been formed in Dublin in 1818. By 1821, there was also an Association for Bettering the Condition of Female Prisoners in Dublin, inspired by Fry's Newgate group of lady visitors; it, in turn, stimulated the establishment of similar associations in the counties. In their survey, entitled 'Report addressed to the Marquess Wellesley, Lord Lieutenant of Ireland by E. F. and J. J. G. respecting their late visit to that country', Fry and Gurney observed that, regarding the condition of women prisoners, where ladies' visiting committees existed, they had achieved

an extensive improvement among the female inmates in Ireland. It was most striking to us, in visiting jails, to observe the contrast between the state of the prisoners visited by Ladies, and that of those who enjoyed no such privilege. The order, decency, and civilisation, prevalent among the former class afford an ample evidence of the salutary influence which it is the power of well educated women to exercise over those degraded and unhappy females.[18]

Once the trip was concluded to her 'relief, peace and satisfaction', Fry felt, on reflection, that it had probably been worth the trouble. But she, too, had been disappointed by the 'serious difficulties, particularly from the Roman Catholics'. She had been overwhelmed, and sometimes terrified, by the excesses of their reception in Ireland.

The great numbers that followed us, almost wherever we went, was one of those things that I believe was too much for me; no-one can tell but those who have been brought into similar circumstances, what it is to feel as I did at such times; often weak and fagged in body, exhausted in mind, having things of importance to direct my attention to, and not less than a multitude around me, each expecting a word or some mark of attention. For instance, on one occasion a General on one side, a Bishop on the other, and perhaps sixty other persons, all expecting something from me. Visiting prisons, lunatic asylums and infirmaries, all expecting something from me . . . and many came in consequence to our Public Meetings, however these things proved too much for me, and tired me more than any part of our service.

Such was proving to be the price of fame.

Shortly after their return from Ireland, in July 1827, Joseph Gurney married again. But there were no festivities this time since tragedy was again looming. In

September, after a lingering illness, Fry's unmarried sister Rachel, the favourite of her childhood and her biggest support in adult life, died. Meanwhile at Earlham, with the loss of a sister and a change of mistress following Joseph's marriage came a change of tone. Fry's eldest sister Kitty, who had run the household for most of the last 25 years with Rachel, was ousted once again; and although she still felt 'the benefit of having a decided home', life was never going to be the same again. 'My spirits are apt to be depressed', she wrote. 'It is impossible that Earlham should ever again be to me what it once was. The chain is gone forever.'

In going to Ireland, Fry had removed herself from the scene of the difficulties facing her husband's business interests. But they were still there when she returned home. This time the Gurney brothers could not – or, more likely, would not – bail him out, and in November 1828, Joseph Fry was declared bankrupt. The Society of Friends, which had issued previous warnings, disowned him the following year, and he would not be reinstated until 1838. Business lapses were very seriously regarded by Friends because of the implied betrayal of trust towards one's clients. Hard evidence as to what actually happened to the Fry businesses is scanty. It has been suggested that some responsibility for the Fry banking fiasco must be attributed to the Gurney brothers, who encouraged the Fry brothers in 1806 to enter the banking business despite the fact, as it transpired, that such an activity was beyond their competence.[19]

As a result of their businesses' failing, the Frys had to leave Plashet for good. They went first back to St Mildred's Court to live with their son and daughter-in-law, and then to a much smaller house in Essex. The Gurney brothers salvaged what they could of the Fry tea business, and installed Joseph as manager on an annual salary of £600. On their sister they settled an allowance of £1,500 a year, although they regularly gave her more, without Joseph Fry's knowing. What effect this had on the dynamics of the Fry marriage is not recorded.

Fry was very bitter about what had happened. 'I do not like to pour out my sorrows too heavily upon thee', she wrote to her daughter Rachel on 27 November, 'nor do I like to keep thee in the dark as to our real state'.

This is, I consider, one of the deepest trials to which we are liable; its perplexities are so great and numerous, its mortifications and humiliations so abounding, and its sorrows so deep. None can tell but those who have passed through it, the anguish of heart at times felt.

She struggled to rise above the situation, but it was 'when secondary things arise' that she was undone: 'parting with servants, the poor around us, the schools, and our dear place'. It was also at this time that she destroyed the first 17 years of her diary, and substituted a résumé.

By mid-December, the Frys were preparing to leave Plashet forever and move temporarily back to St Mildred's Court. Fry continued in

> the low valley, and naturally feel too much, leaving this sweet place, but not being well makes my spirits more weak than usual . . . I am sorry to find how much I cleave to some earthly things – health, ease, places, possessions. Lord, Thou alone canst enable me to estimate them justly, and to keep them in their right places.

With so much upheaval on the domestic front, Fry suspended her prison work for a while. It also seemed wiser that she should remain out of the public eye for the time being. There had been rumours, totally unfounded, that her philanthropic work had perhaps been subsidized by the Fry bank. Certainly, donations had, quite naturally, been processed by the Fry bank. But since the early days of her marriage, the generosity of two younger brothers had been an important element in securing her a comfortable life.

Joseph and Samuel Gurney were both rich bankers: Joseph in the family firm, which he entered in 1805 at the age of 17; Samuel in the bill-broking firm (which by the time of the 'crash' had become the highly respected Overend, Gurney & Co.), in which he was able to buy a partnership in 1807, at the age of 21. The brothers were self-conscious about their wealth, both for the responsibilities it brought, and for the image it created within the Society of Friends where affluence was often seen as next to worldliness.

They were both extremely generous within the family and outside, not just initiating specific philanthropic projects, but more generally: providing direct financial support for the local unemployed in times of economic recession, for example.

Joseph felt particularly uncomfortable about being rich, and regularly in the 1820s tried to persuade Samuel to give up his partnership at Overend, Gurney & Co. in London and come to replace him at the family bank in Norwich. In 1812, he had become a plain Quaker, like his sister Elizabeth (and later also his sister Priscilla), and six years later, like them, he was acknowledged as a minister. His first wife had died in 1822, and his burning desire was to give up banking and become an itinerant minister. As the financial crisis of the mid-1820s was gathering steam, he wrote – not for the first time – to Samuel, encouraging him to take the step that would liberate him. He felt he no longer had the stomach for commerce.

Samuel was more pragmatic. In a letter to Joseph some years later, when his brother was trying yet again to persuade him to return to the family bank, so that he himself could retire, Samuel reminded him of the great power of money to do good, when properly spent.

> Business has an important controlling influence even in religious duties. The income it affords, with its consequent influence and power, is no means to be despised. Is it not a talent that is to be turned to good account? And are *we* to say *when* such a talent in the prime of our lives is to be laid aside?[20]

Despite the fact that she could prove that her philanthropic activities were funded by her brothers, Fry was in no state to return to public life. Her debilitating depression still lingered and prevented her from much public activity. She looked forward, nevertheless, to returning to Newgate one day.

> I trust that I may be permitted to enter this interesting work again, clothed as with fresh armour, both to defend me, and qualify me for fresh service, that my hands may be taught to war, and my fingers to service!

The summer of 1829 saw the family re-established in a permanent home at Upton Lane in Essex, next door to Samuel Gurney's residence at Ham House. It was small by her standards but 'pleasant and convenient, and I am fully satisfied'. She had been 'harrassed and tried' by the 'extreme disorder into which our things have been brought by all the changes – the pain of leaving Plashet – the difficulty of making new arrangements'; but she was resigned to the new home. What she was not resigned to was the pain and humiliation of her husband's disownment by the Society of Friends, which had also led to her own being shunned in some Quaker circles. In an uncharacteristically bitter letter to her niece Priscilla Buxton in September, she commented that 'if there were more perfect dedication in the church of late, there would be fewer spiritual dwarfs and more men of stature'.

But there was also support from the most influential of quarters. William Wilberforce had always been a strong advocate of Fry's work. He had written to sustain her spirits in the early Newgate days, when her practice of visiting condemned women before they were hanged had caused her such mental anguish. An opponent of transportation, regarding convict labour as virtual slavery, he had accompanied her on a visit to a female convict ship about to sail from Woolwich.[21] And, when the news of the Frys' financial disaster unfolded, he had written to assure her of his warm sympathy and 'may every loss of this world be more than compensated by a larger measure of the . . . riches of Christ'. In 1829, she confided to him her fears.

> Advise me as with a child if thou hast any hint to give me in my new circumstances. At present I only attend my place of worship, or pay visits of duty, where I am wanted by my friends; but I look, before long, once more to entering the prisons. The cause is near to my heart, and I do not see that my husband having lost his property should . . . prevent my yet attending to those duties. In this I should like to have thy advice.

Having confided to Wilberforce her reservations about returning to prison work under the circumstances, she eagerly awaited his response. He wrote back:

> I do not see how it is possible for any reasonable being to doubt the propriety . . . [even] absolute duty, of your renewing your prison visitations. A gracious Providence has blessed you with success in your endeavours to impress a set of miserables, whose character and circumstances might almost have extinguished hope. And you will return to them, if with diminished pecuniary powers, yet . . . with powers of a far higher order unimpaired.[22]

He was sure she would continue to be 'the honoured instrument of great and rare benefits to the most pitiable of your fellow-creatures'.

PART THREE

Spreading the word

8

A manifesto for reform

Ten years after the Newgate experiment began, before her husband's ultimate financial ruin, and about the time that Joseph Gurney was compiling their Irish report for the Viceroy, Lord Wellesley, Fry had been putting together a handbook of her own. Called *Observations on the Visiting, Superintendence and Government of Female Prisoners*, it was published in London in 1827. It was a comprehensive practical manual for good prison management which drew on a decade's experience gathered by the British Ladies' Society for Visiting Prisons, the umbrella group for the growing armies of female prison visitors throughout the country. It was nothing less than a manifesto for reform which Fry would distribute to all interested parties – politicians, reformers, prison governors and heads of other welfare establishments, and potential lady visitors – not just in Britain but in America, Australia and Continental Europe. Fry introduced *Observations* with a reference to her lifelong dyslexia, admitting that 'well knowing my incompetency for the task of writing for the public, I have felt considerable reluctance in sending to the press the following brief observations'. But a greater good prevailed, and 'my long experience ... and the numerous applications made to me for further explanation and information on this interesting subject, induce me to make an attempt, on which I should not otherwise have ventured'.

She stressed the absolute importance, first and foremost, of having women in prison supervised exclusively by women. 'No persons appear to me to possess so strong a claim on their compassion, as the helpless, the ignorant, the afflicted, or the depraved, *of their own sex*.'

> During the last ten years, much attention has been successfully bestowed by women on the female inmates of our prisons; and many a poor prisoner, under their fostering care, has been completely changed – rescued from a condition of depravity and wretchedness and restored to happiness, as a useful member of the community.[1]

Nor was this requirement confined to prisons; it applied equally to any establishment where women were cared for.

> A similar care is evidently required for our hospitals, our lunatic asylums, and our workhouses. It is quite obvious, that there are departments in all such institutions which ought to be under the especial superintendence of females. Were ladies to make a practice of regularly visiting them, a most important check would be obtained on a variety of abuses, which are far too apt to creep into the management of these establishments ... The Roman Catholic ladies, in many parts of the continent of Europe, have set us, in this respect, a bright and useful example; and the result of their care and attention, particularly in the hospitals, has been found, in a high degree, salutary and beneficial. Nor have similar effects failed to be produced in the comparatively solitary instances in which women, in our own country, have been in the habit of regularly visiting the public abodes of poverty and disease.[2]

Fry remained open-minded about the sort of charitable activities to which women should devote themselves, taking into consideration their age and circumstances. Prison work, for example, would not suit all and 'among the most interesting exertions of female benevolence, will ever be numbered the visiting of the poor in their own habitations, the necessary attention to the supply of their temporal and spiritual wants and, above all, the diligent promotion of the education of their children'. All these were activities which Fry herself had pursued as a young woman, before the Newgate days. These more gentle pursuits could be a useful training ground for bigger things, she insisted.

> For example, a young lady may be well employed in attending to a school, or in visiting a sick neighbour, who would be far less suitable than the more elderly and experienced for the care of the hospital, the workhouse, the asylum or the prison; and yet, the one service will in time form an admirable preparation for the other.[3]

Time and again, Fry returned to the absolute necessity of ensuring that it must be women who are responsible for the moral management of women in public institutions. Putting vulnerable women in the care of men of unknown character (as such warders often were in these institutions) was not an appropriate procedure, since the scope for abuse was unconscionable.

> I must now express my conviction that few persons are aware of the *degree* in which

the female departments of them stand in need of the superintending care of judicious ladies. So great are the abuses which exist is some of those establishments, that *modest* women dare not run the risk to which they would be exposed, did they attempt to derive from them the relief which they require. I would have this subject occupy the serious consideration of the benevolent part of the community.[4]

The only safe way for women to be supervised was by their own sex, whenever they were in a vulnerable position.

All reflecting persons will surely unite in the sentiment, that the female, placed in the prison for her crimes, in the hospital for her sickness, in the asylum for her insanity, or in the workhouse for her poverty, possess no light or common claim on the pity and attention of those of her own sex . . . May the attention of *women* be more directed to those labours of love; and may the time quickly arrive, when there shall not exist, in this realm, a single public institution of the kind, in which degraded or afflicted females who may happen to be its inmates shall not enjoy the *efficacious superintendence* of . . . their own sex.[5]

While acknowledging the valuable contribution to be made by individual women visiting prisons, Fry still felt that the greatest impact could be achieved by women working in groups, hence her advocacy of committees. For one thing, there was the question of mutual support and strength in numbers, so that 'if one labourer fails, the work will not cease, and others will be ready to supply her place'. For another, there were different aspects of prisoner care which required different qualities in the visitor, more likely to be found 'in a variety of persons'. Most of all, 'a committee will often arrive at sounder and wiser conclusions on any practical question than an individual would be likely to form'. Fry recommended that three committee members meeting monthly was the minimum target for transacting business, and that there should be six visitors a month to monitor each prison. She believed greater success could be achieved by a 'union of forces', when women came together to pool their resources. Under these circumstances, 'the employment of but a small portion of their time would enable them to effect more extensive good than could previously have been thought possible'. And their home life would benefit, too, from their increased energy. 'Instead of being incapacitated for their domestic duties, they would often return to those duties, refreshed in spirit, and stimulated to perform them with increased cheerfulness, propriety and diligence.'

A committee, in any case, carried more gravitas, Fry continued, particularly when it came to eliciting support from 'magistrates or other persons in authority', since in each case it would be necessary, before the 'ladies' could implement their plans, to obtain the sanction of the magistrates under whose authority the individual prison was placed.

The approach that Fry recommended the ladies' associations or committees should take for any particular prison was quite straightforward. The ladies should first call the prisoners together and explain how they hoped to help. They should express their sympathy for the prisoners' plight and 'soothe them with words of gentleness and kindness, and endeavour to hold up . . . the danger and misery of vice . . . and the innumerable advantages which attach to a life of sobriety, industry, honesty and virtue'. Once the prisoners' interest had been engaged, it was not difficult to win their endorsement of the project, since 'experience has amply proved that, when prisoners are tenderly treated, there is a general willingness to submit to such regulations as the ladies who visit them may propose for their conduct and improvement'.

Fry's plan was that a code of conduct should be displayed in each ward of a prison, and that records should be kept as to the behaviour of each woman, on the basis of which small prizes would be distributed. She also recommended adopting the twelve-point rule system that had proved its worth with female prisoners at Newgate. In brief, these rules comprised: appointing a matron in charge of the women's conduct and work; appointing a separate monitor for each class of women; and appointing a keeper of the women's yard, to prevent any disorder, 'and to take care that they do not spend any time at the grating, except with their friends' (thus protecting them from corrupting influences from outside). There was to be no begging, although donations were acceptable, and would be divided among all. There was also to be no quarrelling, swearing, card-playing or other gaming. The women should attend Bible-reading at least once a day. Cleanliness was paramount. Monitors should be ever watchful on pain of dismissal; but anyone who felt herself ill-treated by a monitor had 'full liberty, in a civil, quiet manner, to present her case to a visitor or to the matron'. However, if there was evidence of good behaviour, there were modest rewards to be had. 'For the encouragement of the women in endeavouring to conduct themselves well, the Association distributes several times in the year, to those who prove deserving, some useful article as a reward.'

'The great object which the visitors ought to keep in view is the *reformation* of the prisoners', Fry stressed time and time again. 'To this principal end all their plans must be subservient.' 'Success would depend', she wrote, 'on the spirit in which the visitor enters upon her work'.

> It must be the spirit, not of judgement, but of mercy . . . The good principle in the hearts of many abandoned persons may be compared to the few remaining sparks of a nearly extinguished fire. By means of the utmost care and attention, united with the most gentle treatment, these may yet be fanned into a flame; but, under the operation of a rough and violent hand, they will presently disappear, and be lost forever.[6]

While avoiding excessive familiarity, and in particular not discussing their crimes with them, the visiting ladies must show as much confidence in the prisoners as circumstances will possibly allow, Fry advises. And the reward system is important:

> Marks of approbation and small rewards ought, also, at times, to be bestowed on them as an encouragement to good conduct. To miss these rewards is generally found to be a sufficient mortification for the correction of the disorderly.[7]

Solitary confinement, however, was a deprivation of privilege to which Fry did not subscribe. Although she approved the principle of prisoners being kept apart to sleep, association during the day was much more to her liking since segregation during the day, 'while useful in extreme cases, is, in my opinion, a punishment too severe to be resorted to on any light and trivial occasion'.

Fry warned against any 'endeavour on the part of the visiting ladies to procure the mitigation of the sentences of criminals', even in the case of capital punishment to which she, like most Quakers, was intractably opposed. Fry had the painful personal experience of trying unsuccessfully to have a death sentence commuted for one young Newgate woman.

> Such endeavours ought never to be made, except when the cases are remarkably clear, and then through the regular official channels. Deeply as we must deplore the baneful effects of the punishment of death, and painful as we must feel it to be, that our fellow-creatures, in whose welfare we are interested, should be prematurely plunged into an awful eternity, yet, while our laws continue as they are, unless they can bring forward *decided facts* in favour of the condemned, it is wiser for the visiting ladies to be quiet, and to submit to decrees, which they cannot alter.[8]

Fry believed that it was absolutely essential for female prisoners to be super-vised by other women, since 'females confined in our prisons are, for the most part, persons of light and abandoned character'.

> To place them under the care of *men* is evidently unreasonable, and seldom fails to be injurious to both parties. Male turnkeys ... ought never, in my opinion, to have access to the female department of the prison ... In visiting small prisons, I have frequently observed one or two unfortunate young women – committed, perhaps, for some minor offence (such as running away from an apprenticeship) – placed under the sole care of a man, whose key will at any time unlock their door, and afford him admission to their society. This I cannot but consider a most unwarrantable and deplorable exposure.[9]

One matron, on the other hand, could maintain far greater order that any number of male turnkeys. She was safer in their company, as well as more powerful. She could instruct them in their feminine duties, and provide a role model for a 'modest, regular, and well-ordered life'. Perhaps more importantly, women prisoners could bring their problems to her in safety, and 'pour forth their sorrows to a wise and sympathising friend'.

While such an arrangement would be enough for smaller gaols, 'it is evident that, in our larger jails, or houses of correction, subordinate officers of the same sex will also be required ... and these, like the matron who governs them, ought to be selected with peculiar judgment and care'.

> Let the female criminal in prison behold, in every officer who exercises authority over her, a consistent example of feminine propriety and virtue, and great will be its influence towards a happy change of habit and character in herself. May the time quickly arrive, when not a single prisoner in this enlightened kingdom shall be found under the immediate superintendence of any persons whatsoever, except the sober and virtuous of her own sex.[10]

As to the question of prison accommodation, Fry was insistent that the proper practice was to keep female convicts as far away from men as possible, ideally in separate buildings lest, she said – quoting St Paul – 'evil communication corrupts good manners'. Avoidance of all contact between the sexes in prison would help to promote order and sobriety among the inmates, and greatly facilitate the duties of the officers. Being deprived of male company also added 'considerable weight and effect to the punishment'. As well, employing female officers was cheaper.

Female prison quarters should be arranged on the panopticon principle, with the matron's office so positioned in relation to the cells, day rooms and exercise yards, that she could see the prisoners at work and recreation during the day – and overhear them at night – since 'vigilance and unremitting inspection' was one of the most essential elements of effective prison discipline.

Again, Fry calls for prisoners to be divided into those on remand ('untried') and those convicted ('tried'); and for the convicted to be classified not strictly by the nature of their offence, but according to their general character and degree of criminality. Grouping together a hardened offender and a 'mere novice', simply because they had committed the same crime, risked further corrupting the less experienced prisoner. Classification would therefore depend on the prisoner's conduct, and be at the discretion of the prison officers under the guidance of a ladies' committee.

There should be no need for more than four classes. The top class would include women 'whose crimes are of no deep moral dye, and whose demeanour and conduct in the prison are exemplary'. They might enjoy some advantages, such as better clothing, lighter work and some payment for that work. They could also be allowed a degree of self-supervision, since 'it is wonderful how much confidence may safely be placed in the better sort of female criminals . . . when a good spirit has been infused in their minds'. The bottom class, consisting 'of the most hardened and desperate offenders, and of those persons who have been committed to the prison more than once . . . must undergo peculiar privations and hardships'. Among these privations and hardships, Fry reluctantly included occasional use of the treadmill and handmill for the 'hardened and depraved', but only tentatively, and only short-term, since 'the female character is seldom improved by such rough and laborious occupation'. More important was that members of the bottom class would be allowed to move up into a higher class as and when an improvement in their behaviour warranted it. With regard to prisoners on remand, and therefore innocent until proven otherwise, Fry saw no reason to divide them into classes, except to separate 'modest' women from prostitutes.

Classification should be possible even in prisons where there was no physical segregation, except between the sexes, by having each group or class supervised by its own monitor, chosen from among themselves. Fry recommended the monitorial system pioneered by Bell and Lancaster, or, as she called it, 'the plan of mutual instruction'. The monitors should be given the responsibility of preparing a daily account of the activities and behaviour of every member in their groups, and of passing this on to the matron, or to the lady visitor, who would record it in a register. This register would provide 'a useful check on every kind of improper conduct, and form the foundation of a judicious application of rewards to the most deserving prisoners'.

As to their clothing, Fry recommended that each class should have one plain but distinctive item of clothing – a different bonnet, perhaps – which would indicate to staff where they belonged and also help to promote a sense of group pride. But otherwise there were to be no adornments, no earrings or curled hair, and 'all sorts of finery and superfluity of dress' must be absolutely forbidden. As a plain Quaker accustomed to dressing simply and soberly (though personally she liked her sombre-coloured cloaks made of silk and lined with fur), this would have seemed less of an ordeal to her than it was to the women. Much more harsh, uncharacteristically so, was her advice that female prisoners' hair should be cut once they were convicted, and kept short until they had completed their sentences. While there is evidence that the women found this particularly distressing – among the convicts in New South Wales there was a major riot when the practice was introduced – Fry believed it would be found to act as a 'certain yet harmless punishment', and would promote the humiliation of spirit which, in persons so circumstanced, is one indispensable step to improvement and reformation'.

Each prisoner should have a personal number which would be marked on her seat at table, on her clothing, her bed and bedding, her books and any other property. This practice had worked particularly well on the convict ships, and 'is found by experience to be very effectual in preventing disputes among the prisoners, and in promoting that strictness of discipline which is essential to the order and regularity of the whole machine'.

Only about one-third of women in prison at the time were able to read at all; another third could read a little. From Fry's point of view, the main disadvantage of this was that they were unable properly to read the Bible, and therefore the religious route to a better life remained closed to them. The solution was to read to them from the Bible, and to teach them to read using the Bible, thus achieving two objectives at the same time. Most prisons already had regular religious services conducted by chaplains, who in the case of women prisoners should ideally be 'married men of *established* character, with some knowledge of life'. However, Fry stressed, with some delicacy, 'there is a part of the moral and religious instruction of female prisoners which cannot be communicated to them so well, so safely, or so efficaciously, as by *the ladies who visit the prison*. The instruction to which I allude is all of a private nature.' Beyond that she gave no details. As well as group meetings and Bible readings, there should also be the opportunity for prisoners to be mentored individually.

Since the devil finds work for idle hands, the women's time must be usefully employed, the better to prepare them for life after release from prison. As well as reading, writing and numbers, they should also be taught 'to make a ready and profitable use of the needle'. At a time of rising national unemployment, there was some public resistance to the idea of providing work for prisoners, on the grounds that this took work away from the honest and more deserving poor. Fry's argument was that it was a question of enlightened self-interest, as the long-term benefits to the community far outweighed the minor interference with the labour market caused by the small amount of work done in prisons. If there were less re-offending, as a result of prisoners becoming useful and productive members of the community, the whole of society would benefit.

> Unless the time of these poor females, who have abandoned themselves to idleness and vice, be fully occupied while they are in prison, there can be little or no hope that their confinement will lead to their reformation. Without this important aid to the work of prison discipline, their attention will still be directed to the criminal objects which have previously occupied them, and much of their time will probably be spent in contriving plans for future evil. We cannot promote the reformation of such persons more effectually than by making them experimentally acquainted with the sweets of industry.[11]

The type of work that women prisoners should be taught to do, as they were encouraged to make progress up to the higher classes, should, therefore, involve those domestic skills that would enable them to earn a living. These included needlework, knitting, washing and ironing, housework, cooking, spinning and weaving – many of which activities were essential to the running of the prison. If such work could not be found, there was always the patchwork option – the original activity of the first women's groups at Newgate. By the time that Fry wrote *Observations*, the Newgate women had largely given up patchwork in favour of either knitting stockings for the orphans at the Foundling Institution, or making clothes for the poor which more affluent women would buy at 'sales of work', to distribute among deserving cases locally. But the craft of patchwork was still practised to great effect on the convict ships to Australia. From the modest amounts of money they might be paid for their work, Fry advised allowing them to retain some pocket money for harmless luxuries such as tea and sugar, as this would be found to be 'a powerful stimulus to a steady and persevering industry'. Most of their earnings, however, should be kept for them to use on their release from prison. 'The possession of a moderate sum of money will *then* be found of essential importance, as the means of preventing an almost irresistible temptation – the temptation of want and misery – to a renewal of criminal practices.'

At the time Fry wrote this, the treatment of female prisoners sentenced to transportation had already been considerably improved in Britain as a result of the efforts by the ladies' committees. Perhaps with a view to her manuals being used on the continent, where practices might be less enlightened, she revisited some of these achievements. No woman who was breast-feeding, for example, would be forced into transportation until the child was deemed old enough to be weaned. Mothers could take with them any children under the age of seven years. While being taken from their prison to the convict ship, they were not to be kept in heavy irons or otherwise humiliated, and 'since these rules are often infringed', lady visitors should be vigilant and report all infringements to the relevant authorities.

Women who escaped transportation or execution, and could be expected to be released back in to the community, faced another evil in that they would be 'for the most exposed to a variety of temptations' and would need the continuing support and care of the lady visitors.

> It is often their lot to struggle with much poverty and distress, with the force of habit, and with the insinuations and persuasions of their old companions in crime. Distrusted by the virtuous and respectable, and ridiculed by the vicious and dissolute, the liberated female criminal must have indeed received strong impressions from the instruction bestowed upon her in prison, if she is enabled to encounter all these difficulties, and to persevere in her newly-formed habits of morality and industry. The vigilance therefore of, perhaps, her *only* friends – I mean the members of the Visiting Committee – is evidently needful, in order to protect her from the influence of her old associates, and to introduce her, if possible, to some safe and respectable situation.[12]

Several aspects of the care of women and prison can be adequately and properly discharged by well-meaning people of either sex. However, Fry insists, there are many other aspects 'for which, from their domestic knowledge and habits, and from some of the qualities characteristic of their sex, women are peculiarly, and indeed exclusively adapted'. Those magistrates and other male officials who still resisted the idea of admitting lady visitors to female prisons would, she insisted, 'after a little experience of the plans now proposed, find that they derive a most material assistance from the ladies' committees, in the care of the female officers of the prison, as well as the prisoners themselves'.

> Gentlemen who only occasionally walk through a prison – however praiseworthy their endeavours might be to promote a right discipline – are seldom fully aware of the evil that might be prevented, and of the good which might be effected, by that constant inspection and superintending care which, as far as the female department of the prison is concerned, would devolve on the members of a Ladies' Visiting Committee.[13]

Nor should the world think that these lady visitors – or indeed anyone seriously committed to the movement for prison reform – were sentimental do-gooders and soft on crime, Fry insists.

> Let not the interest manifested by so many . . . in behalf of those who have broken the laws of their country, lead anyone to imagine that such persons [the reformers] are not sensible of the danger and enormity of crime, or of the necessity of its being followed by punishment. Their desire is only that punishment should be of such a nature, that, while it deters others from the commission of crime by the force of example, it should also have a tendency . . . to the reformation of the offenders. They would not save convicted criminals from the necessary degree of present suffering – but they would have that suffering applied on the principles of a *wholesome discipline*, so as to be productive of future good, both to the criminals who are the subject of it, and to society at large.[14]

9

Recovery

With the publication of her *Observations*, Fry was now equipped with a single document that encapsulated all her ideas on prison reform for women, a document that she could circulate among her growing network of contacts at home and abroad. For, while maintaining a low profile in public until the notoriety of her husband's bankruptcy subsided, she continued to expand her overseas connections. Her Australian correspondents have already been documented; her German acquaintance Nicolaus Julius wrote to say that a ladies' committee had been formed to visit prisons in Berlin; and there was news of similar efforts in Paris from her correspondent there, Madame la Marquise de Pastoret, wife of a noted politician and abolitionist; from Turin, Madame la Marquise de Barol reported the establishment of a refuge for penitent women. Contacts in Potsdam and St Petersburg wrote of similar initiatives there. Indeed the improvements carried out at the government lunatic asylum outside the Russian capital were directly attributed to advice given by Fry, who was sent a copy of the plans for her inspection.[1] Fry was not yet ready to embark on any ambitious trips abroad; but she was prepared to expand her geographical horizons within Britain now that the time seemed right to re-launch her prison career.

The initial excitement over the Newgate experiment and the strangeness of women visiting prisons had given way to a steady movement towards improvement throughout the criminal justice system. Robert Peel succeeded in persuading the House of Commons to abolish capital punishment for forgery offences; and although this was overturned in the House of Lords, public opinion was so strong that the death penalty was never again applied in such cases.

By the 1830s, Fry was firmly back in the public arena. In June 1830, she was presented with a bedspread made by the female inmates of the House of Correction at Kirkdale in Liverpool in gratitude for her kindness and concern for their welfare. In April 1831, she published a small book of brief devotional texts for every day of the year, as a way of making the messages of the Bible more accessible to a wider readership. She would give away thousands of them over the next few years. That same month, she was greatly encouraged by an invitation to visit the Duchess of Kent and her daughter, the Princess Victoria. A few days later, an invitation to meet the Duchess of Gloucester followed; and, in June, she was introduced to Queen Adelaide herself and other members of the royal family at a charity sale of work. Her rehabilitation was complete. And yet, delighted though she was at the opportunity to talk to them about her work, she was concerned that vanity, too, played a part in that pleasure.

> The Queen paid me very kind and marked attention. [We talked] almost entirely on benevolent objects . . . It was a very singular opening, thus to meet those, some of whom I much wanted to see. I had it on my mind to endeavour to see the Queen, and by night and day seriously had weighed it, lest my motives should not be right; but . . . I felt that if there should be any opportunity to put myself in her way, I had better do it. It was striking how the whole thing was opened for me . . . Afterward, I felt as I mostly do after anything of this kind, rather anxious; and extremely fearful for myself, how far it was safe for me thus to be cast among the great of this world . . . and how far others would judge me for it.

In the summer of 1833, the Frys decided to take an extended holiday on Jersey. Family life had been through a hectic and turbulent period, and the pressure of public demands was again weighing heavily on Fry herself; so, despite her fear of the sea, the Channel Islands were agreed on as providing the ideal place to calm jangling nerves. It was a time to enjoy peace, pure air and fine scenery; for rest, recuperation and quiet picnics at secluded beaches.

But Fry was not one to let philanthropic opportunities pass her by. Before long, visits were arranged to the hospital, workhouse, lunatic asylum and prison, and their conditions noted. British jurisdiction does not extend to the Channel Islands, and so the prison reform measures introduced in the mainland did not apply. Fry therefore took it upon herself to address the island authorities directly in a report that offered 'some strong and decided observations on their condition and management'.

> Our protracted residence in this beautiful and interesting island has afforded me a full opportunity of observing the manner in which the defective system pursued in the management of the prison appears to operate upon its inmates; and I feel it to be my duty to represent the effects which my experience has taught me must necessarily result

from its operation, as being nothing less than a gradual but certain demoralisation of the lower, and some of the middling classes of society, and the increase rather than the diminution of crime.[2]

She identified the objectives of a prison – safe custody, fair punishment, deterrence and reform – and pointed out that the Jersey establishment achieved only the first. She stressed the importance of employment, earned privileges, proper diet (and no alcohol), classification of prisoners, segregation of the sexes, a decent uniform, clear rules, regular independent inspection, religious instruction and literacy classes. She made practical suggestions as to how the existing premises might be modified to accommodate some of her recommendations and drew the authorities' attention to the provisions of the 1823 Gaols Act that applied on the mainland. However, as on the mainland, there were no funds available to overhaul the system and it would be some years before reform would begin in Jersey.

As autumn approached, the family party crossed from Jersey to Guernsey, where Fry embarked on an inspection of the local prison there and found it substandard in almost every respect: debtors and felons associated freely, there was no education or employment, and the gaoler earned his living by selling alcohol to the inmates. In short, as in Jersey, the system was entirely defective and prone to encourage rather than to prevent crime – a worrying prospect on a small island.

By now it was October. There had been visits to the smaller Channel Islands of Sark and Herm – no prisons there, but always the opportunity to distribute tracts, and to set in motion the establishment of one of the many district societies that Fry always left in her wake. At least these societies, which aimed to foster good habits of thrift, saving, morality and sobriety among the less well-off, proved a tangible and immediate success.

Meanwhile there was worrying news from home. One of Fry's daughters was seriously ill and her presence was needed. There was some debate as to whether she should return to England by the slower, predominantly overland route through France, with her husband and other family members; or risk the long but quicker sea voyage directly from Jersey to Southampton and be with her daughter sooner. The weather was particularly stormy that autumn, and many ships had been lost in the Channel. Among them was the *Amphitrite*, which was bound for Australia carrying many Newgate women convicts known to Fry. In the event, she braved the storms and was back in London within the day.

It was often said of Fry that if she didn't have a current cause, she would find one. The coastguard library project was one such cause. The idea had occurred to her several years earlier, but it was not until 1834 that she decided to expand it into a nationwide initiative. Her approach was a model for all her philanthropic activities: identify a problem; quantify the problem by personal research; publicize it; call in influential contacts; establish a committee; delegate effectively; and, most of all, persevere doggedly until a successful outcome is achieved. The coastguard library project was also typical of the times in that, once it proved a success, it was taken over by the establishment.

At the time, there were nearly 4,500 coastguards, or 'blockade men', staffing the 498 on-shore stations around the shorelines of England, Scotland and Ireland. Their wives and dependent children brought the total coastguard community to over 20,000 souls. Fry's interest in their welfare went back to 1824 when she was holidaying in Brighton for her health. She was suffering from fainting fits, and had taken to sitting by an open window in the evening to draw benefit from the cooler air. Every evening, she noticed a solitary coastguard patrolling the beach. One day, when driving past the Brighton coastguard station, she stopped to speak to the duty officer who told her, politely, that they were not permitted to speak to strangers; but he accepted her visiting card. The coastguards were not popular at the time in their localities. They were employed by the customs authorities and their objective was to prevent smuggling (and its benefits to the local community). It was not until 1856 that they were transferred from the customs authorities to the Admiralty, and became a general police and coastal defence force, and thereby more socially acceptable. In Fry's time, they represented a serious threat to the local black economy.

Some days after Fry's call at the coastguard station, its commander paid her a visit. They discussed the unhappy situation of many of the service's men and officers and how it might be improved. They agreed that the supply of some Bibles and other books might help to while away the solitary hours.

Meanwhile, when she had time, Fry took the opportunity to visit the naval hospitals at Haslar and Plymouth where, despite initial resistance, she succeeded in having modest libraries installed for the invalids. The exercise gave her some idea of the scope and limitations of a coastguard library project which, once begun in earnest in 1834, was successfully completed within two years.

Her first step was to visit as many as possible of the coastguard stations to discuss the project with the officers and their families, which included thousands of children who, at the time, had no access to education because of their remote location. This was a particularly serious problem in Scotland and Ireland, where few stations had schools or churches within four miles. Many were up to ten miles away. Five stations were 20 miles from any place of worship or education. While their menfolk at least had their work, women and children were almost completely cut off from the outside world.

Having gathered her information, Fry set herself a goal of furnishing every coastguard station with its own library in order that 'by this means, the minds of the seamen might be instructed, and [those] of their wives be excited to seek the instruction of their numerous children'. Each library would cost £3, a total of about £1,500. In the summer of 1834, Fry wrote to the then Chancellor of the Exchequer, Lord Althrop, asking for a start-up grant of £500. While approving the proposal in principle, he declined to grant the funds as he was unsure whether he would be staying in office; but he promised to commend the scheme to his successor. When Sir Robert Peel's government eventually took over in early 1835, funds were made available for the project, pending confirmation from the coastguard authorities that the establishment of such libraries warranted the advance; and on the strict understanding that there would be no public endorsement of the scheme.

The inevitable provisional committee was set up. It included Edward Parry, whose exemplary administration of a convict settlement in Australia had originally brought him to Fry's attention; and also a clergyman, Thomas Timpson, honorary secretary of the British and Foreign Sailors' Society, who offered his association's support as well as his own skills to manage the project and organize the fund-raising for it. Agreeing on suitable books presented something of a challenge; but eventually a list was drawn up with the approval of all interested parties.

It was a noble project; but it was slow to attract donations. In June 1835, Fry wrote to Timpson, as secretary of the committee, calling the 'great lack of subscriptions truly discouraging, so very few except from some of our relations or particular friends', and exhorting the committee to 'bestir themselves'. The problem was that many people felt that the provision of libraries was a public service that should therefore be paid for from public funds; and that to provide subsidies from private money would be to absolve the government of its responsibility. Fry herself, meanwhile, concentrated on getting a fund-raising leaflet published and trying to obtain newspaper coverage for the project.

Finally, all the books were bought, labelled, packed up and delivered to the nearly 500 coastguard stations. Each consignment comprised at least 52 volumes – one for each week of the year, a total of nearly 26,000 volumes. As well as Bibles and other religious books, they included biographies and temperance tracts; and nearly half were travel books, covering regions as far apart as the Americas, south-east Asia, Africa and the Arctic (including works by committee member and Arctic explorer Edward Parry).

By the autumn of 1835, the project was largely completed. But Fry's ambition did not end there. Anticipating the probability that some coastguard stations would work through all the books, she arranged for an additional and larger library to be installed at each of the 74 district headquarters, to which each individual station might apply for an exchange of books. She also proposed installing a library on each of the 48 revenue cutters or sailing boats employed by the customs authorities to patrol Britain's coastal waters.

All aspects of the extended project were completed by April 1836. Even the committee expressed its delight and surprise at the scope and success of this massive undertaking. At the final count, Fry's initiative had provided the following: 26,000 volumes for 498 on-shore coastguard stations; 12,380 volumes for 74 district station libraries; 1,867 volumes for 48 libraries on revenue cutters; 6,464 schoolbooks for the children on the coastguard stations; an extra 5,357 various pamphlets and tracts. This was a total of well over 52,000 items, all bought, packaged and delivered for just £2,700 – less than half the going rate, thanks to Fry's extended network of friends and well-wishers.[3] On completion of the project, the libraries became government property under the care of the coastguard department, and the government published a testimonial taking credit for the success of the project it had initially declined to endorse. Just two years later, in September 1838, the government extended Fry's library scheme to the Royal Navy as well, when the Admiralty issued an order to supply all Her Majesty's ships with libraries of entertaining, useful and religious books, using the catalogues of the coastguard libraries for guidance.

Once she had launched the coastguard library project, in July 1834 Fry set off on a second tour of Scotland. Her husband and two daughters had gone on ahead on holiday, and she met up with them in Dunkeld. The party then travelled by Aberfeldy up to Loch Tay. The previous year, Parliament had passed an Act to abolish slavery. The movement's champion, William Wilberforce, whose anti-slavery campaigning baton had been taken up by Fry's brother-in-law, Thomas Fowell Buxton, had died three days before the Bill was passed. The first day of August 1834 was appointed for the liberation of slaves in all the British colonies. Fry knelt by the side of Loch Tay and prayed for their welfare.

Rain set in for a prolonged period in the Highlands, and towards the end of August Fry left her husband and daughters to travel, via Loch Lomond, to Edinburgh to accompany a son who was returning to England. This also gave her the opportunity to revisit the city's prisons, 'under the belief that duty called me to do so'. Her son being dispatched southwards, she returned to the family party, but Edinburgh remained with her. She was convinced that much more could be done there. Her mind was never off the job; her preoccupation dampened the holiday mood.

I find [in Edinburgh] a field for much important service for the poor, and [the need] to make more arrangements for the Ladies to visit the prisons. I desire, and earnestly pray, to be preserved from an over-active spirit in these things; and, on the other hand, faithfully, diligently and humbly . . . to do whatever my Lord gives me to do that may be to His glory, or the good of my fellow-creatures.

She was itching to return to work. She seemed to find holidaying trivial. Her frustration cannot have failed to be picked up by her family.

We have passed through very lovely country; but the sun has not shone much upon us; and the atmosphere of my mind has partaken of the same hue, which is not so pleasant as a more lively colouring over the mind. But I am ready to think it more profitable, and perhaps more likely to qualify me for the weighty duties before me.

From Loch Katrine, the party travelled to Balloch, Luss, Inverary, Loch Awe, Oban, Dunbarton, Glasgow, Edinburgh, and then home, On her return, Fry wrote a report for the Scottish authorities on the state of their prisons; then she resumed her Newgate visits.

By 1835, the treatment of women in Newgate had improved beyond all recognition. Charles Dickens visited one of the women's wings with his publisher in the autumn of that year, and described what he saw in *Sketches by Boz*.

It was a spacious, bare, whitewashed apartment, lighted of course, by windows looking into the interior of the prison, but far more light and airy than one could reasonably expect to find in such a situation. There was a large fire with a deal table before it, round which ten or a dozen women were seated on wooden forms at dinner. Along both sides of the room ran a shelf; and, below it, at regular intervals, a row of large hooks were fixed in the wall, on each of which was hung the sleeping-mat of a prisoner; her rug and blanket being folded up, and placed on the shelf above. At night these mats are placed upon the floor, each beneath the hook on which it hangs during the day; and the ward is thus made to answer the purposes of a day-room and sleeping apartment. Over the fireplace was a large piece of plasterboard, on which were displayed a variety of texts from Scripture, which were also scattered about the room in scraps about the size and shape of the copy-slips which are used in schools. On the table was a sufficient provision of a kind of stewed beef, and brown bread, in pewter dishes, which are kept perfectly bright and displayed on shelves in great order and regularity when they are not in use.

Dickens was clearly impressed by what he saw when he entered the women's wards at Newgate.

The women rose hastily on our entrance, and retired in a hurried manner to either side of the fireplace. They were all cleanly – many of them decently – attired, and there was nothing peculiar either in their appearance or demeanour. One or two resumed the needlework which they had probably laid aside at the commencement of their meal; others gazed at the visitors with listless curiosity, and a few retired behind their companions to the very end of the room, as if desirous to avoid even the casual observation of strangers.[4]

Her work at Newgate being largely completed, on 22 May 1835, Fry was called on to give evidence to a Select Committee of the House of Lords on the state of all gaols, Bridewells and houses of correction in England and Wales. The panel was chaired by Charles Gordon-Lennox, fifth Duke of Richmond. Fry was accompanied by three co-workers: Elizabeth Pryor, whose special concern was the welfare of the women on the convict ships, and Jane Pirie and Catherine Frazer who were involved with the Newgate project.

The committee had already heard evidence from Matthew Cope, the keeper of Newgate, that Fry's continuing weekly visits did 'a great deal of good' among the female prisoners. He was particularly pleased to report that the conduct of 65 women escorted on board the latest convict ship for transportation was 'much better than any of the others', since 'a great deal of pain was taken with them'.[5]

Dozens of witnesses were called to testify to the committee: prison governors, turnkeys, magistrates, chaplains, surgeons, accountants, charity representatives, even two former prisoners. As well as Fry and her colleagues, two other women gave evidence to the Lords' committee. Rebecca Bourhill offered the benefit of her experience as matron of the asylum for women at Chiswick (later the Royal Victoria Asylum). And Mrs Benjamin Shaw reported on the School of Discipline for young girls in Chelsea, which she had set up at Fry's suggestion some ten years earlier. This small establishment sought to reform young girls up to the age of 13, before they turned to serious crime, and to train them as domestic servants. The girls were originally transferred from the women's prison at Newgate; later they were referred to the school by magistrates.

On her first Select Committee appearance, Fry's prison experience had been of short standing, and confined to the women's ward at Newgate. Since then, she had travelled widely throughout England, Scotland and Ireland, and occasionally Wales, as well as all the Channel Islands. Most of the prisons that had attracted her interest she had visited more than once – she always felt that the second visit was more productive – on trips lasting from a few weeks to four months.

No one since John Howard six decades earlier had amassed such an extensive understanding of different prisons and their regimes, of good and bad practice, of what worked and what did not. Her knowledge of the whole prison system – and not just the women's side of it – was infinitely greater than any of those involved in the legislative process to improve and reform.

The 1823 Gaols Act had enshrined in statute many of the recommendations that Fry had made the first time around. These included: regular visits by prison chaplains; the banning of chains; and the recruitment of women warders for women's prisons. An absence of funding meant that these recommendations were only partially implemented; however, their validity was established, and the 1835 committee was therefore able to look at broader matters, nationwide. There were three major issues on which it wanted Fry's views: the employment of female prisoners, religious instruction, and the provision of matrons both in prisons and on the convict ships.

With regard to the employment of female prisoners, Fry thought that 'a very great good results from their being occupied in things suitable for their sex'. She was even in favour of the crank-handle or handmill (though not the treadmill) for women, since it provided some form of exercise for otherwise idle hands. But there were better ways of keeping those hands busy.

Many women come into prison wholly unable to work at the needle, and in giving a poor woman a knowledge of how to cut and make up articles of clothing, she goes out better able to perform her domestic duties; and there are several other things of that sort – teaching her to wash [laundry] properly, and to iron and to mend; all those things help her after she quits the gaol.[6]

Although it was difficult to find enough work for all the women in prison who would benefit from it, it was worth persevering, she added, since her experience was that, among women given employment at Newgate, re-offending was reduced by one-third.

As to the question of religious education, Fry reiterated the firm belief she had held since the start of her Newgate experiment: that it provided a very great advantage except, categorically, when it was given in private by a male cleric to an unaccompanied woman. The best solution was for women to instruct women but, if that was not possible, the male chaplain or priest should always have a female attendant as chaperone. As to the effect of religious instruction, Fry explained, at some length, how 'tractable' and 'tender-spirited' the prisoners became towards the lady visitors who provided their instruction, compared to those who were continually chastised and who became even more hard-hearted. And the Newgate women came to cherish the comradeship of the classes in which they were instructed. One of these groups, which had been together for three months, wrote to Fry, on leaving to go to New South Wales, with a plea that they might not be separated.

> We do humbly request we may be together on board the ship, and do humbly pray we
> may be permitted to read together, as we have been accustomed to do in the ward; and
> likewise return our most humble thanks to the Ladies.[7]

As to the appointment of female officers in women's prisons, as provided for in the 1823 Act, Fry reported with regret that the implementation of this clause left a lot to be desired. Indeed, the practice was open to serious abuse, but she thought the intervention of the ladies' committees could be of assistance, would the magistrates but call on their assistance. At one prison she visited, she found that

> a little girl of sixteen had care of all these women, some of them of very bad character. I
> found she was the gaoler's daughter, on enquiry, and that the magistrate had adopted the
> system of the gaoler's being allowed so much a year to pay any officers . . . It appeared a
> very simple plan to put his daughter in the situation of matron, but it was a likely means

to destroy the morals of the daughter. I find in some of the prisons the matrons live out of the gaol and attend only a certain number of hours to give the poor women some assistance; whereas some of the women [prisoners] are superior to themselves in point of power and talent, so that they [the matrons] have scarcely any influence over them.

Much depends upon the proper appointment of the matrons and female turnkeys. It requires a very judicious choice; and though I would not take too much to ourselves, I think it would be advantageous if the magistrates would now and then consult the Ladies about it; they are in the habit of hiring female servants, and I think that their knowledge of their character would be useful.[8]

The committee wished to know what success Fry and her co-workers had achieved in appointing matrons to supervise women convicts on their voyage out to Australia. Elizabeth Pryor, who by then had visited 60 such ships prior to their departure (she would visit all but one during her lifetime), stressed how desirable it was that 'a lady of competent talent and religious views' should accompany each ship, but that the cultural obstacles militating against such appointments were considerable.

The prominent difficulties we had to look at have been their being confined in the society of the captain and the surgeon, whose characters are often unknown to us. And we do not know how to reconcile a lady going out in their company and perhaps being prevented attending to those duties required of her as a matron. We have felt great difficulty attending to that point. And what is to become of a lady when she gets over there, or how is she to be got back if it is her wish.[9]

In fact, only one matron had been sent out so far, and she was the wife of a Baptist minister. They were going out as settlers on the *George Hibbert*. The couple had been highly praised by the captain for their attentions to the female prisoners, several of whom had been taught by them to read and write on the outward journey, 'and all of whom will have to acknowledge to the end of their days that the *George Hibbert* has been a comfortable home to them'. Employing more settler missionaries' wives in the post of matron on the convict ships would be an ideal solution, could more ships be persuaded to take them.

Pryor reminded the Select Committee of the materials that the ladies' committees had been providing for many years for departing female convicts – the clothes and other personal articles, patchwork pieces, sewing kits and spectacles for those who needed them. Psalm books and Bibles were given to all; even, for the sake of fairness, to those not yet able to read them. Whereas the ladies' committee and their friends had previously paid for these materials, the cost was now borne by the government, with the ladies being responsible for the logistics of supplying them. Lending libraries were also being introduced, both for sailors and for women prisoners.

Asked for her overall view of the state of prisons in England and Wales, Fry replied that 'in many instances their condition is melancholy . . . they may truly be called schools for crime'. Despite the recommendations of the 1823 Act, there were 'several that have no instruction, no employment, no inspection, no classification . . . and they get into a most low and deplorable state of morals . . . I would not say that all are in that condition, but I fear many are'.[10] Without naming individual prisons, she highlighted specific problems such as the gaolers selling alcohol to prisoners as a sideline, overcrowding so intense that 'the contamination must be dreadful, religiously, morally . . . for the health also'. Accustomed as she was to the stench of prisons, some were 'so offensive . . . I hardly knew how to remain there'. Prisoners were still kept in heavy chains in town gaols, although this had been made illegal in county gaols. Town councils felt justified in blaming their lack of expenditure on prison improvements on the fact that the money had been spent on other projects, such as a new civic theatre and hotel. Most remarkable of all was how little had changed since Fry's last report except, however, that there remained very few prisons where men and women were not now, at last, segregated.

Fry answered in considerable detail all the questions put to her. And then shortly before the end of the interview, she proposed a plan that she had seen work well in Ireland and would like to see introduced in England. Having taken so much of her time, the committee was hard placed to deny her its attention. Her idea was that all female prisoners sentenced to transportation, from throughout the country, should be confined together in a separate wing of the new Millbank penitentiary,

and it should be superintended by Ladies, and the same plans to be adopted that are to go on in the voyage; they would then come trained to the ships, and would be far more likely to turn out well when they got to the colony. [This] is of importance as it respects the prisoners and as it respects the colony, for the effect of the conduct of the female convicts there is no light consideration, and we have had great satisfaction in our commendation with the late Governor General Darling's wife . . . and we have received information of several of our late prisoners turning out valuable servants.[11]

Newgate, where the London transport convicts were contained, was not fit for this purpose, Fry explained, echoing John Howard's assessment of the place as 'so very faulty a prison that it can never be effectual'. Indeed, the inadequacies at Newgate, the ladies agreed, 'manifestly tend to the extension rather than the suppression of crime', with overcrowding that was 'ruinous'. While they were doing the best they could, it was a 'very bad system; everything is as badly arranged there as is possible with regard to moral improvement'. Millbank, however, offered real potential. It offered space and separation but also the opportunity for a period of calm and assessment of the individual needs of female convicts, some of whom were too old, infirm, or of unsound mind, to be shipped out directly from the county prisons. It was 'a terrible thing', Fry told the committee, to see the state in which some women were sent from the county prisons to the convict ships, scenes which 'every Peer present would deplore to see'. Some women arrived on the point of giving birth, others 'in a very improper state'. Moving the female transport convicts to Millbank would have the added advantage of freeing up space at Newgate, rendering it effectively a remand-only prison.

Finally, the Select Committee asked Fry's opinion on a number of general issues which she wholeheartedly endorsed: that a uniform system of prison discipline should be established throughout England and Wales; that gaol regulations should be submitted for approval not to local authorities, but to the Home Secretary; that prison inspectors should be appointed and report directly to the Home Secretary; and that those acquitted at trial on grounds of insanity should not be kept in prison, but in lunatic asylums. All these recommendations were included in the committee's report and went on to form part of the 1835 Prisons Act. Eventually, Millbank ceased to be a penitentiary and became a holding centre – not just for female convicts, as Fry had requested, but for all prisoners awaiting transportation.

Towards the end of March 1836, Fry applied successfully to the Society of Friends for a certificate giving her permission to revisit Ireland as a minister, for a period of one month. There were Quaker Meetings to attend in Lancashire and Ireland, and the contentious question of religious instruction in Irish schools to address. But her main interest was the establishment of the new experimental women's prison at Grange Gorman Lane in Dublin on the site previously known as the Richmond penitentiary. This experimental gaol was to be the first all-female prison in the United Kingdom and, as such, Fry was concerned that it should be organized as efficiently as possible. She left London for Dublin, furnished with a letter of introduction to the new Viceroy, the Marquis of Normanby, from the current Whig Chancellor of the Exchequer, Thomas Spring-Rice (later Lord Monteagle), who added a gentle note to Fry that he thought the esteem in which she was held for her philanthropy rendered any introduction from him superfluous.

Lord Normanby listened carefully to her recommendations and the Grange Gorman Lane women's prison, formerly the Richmond General Penitentiary, was opened the following year. The specific details of what Fry advised are not known, but they would have been consistent with the system outlined in her *Observations* manifesto of 1827, written the same year that she first visited Ireland. These covered separation, classification, supervision, religious education and practical training, employment and reward – all with a view to reformation and rehabilitation. One concrete recommendation that she made was that her protégée Marian Rawlins be installed as matron of the prison. She had previously been a warder at Cold Bath Fields house of correction in London. In effect, matron Rawlins acted as a governor, although such a position was not officially open to women at the time, and she was required to act under the supervision of a male governor.

On the tenth anniversary of the establishment of Britain's experimental first all-female prison (and two years after Fry's death), the Irish prisons' inspectorate published a report in which it praised

> the high and superior order with which the prison was conducted. The matron, Mrs Rawlins, upon whom the entire responsibility of the interior management devolved, was selected some years since, and sent over to this country by the benevolent and philanthropic Mrs Fry, whose exertions in the cause of female prison reformation were extended to all parts of the British Empire . . . She has nowhere left a more valuable instance of her sound judgment.[12]

So successful had the experiment been that several other women-only prisons had been opened since in Scotland and Australia. Marian Rawlins added:

> Mrs Fry had long wished to have a trial made of an exclusive female prison. That Mrs Fry's plan has completely succeeded, every authority, both city and government, have borne ample and unqualified testimony . . . She never personally saw the fruit of her labour, not having visited Ireland since my residence here, but to her wise, judicious, and maternal counsel I entirely ascribe the success that has attended our exertions.

I never took any material step at the commencement, without consulting her, and at her own request, at least every week, I wrote an account of my movements; and many obstacles that at first arose, she settled in her own quiet way by her influence with the government.[13]

Fry returned home from Ireland on 13 May 1836, pleased at what she had achieved, but also relieved that she had managed to overcome the fear of Ireland instilled by the bad experiences of her first visit in 1827. 'The fear of man was much taken away in Ireland, when I had to tell them what I believed to be home truths.' Faith in the validity of her own experience had given her increasing confidence. Things seemed to be more harmonious at home, as well. In her absence, her husband had made a serious effort to make her feel valued. In her journal, she described her homecoming, and a welcome she felt almost guilty in enjoying, so intense was her desire sometimes to be away from home.

I arrived home safely yesterday afternoon. I think I have never had so happy and so prosperous an arrival – I wept with joy; the stream seems to have turned for a while. My tears have often flowed for sorrow; and now my beloved husband and children have caused them to flow for joy. I found not only all going on well, and having done so during my absence; but to please, comfort and surprise me, my dearest husband had my rooms altered and rendered most comfortable, and my children had sent me nice presents to render them more complete. Their offerings of love quite gladdened my heart, though far too good for me; I felt utterly unworthy of them, I may say peculiarly so. I have seldom returned home more sensible of the hidden evils of my heart.

Life back in England was as hectic as ever, with the pressure never letting up. In mid-June, Fry wrote in her diary that 'I have felt a good deal pressed in spirit in these last few days. The day before yesterday, I counted twenty-nine persons who came on various accounts, principally to see me; there are times when the tide of life is almost overpowering.' Her thoughts were also returning to the state of prisons in the Channel Islands. On the mainland, the 1835 Prisons Act had reinforced the sentiments of the 1823 Gaols Act, and conditions overall were improving, if not at the rate that many would have wished. In the Channel Islands, however, little or no improvement had been attempted since Fry's visit in 1833, since there was no legal requirement to do so. In order to ascertain what could be done to encourage the islands to move voluntarily towards a more liberal regime, the prison inspector for the south of England, Dr Bisset Hawkins, himself a great Fry supporter, paid the Jersey prison a visit. In a report to the then Home Secretary, Lord John Russell, Hawkins described it as being in the most neglected state and failing in every area. Hawkins also unearthed forgotten legislation that entitled Jersey to raise a tax on alcohol specifically to fund a prison. The scheme was backed by Russell – who had consulted about the prison with Fry – and it was accepted by the Jersey authorities.

Encouraged by her Jersey friends to visit the island again before building work began on the new prison, and particularly anxious that proper provision should be made for female prisoners, Fry, her husband and some friends set sail once more from Southampton at the end of July 1836, just two months after her return from Ireland. The visit was a total success. The district societies which she had helped to establish were going from strength to strength; and she was reassured that the new House of Correction was to be established on the best principles, and the project supervised by one of her staunchest supporters.

10

Continental campaigns

The years between 1838 and 1841 were the great period of Fry's campaigning in Continental Europe. Not that she neglected her work in Britain: there was a major inspection tour of Scotland in 1838, as well as regular shorter trips to various parts of the country. But she had acquired, quite by chance, a taste for foreign travel, and this opened up for her a whole new array of prisons to visit and people to influence. There were four major trips in all – in 1838, 1839, 1840 and 1841, most lasting two to six months' duration, plus a short follow-up visit to France in 1843. She made three visits to both France and Germany; two to Holland and Belgium; and one visit each to Switzerland and Denmark.

Her first sortie across the Channel was completely unscheduled. In the autumn of 1836, her husband Joseph and their eldest daughter Katherine were on holiday in Normandy when the carriage in which they were travelling crashed down a precipice. They survived the accident but her presence was required; so she and her son William sailed across on the first available packet-boat. Having established that husband and daughter were bruised and shaken but not seriously hurt, she went off to find the nearest prison and hospital. Despite her initial disinclination to visit France – the reason is not clear – she found herself very taken with the country; and, a month later, she and William returned to spend a couple of days at St Omer.

In 1837, Fry's brother Joseph, who had been recently widowed for the second time, decided to embark on a three-year ministry in America. Initially, Fry considered going with him, despite her fear of such a long voyage by sea. On 25 January, she wrote in her diary:

My heart and mind have been much occupied by my brother Joseph writing to inform me that he apprehends it will be his duty to go to America this year, upon religious duty. The subject is deeply important and weighty, yet I desire to rejoice in his willingness to give up all for the service of his Lord. Though some fears have arisen from a sort of floating apprehension I have had for many years that I ought or might go with him if ever he visited that land. [However] I do not at present see any such opening. As far as I can see, home has my first call of duty.

Her husband Joseph appeared not to share his wife's view that she was giving first priority to her home life. Her daily schedule at the time was, indeed, hectic. On one day alone, 12 March 1837, she recorded in her dairy:

> Went to the Colonial Office to meet Sir George Grey, on subjects respecting New South Wales, and the state of the female convicts; to the Irish Office, and saw Lord Morpeth respecting national schools and prisons, and then to the Home Office, about Jersey prisons, &c. In every one I met with a most cordial reception. So the Lord makes my way with those in power.

Joseph Fry made it clear to his wife that he felt neglected by her pursuit of good works and commitments within the extended family.

> This morning, my dearest husband really feelingly expressed his deep feeling of my constant engagements – calls of duty from home. I deeply felt it, for much as I make a point of always dining at home, and spending every evening and morning with him and my family, yet my mornings are much occupied by public and relative duties – ministerial, public, children, brothers and sisters, their children and others in illness and sorrow. I felt greatly cast down at his remark, desiring greatly to be a faithful and loving wife.

In mid-July 1837, Joseph Gurney prepared to set off alone for his missionary tour of America. Fry, her brother Samuel and his wife Elizabeth travelled around the country with him as he said goodbye to family and friends, and accompanied him to Liverpool to see him off. Fry was in a state of some agitation, unable to enjoy the farewell trip to the full, knowing that she was wanted back home.

> I am very sorry to say, my mind has too much the habit of anxiety and fearfulness. I believe this little journey would have been much more useful to me, but from an almost constant cloud over me, from the fear of being wanted by some of my family. I think it would be better for myself and them, if they did not always cling so closely round my heart, so as to become too much of a weight upon me.

Fry was very close to her brother Joseph. It may be no coincidence that her own period of travelling ministry in Europe began as a means of filling the gap while he was away; for, before the year was out, she had applied to the Society of Friends for a certificate to visit France for a few weeks. Permission was granted, and in January 1838 she set off with her husband Joseph, the philanthropist and educationalist Josiah Forster, and young Lucy Bradshaw, niece of another Quaker philanthropist, William Allen; Lucy had accompanied Fry on a visit to Jersey two years earlier. Since her first trip to France, Fry had learned a little more of the language, so that she could read the Bible to the hotel staff, and also 'in some degree convey my feelings and sentiments, enough to produce sympathy and interest. In our visits to prisons, hospitals and convents, I found this to be the case.'

Once they had settled in at Paris, and Fry had overcome the nervous exhaustion which habitually accompanied the start of a new adventure, their first visit was to the St Lazare women's prison which held nearly a thousand inmates and presented 'a very melancholy sight'. Then they inspected a young offenders' institution which they found 'well ordered but still capable of improvement'. There followed the La Force prison for men, and the military prison at St Germain which they found on the whole well conducted and 'in tolerable order; books they found to be greatly wanted'. The central prison at Poissy they considered 'not sufficiently penal, too much like a manufactory for different trades, instead of a place of punishment'. At the prison of the Conciergerie, they saw the room where Marie Antoinette had been confined. Infant schools and foundling homes were also visited. In one, Fry left money to treat all the children to a bun for tea; in another, she offered advice as to how the babies' clothes could be modified to give them greater freedom of movement. They also visited the Sâlpetrière hospital, home to five thousand people who were 'old, infirm, idiotic or insane', where they were impressed by the great kindness shown to the inmates and the liberty with which they were permitted to move around, but shocked at 'the absence of all religious instruction'. Wherever they went, they distributed bibles, textbooks and tracts to make up for that lack.

Evenings were taken up with the usual round of meetings: with prison officials, to share their findings; with local dignitaries, to foster goodwill for reform; with philanthropists able to finance improvements; with royalty even, whose endorsement added *gravitas* to the work; and, of course, with women willing to form ladies' committees to continue the practical task of prison visiting.

One such meeting was held on the second of Fry's three visits to the women's prison at St Lazare. She had requested that the inmates be brought together, and the gaolers left outside, but they crept back in. After a passage of the Bible was read to the women in French, Fry explained the reading to them through an interpreter. She then asked them, exactly as she had done at Newgate, whether they would like ladies to visit them, read to them, and 'sympathise' with them. The response was an overwhelming 'oui'. It is said that even the gaolers were moved to tears by the magic of her voice.

The event caused quite a sensation in Paris. Her miraculous effect was attributed to her exceptional voice and manner, her skill in holding the audience's attention, and her power to touch their hearts. It was simply the effect of the word of God being spoken, she replied.

It had been a hectic but successful few weeks, and Fry was exhilarated but exhausted.

> At times our business has been so great, as almost to overwhelm us – callers almost innumerable, and out and in almost constantly ourselves, so that I have sometimes felt as if I could not long bear it, particularly when I could not obtain some rest in the afternoon.

One afternoon, she sat down on a chair and simply wept with fatigue. She was, after all, now 58 years old. But as the party set off back for England, she was already planning a return trip to France. The summer was taken up with re-inspecting prisons in Scotland, but before Christmas she had again applied to the Society of Friends for permission to return to minister in France and beyond. Once more she wondered whether she should join her brother Joseph in America instead; once again the pull of the Continent, and of duties at home, was greater.

Fry was quite simply entranced by the contradictions she had observed in contemporary France:

> Such a nation! Such a numerous and superior people! Filling such a place in the world! And Satan appearing in no common degree to be seeking to destroy them: first by infidelity and so-called philosophy; secondly by superstition and the priesthood rising with fresh power; thirdly, by an extreme love of the world and its pleasures; fourthly, by an unsettled, restless and warlike spirit. Yet, under all this, there is a hidden power of good amongst them; very many extraordinary Christian characters; bright, sober, zealous

Roman Catholics and Protestants; education increasing; the Holy Scriptures more read and valued; a general stirring to improve the prisons of France.[1]

And the French seemed to have been entranced by Fry, by the 'witchery of her voice, her appearance and manner, which overcame all difficulty of language'. After her meetings, people clung to her and could hardly bear to let her go, her niece Priscilla Buxton wrote to her brother.

> Everyone wanted a few private words and they wished to make her a kind of Mother Confessor. Sometimes those who could speak no English would beg [for a private interview] with her – the difficulty of getting on you can imagine – but I can fancy that there would be some edification in only looking at her and hearing her voice.[2]

At the beginning of March 1839, just days before she was due to set off for the Continent, Fry made a new acquaintance. He would furnish her with valuable introductions to important people in Germany. He would also become one of her staunchest supporters, and, some years later, a relative by marriage.[3]

Christian von Bunsen was a close friend of, and adviser to, the Crown Prince of Prussia; after the Prince's accession as King Friedrich Wilhelm IV in June 1840, Bunsen would also become the royal diplomatic representative in London. Bunsen had gone to Crosby Hall in Bishopsgate for a sale of books and handicrafts for the benefit of female prisoners and convicts.[4] As he entered the hall, he saw Fry in the middle near the front stall, and was introduced.

> [She was] a tall, large figure, about 60 years of age, with eyes small but of sweet and commanding expression – a striking appearance, but plain, rather grand than handsome. This was Mrs Fry, my favourite saint. She promised, when we had finished our circuit, to find a place in which we could have conversation; and this she did, in a gallery overlooking glorious Crosby Hall. When she stopped speaking, I said something expressive of my feeling as to her work of love, and further ventured to say: 'I have for many years wished to convince myself why you could and should not devise measures for making such great and blessed efforts as yours, for so grand an object, independent of yourself – to form something that might survive you.'[5]

Fry suggested that Bunsen should read her book that he had just bought, after which he should visit her at home at Upton to talk more; she also invited him to go with her to Newgate. The following Sunday, he received a note from her,

announcing her intention to leave for the Continent in a few days' time, and
wondering if he might be able to help her with letters of introduction or travelling hints. He called on her at St Mildred's Court that same day.

> At Mrs Fry's door, the servant protested that she could not see anybody; yet we were
> let in. Mrs Fry came, much fagged but friendly. I began my statement of a plan for her
> journey, quite different to that which had been made out for her; she took my hint
> instantly. I gave her a picture of country and men from Stuttgart to Elberfeld, and before
> I reached Heidelberg she said: 'That is settled, I must go that way'. Then I took courage
> and told her of [the] establishment for lost children in Berlin, and of the deaconesses at
> Kaiserswerth.[6]

Fry was deeply impressed by all he told her, adding: 'I ought to have seen more
of thee – thou shouldst have been under my roof . . . I am sorry for what I have
missed; shall I ever see thee again?'

> Then, having put on her long black cloak to go to their meeting, she took my hands and
> said, 'Farewell, may God be with thee in all thy ways, and prosper all that thou doest'.
> It was an impressive and solemn interview, and we all felt the power of her character.[7]

As well as helping to plan the journey, and furnishing letters of introduction,
Bunsen also had printed for Fry a pamphlet in German, as if written by her. It
outlined her prison work, and the steps taken as a result at government level in
Britain for the improvement of prison life. The pamphlet further listed practical measures that could be introduced, including the promotion of literacy for
prisoners.

So on 11 March 1839, Fry was off again; this time the trip would last six months.
Her husband accompanied her on this occasion, as did their old friend Josiah
Forster. Various members of the family, and friends, came out to join them for
some part of the tour. By now, Fry's fame was firmly established in Europe. No
sooner had they reached Boulogne on the north coast of France, *en route* to Paris,
than people came wanting to consult her. She briefly visited the local prison which
she found to be 'in a very deplorable state', and had a meeting with the ladies of a
district society that she had helped to establish on her previous visit. Wherever
she went, people were clamouring for Bibles, religious books and tracts.

Soon the party arrived in Paris and began renewing acquaintances, revisiting
some prisons in order to review progress, and inspecting others for the first

time. But on this visit, the focus of her attention was more on hospitals. Her guide was the elderly Roman Catholic Baron Joseph-Marie de Géronda, philosopher, philanthropist, and co-founder of the movement that introduced into France the monitorial system of education that had been pioneered in Britain by Joseph Lancaster. Géronda had been trying to raise funds for a penitentiary for fallen women, but with no great success. He complained that, while it was comparatively easy to induce people to help feed the starving, clothe the naked and administer to the sick, 'moral reforms, the benefits of which are less immediately obvious, but of such infinitely greater importance, are too often neglected'.

Together, Fry and the baron first visited the ancient foundation of the Hôtel Dieu, a vast hospital located on both sides of the river Seine, connected by a covered bridge. The hospital contained 1,260 beds, in wards of a hundred or more. Other hospital visits followed.

One of the topics most hotly debated during Fry's stay in Paris was the issue of solitary confinement. Before she left the capital, Fry asked her husband to draw up a list of the arguments for and against, for the benefit of those interested in the question of prison reform. Her own preference was for productive association during the day, and segregation at night for the sake of peace and propriety. In a letter written by her husband and addressed to her influential reformer friend Alphonse de Béranger, Fry gave four brief reasons in support of the practice, and seven lengthy ones against it. The most powerful arguments in favour of solitary confinement were:

> *First*, it prevents . . . all contamination from their fellow-prisoners.
>
> *Secondly*, it prevents the formation of intimacy . . . with persons who may prove highly injurious associates in future life.
>
> *Thirdly*, it affords more opportunity for serious reflection and . . . it may lead to a greater dependence on God.
>
> *Fourthly*, the privacy of confinement may prevent that loss of character . . . which is the general consequence of imprisonment, as now inflicted.

The arguments against adopting the system were, in her experience, both in Britain and France:

> *First*, the extreme liability to its abuse . . . according to the will or caprice, partiality, dislike or neglect, of the persons who have the management of them.
>
> *Secondly*, the . . . difficulty of obtaining a sufficiency of either men or women officers,

of that high and upright principle, as by their impartiality and firmness, with proper kindness and due attention to the welfare of prisoners, would be *fit* persons to be entrusted with so weighty a charge.

Thirdly, prisoners so confined are rendered almost *irresistibly* subject to the moral contamination of officers.

Fourthly, . . . expense ought to be a very secondary consideration, yet it ought not to be overlooked. The expense of providing proper cells, and a sufficient number of properly qualified officers, for so large a number of prisoners, would be enormous; and the difficulty, of so building as to prevent the communication of sound, very great, and its attainment uncertain, besides the liability of the prisoners from not being able to make themselves heard in case of necessity, arising from sudden illness or accident.

Fifthly, although for short periods, neither the powers of the mind nor body might suffer essentially, yet after a long and too solitary confinement, there is *unquestionable danger for both*. Too much silence is contrary to nature, and physically injurious both to the stomach and lungs . . . amongst the monks of La Trappe, few attained to the age of sixty years without having suffered an absolute decay of their mental powers, and fallen into premature childishness.

Sixthly, there is reason . . . to fear, that a large proportion of those who are confined in jails, are so deeply depraved, that when left to themselves they would be *more likely* to consume their hours in ruminating over past crimes and exploits, and in devising and planning schemes for the commission of new ones.

Seventhly, and the most weighty objection of all, is this: that as the vast majority of those who enter a prison are likely to be returned to the bosom of society, it is a most important and paramount consideration, that as man is a social being, and not designed for a life of seclusion, such a system of prison discipline be adopted, as may best prepare those under its correction, for re-entering active life, and all its consequent exposures and temptations. This can never be effected in solitude or separation: it can only be achieved by such regulations, brought to bear on everyday prison life, as may most easily, and with the best chance of success, be afterwards carried out and realised in daily practice, upon their restoration to liberty.

The letter continued with recommendations on the best way of dealing with untried prisoners. Above all, it was important that they should not be demoralized or brutalized through contact with hardened offenders. It could take many months for a case to come to even a preliminary hearing. During this period, there was the serious danger of the untried prisoner's being corrupted by association, since opportunity is thus afforded to the profligate villain, to harden, to season and to imbue the mind of his unpractised victim, for re-entering society depraved, debased and ripe for the commission of crimes, at which he would have shuddered, when the act of law, by placing him in public detention, first exposed him to irretrievable degradation and ruin.

The solution was to keep the untried separate from the convicted, and allow them as normal a life as possible, for as short a period as possible before their trial. They should be able to see their friends; consult their solicitors or other legal advisers; and have extra comforts such as bedding and food sent in from outside at their own expense. If found guilty, first-time offenders should be organized into small, manageable groups, and given regular instruction and Bible readings. For repeat offenders, isolation might be the only solution, she admitted. But, in the case of women, she insisted that

in no case should women be separately confined, unless under the care of officers of their own sex; nor should any man, not even the chaplain or physician, be allowed to visit them under any pretext, unless accompanied by a female officer.

This letter was written as Fry was about to leave Paris. At that same time, it came to her notice that the Archbishop of Paris had expressed his annoyance at the measures she had recommended be introduced at the women's prison at St Lazare, and at Baron de Géronda's acting as her guide on a tour of the hospitals. Her promotion of the Bible as the source of all moral authority, and her propensity for handing out New Testaments and other tracts wherever she went, had been interpreted as a direct challenge to the authority of the Roman Catholic Church. Also, the very simplicity of the Quaker faith, the absence of a priesthood, and the idea that God spoke directly and personally to men and women through the medium of Holy Scripture, must have seemed quite shocking to the religious establishment.

Visiting prisons and hospitals as they went, the party travelled from Paris to Melun and Fontainebleau, and thence to Chalons-sur-Saône, from where they took a boat down the river to Lyons. Tracts were distributed as usual – one fellow traveller gave Josiah Forster an antique Sèvres wine flask in exchange for a pamphlet by Joseph Gurney. Generally, however, they found that there was not the same thirst for books in the south as in the north, 'partly arising from comparatively few of the people being taught to read'.

The further south they travelled, the more they found that charitable institutions like prisons and hospitals were run by religious orders. At La Perrache, delinquent boys were cared for by the brothers of St Joseph, while sisters of the same order ran the Maison d'Arrêt for women – where Fry 'saw with pleasure the beneficial effects of women placed under the care of persons of their own sex' – as well as a refuge for discharged female prisoners and vagrants. Fry wrote to her children that the order

> believe it their duty entirely to take care of prisoners and criminals generally. They do not visit as we do, but take the entire part of turnkeys and prison officers, and live with the prisoners day and night, constantly caring for them. I thought the effect on the female prisoners surprisingly good.

During a brief stay at Avignon, Fry inspected the remand prison where inmates were kept busy making coarse cloth used for packing madder plants (a source of red dye) grown in Provence for the English textiles market. The party then proceeded to Nîmes. They were to spend several weeks in the area and not because of the attraction of its prisons. Fry was 'a great friend of not stopping too long in a place', but the Nîmes region was different, since it was the home to 'a scattered body of people protesting the principle of the Society of Friends'. These people were the descendants of the French Protestant Camisards who were persecuted, and fought back against their persecution, following the revocation in 1685 of the Edict of Nantes, which had granted them religious freedom. They had ultimately found their spiritual home within the Quaker movement, and a sojourn with them at Nîmes provided Fry and her companions with a welcome break, although work was not entirely forgotten.

The central prison in the town was built on the site of the former citadel, and housed 1,200 men who worked in total silence, in vast workshops. Fry asked especially to see the dungeons where prisoners were kept who had committed additional crimes while in prison, or had proved particularly unmanageable. In one cell, which was completely dark, she found two men, one of whom was chained both hands and feet. The visitors – Fry, Forster, the chaplain and the prison surgeon – asked that their armed guard of five soldiers should remain outside while they entered the cell alone. Fry told the men that she had sometimes pleaded for prisoners to be unlocked from their irons if they promised to behave well in future. The prisoners promised, the chains were unlocked and the men were released from the dungeon. On a later visit, Fry attended a service in the Protestant chapel, 'filled by depraved-looking men in their rough prison dress'. She spoke of redemption – and then of its dreadful alternative – and reminded the men that the choice was theirs. As she made to leave, a warder brought two men out of the workshop to speak to her. They told her they prayed for her each night. They were the men from the dungeon.

Some days later, Fry also received a letter from another of the prisoners, thanking her for her visit which had been

> a great source of consolation. Your words of kindness and goodness are deeply engraved on our hearts. We are so unaccustomed here to see outsiders – particularly one so very distinguished – plead our case, and offer us sympathy, that we are very sorry we shall not be able to be honoured often by a visit from you.

The first institution that Fry visited at Marseilles, their next stop, was a closed convent which took in 'penitents' and impoverished young women as well as novices. Most of those who did not become nuns became servants. None were compelled to stay against their will, but some had been there as long as nine years. They were not taught to read or write, nor permitted to exercise those skills if they already had them, for fear that they might communicate with the outside world. They spent their days working, sewing, praying and reciting psalms. Fry was very uncomfortable with the idea of either prisoners or 'penitents' being committed to the exclusive care of religious orders without their being accountable to the secular superintendence of magistrates. The Marseilles home for children orphaned by cholera Fry found to be in excellent order, as she did a small penitentiary in the city for delinquent boys. In the local hospital, she found four English sailors, one of whom recognized her from one of the female convict ships, and greeted her as an old friend.

At Toulon, Fry and her company were taken to visit the *bagnes*, or prisons for galley slaves, and were appalled.

> They work hard, sleep on the boards, and eat only bread and dry beans, with half a bottle of wine to those who work. Many of them die . . . from the close communication, the contagion of evil is fearful. A man who is vicious when he goes in, inevitably comes out more so. They sleep in vast galleries, a hundred or two hundred in each, chained to a long iron rod which runs the whole length of the foot of the sleeping board. There is a *salle*, which contains four hundred, for those who have improved in conduct, and to

them mattresses are allowed and rugs. In their leisure hours, they are allowed to make and sell little toys and netting. Their look is generally unhealthy.

The next stop on the prison visit schedule was the Maison Centrale women's prison at nearby Montpellier, which housed five hundred women. A law had recently been passed in France, stipulating that female prisoners should be supervised by female officers and it was meeting some resistance from the female prisoners themselves! Fry visited the prison on two consecutive days, and met with a number of Protestant ladies willing to form themselves into a committee to visit women both in prison and in hospital.

By now Fry was flagging. Her perseverance was as great as ever but physically and emotionally, she was running out of strength. At the end of June 1839, she wrote to her children: 'My attraction homewards grows stronger and stronger, but I desire patiently to wait the right time – the openings for religious service are greater than I expected'. Leaving her husband Joseph behind in Toulouse, where he was suffering from the heat, she and Josiah Forster accepted an invitation to visit France's only Protestant training college, at Montauban, for what she thought would be a quiet evening's discussion in a private house. But when they arrived,

> we found, to our dismay, all arranged to receive us in the college . . . the whole of the collegians were assembled, in all at least a hundred. It was fearful work. There were also numbers of people of the town; we thought about three hundred.

Undaunted, Fry spoke of her prison experience and told them a little of what she had discovered in the prisons of France. The audience was deeply appreciative, so in the end it had been worth the effort, and, as they returned to Toulouse, she 'had seldom felt sweeter peace in leaving a place than Montauban'.

The otherwise relentless schedule of prison and hospital visiting was broken up by excursions to mountains and lakes, waterfalls and other beauty spots, and an occasional few days' rest to write a report for the French interior minister on the state of his prisons and her recommendations for their improvement.

Travelling south towards Switzerland at the beginning of July, the party stopped at Grenoble where Fry found evidence of the benefits that a committee of visitors could bring to a prison. The Grenoble gaol was old and badly constructed, but kept very clean, and its defects and the wants of the prisoners as much remedied as possible, by an active committee of ladies and gentlemen, who pay much attention to the bodily wants of prisoners . . . The funds of these committees are chiefly derived from money dropped into a box at the gate, by the peasants and lower class of persons, to obtain the prayers of the prisoners, which are considered by them particularly efficacious in releasing souls from purgatory: these alms are chiefly expended in linen for the prisoners' use . . . The government and authorities have tried to put this system . . . entirely down, but have been successfully opposed by the committee, on the ground that they have neither power nor right to interfere with private almsgiving, its purpose or appropriation.

Fry was reluctant to visit Switzerland, just as she had not originally wanted to go to France: 'Our returning home through Switzerland, I still view very doubtfully. Unless thy presence go with us, oh Lord!, take us not there.' But once there, as with France, it proved a 'very interesting time, from various and important openings for religious service, in large parties, in prisons, etc. My belief is that we were sent to this place.' Her contacts at Geneva were very welcoming and hospitable, and the addresses she gave on the reformation of prisoners through religion seemed to make a deep impression. One evening, she was the guest of a Colonel Tronchin at a gala dinner and lecture at his villa at Beseinge outside Geneva, in whose grounds he had established a convalescent home. A group of young students from Geneva University had turned up uninvited, out of curiosity. While the invited guests dined inside, the students ate their picnics in the gardens before creeping into the house to hear Fry speak, crowding up the staircase and spilling over into corridors, as one student recalled,

eagerly hanging on such parts of the beautiful exhortation as we could catch by the most breathless attention. After she had concluded, she kindly came out among us, and expressed her regret that we should have been so inconvenienced. I can see her now, her tall figure leaning on Colonel Tronchin's arm . . . her dignified, animated yet softened countenance bending towards us. I can never forget it. Such occasions are very rare in life; they are very green spots in the garden of memory.

At the Maison Pénitentiaire at Geneva, Fry had the opportunity of meeting the brother of her old friend Stephen Grellet, who had first introduced her to Newgate. It was a small prison with just 50 long-term prisoners, and Joseph Grellet was its deputy governor. As might be expected, it was a model establishment, with inmates divided into four distinct classes, with association during the day and segregation at night in individual cells, each furnished with a bed, chair, table, shelf and some books.

After Geneva, the party visited Lausanne and Berne, where the prison facilities were generally found to be excellent. At a reception in Berne, a young woman offered to interpret Fry's address into German, and later produced a lengthy German-language tract, based on the address, which was widely circulated in Swiss prisons. From Berne, Fry and friends travelled to Thun 'in the midst of mountains and waterfalls'. It was now August 1839, and they had been away from home for five months. She wrote home: 'Switzerland is certainly a wonderful country, and very attractive . . . [but] sweet as it is, the flats of East and West Ham look to *us* sweeter. I have much felt on this journey, that life itself is but a journey.'

For now, the journey took them onwards to Zurich, Stuttgart and Ludwigsburg, where Fry had intended to speak on prisons but found herself diverted to voicing her support for the Protestant Church in France. She inspected the local female prison, and called on the chief magistrate to report on 'the evils I had observed', before meeting with local ladies to discuss the establishment of a prison visiting system. From Ludwigsburg they went to Cologne, and thence to Frankfurt, and then straight home to Upton Lane where she arrived on 13 September 1839 to find the family well and prospering, and 'nothing appears to have suffered from our absence'.

As the year drew to a close, Fry was able to look back with pleasure at having received

> very satisfactory letters from the Continent, in which it appears, in various ways, that our visit has been blessed in many places: committees formed to visit prisoners, prisons improved. The minds of prisoners appear to have been seriously impressed, encourage-ment given to some who wanted it, and, I trust, by what I hear, many stimulated in their progress heavenward.

The year 1840 began with public excitement at the announcement that the young Queen was to marry Prince Albert of Saxe-Coburg-Gotha. To cele-brate the betrothal, Victoria sent Fry a gift of £50 towards the upkeep of the Chelsea refuge for young girls which she had helped to found. Privately, Fry was more excited about the prospect of another trip abroad, and an invitation to Buckingham Palace in February provided the opportunity to discuss with the monarch both the refuge and the impending Continental tour.

This time, her husband Joseph decided to remain at home; her brother Joseph was still in America. Her companions were to be brother Samuel, his daughter Elizabeth – who kept a refreshingly frank, if sometimes irreverent, account of life on the road with 'the elders' – Josiah Forster, William Allen and his young niece Lucy Bradshaw.

William Allen (1770–1843) was a Quaker philanthropist who championed many areas of social reform, including the abolition of slavery, prison reform and the education of girls – particularly in science subjects. He had been an acquaintance of Fry and her brothers since the early 1820s. He was much taken with the ideas of Joseph Lancaster and became an influential member of the Royal Lancastrian Society (later the British and Foreign School Society), which sought to promote progressive education in Britain and abroad, in which capacity he had travelled extensively throughout Europe with Stephen Grellet in 1818–20. Also an eminent scientist and researcher, he was a founder and first president of the Pharmaceutical Society (later, the Royal Pharmaceutical Society), and owner of what became one of Britain's leading pharmaceutical companies, Allen & Hanbury.[8]

Allen's life was dogged by personal tragedy. At the time he joined the Fry party in 1840, he had been widowed three times and suffered the loss of his only child, a daughter, who died giving birth to his grandson; after which he devoted his considerable time, energy and resources for the rest of his life to promoting the causes that he held dear.

The journey began in February 1840, when the party set sail from Dover. The plan was that Fry would talk about prisons, Allen and Forster would advise on education, and Samuel Gurney would speak out for the abolition of slavery; although in practice the boundaries were blurred and all were competent in all subjects. They would visit and report on prisons, orphanages, workhouses, schools, convents and lunatic asylums.

The first country on their schedule was Belgium, stopping at Bruges and then Ghent, where they met English labourers working to make steam engines for the region's cotton mills. In Brussels, they were invited for an hour-long audience with King Leopold, uncle of Queen Victoria. Leopold's sister and Victoria's uncle, the Duchess of Kent (formerly the widowed Countess of Leiningen), had written to Leopold informing him of Fry's impending visit, and had furnished her with a letter of introduction.

From Belgium, they crossed the border into Holland, where in Rotterdam they met the 'Howard of Holland', Willem Hendrik Suringar. At Leuwarden in the north of Holland there was a model prison that Suringar's father had shown to John Howard a generation before, and Suringar had 'wished for many years to have the honour that his father had, and show it to Mrs Fry'.

By now they were a month into the campaign and although Aunt Fry was usually 'bright and cheerful and loved wherever she goes', she was beginning to flag a little and found no time to write home to Joseph. As her niece observed in her travelogue, 'She has begun one letter and written as far as "My dear husband", but she gives up without adding another word'. At Gouda, the inmates of a women's prison, where an informal 'committee' of two lady visitors had for some years been attending to their welfare, 'were beautifully addressed by our Aunt. They seemed deeply affected by what she said and wept bitterly'. Whether an interpreter was present is not recorded. It seemed not always to matter. The tone of Fry's voice and the manner of her delivery were known to elicit tears even among those who had no knowledge of English. After Amsterdam, Leyden, Zwolle and Utrecht, the party crossed into Germany, much to the relief of Samuel Gurney who by now was openly expressing himself bored with water and windmills.

Their first stop in Germany was at the spa town of Pyrmont in Lower Saxony. Pyrmont was the centre of Quakerism in Germany, and here Fry met the influential Seebohm family – Benjamin Seebohm was the colleague and biographer of Stephen Grellet. It was in Pyrmont, too, that they became acquainted with – and were rather taken aback by – the German kissing culture. Elizabeth Gurney wrote:

> Not content with one smack, they give you at least four – that is, two on each side, for a German kiss is never completed until both cheeks have been attacked, so that when you are in a room with a dozen ladies, it is hard work to accomplish the parting. Aunt Fry bears it heroically. (I think she rather likes it.)[9]

Possibly as a result of kissing too many strangers, Fry, who was nearly 60 years old by now, developed a serious chest infection 'and is not at all strong, hardly able to go out at all on account of the cold'. Nevertheless, the work carried on and there was a productive meeting with local dignitaries about the possibility of forming a local district visiting society.

From Pyrmont, the party continued to Hanover, where the condition of the poor was observed to be 'about on a par with the Irish'. They visited a large military prison but found it 'in a sad state, the prisoners so heavily chained and scanty provisions'. In Britain, the Gaols Act of 1823 had outlawed the use of leg irons and manacles in prisons, as Fry pointed out to the governor when he dined with them that evening. Seeing the state of the prisons in Hanover, 'our feelings in them have been painfully excited . . . men chained to the floor and confined with very little intercourse with their fellow men, until their faculties are evidently impaired'. They were unable to make representations to the King of Hanover, Ernest Augustus, Duke of Cumberland (who acceded to the throne in 1837, since his niece Queen Victoria was prevented by local Salic law which precluded female inheritance). The King was indisposed, and they made little headway with the Crown Prince, who was 'quite inclined to talk about many objects, but I fear not to much purpose as he is so riveted to his own views'; he was also only twenty years old. Fry expected little success from the visit.

By early April, they were in Berlin, then the capital of Prussia, and comfort-ably installed at the splendid Hôtel de Russe, where again they were fêted by the great and the good, including the British Ambassador Lord William Russell, brother to the more famous John. Elizabeth Gurney wrote that Aunt Fry

> still complains of her chest, and yet it is wonderful to see her extraordinary power of body and soul when necessary labours of actual business for the religious or moral welfare of her fellow creatures come in her way. But the weather is now much finer and signs of spring beginning, and so we may look forward to her being better.[10]

That stamina was soon to be called on, since the following day – 12 April 1840 – a message arrived from Princess Wilhelm, sister-in-law of the late king, to say that King Friedrich Wilhelm III had granted her permission to accom-pany Fry on a prison visit at noon that same day. The Princess and her daughter arrived in a gilded carriage, with footmen in blue and gold livery, to collect her, but Fry was not to be outdone. Her niece wrote:

> Our Aunt looked like a princess herself, in a beautiful full silk cloak that Papa [Samuel Gurney] had given her and that [we] have managed to have made for her here, and then a pair of light gloves and a new cap. She looks fit for any court in Europe. They pranced off in fine style and we followed, as their humble servants, in our own carriage.[11]

In the event, the outing seems to have been more of a royal public relations exercise than a serious fact-finding visit.

Neither of the Princesses had ever visited a prison before, which made it all the more interesting to hear the remarks that Princess Wilhelm made to the prisoners and to see how curious they were to learn all about it. It was not to our idea a very satisfactory visit, as the numbers of governors and officers, all in full dress, made it next to impossible to move through the long narrow passage. The Princess kissed our Aunt on taking leave ... of course, a vast crowd was attracted outside by her carriage, but I think our Aunt excited the most attention.[12]

The next stop on Fry's schedule after Berlin was Frankfurt, for which part of the journey the party expected to take 'perhaps a week, as we cannot take very long stages, for our Aunt must rest in the middle of the day. We feed her up with porter and ale where we can get it', her niece observed.

Wherever they went, Fry began her public talks with a description of her entering the 'horrid abodes' of Newgate, the

clamour that was raised by all parties on her venturing to go in unprotected. The awful state of filth and depravity they were in and the prisoners, the females especially, so violent that even the turnkeys hardly dared venture in; the quiet way herself and her companion were received; their taking clothing for the children; the respect with which the prisoners treated them. Then she went on to express her own feelings about introducing Christian doctrine to them.[13]

She gave examples of the good that had been achieved by the efforts of her lady visitors and herself, and she entreated her audience in the warmest terms 'to seek to turn poor prisoners from the error of their ways and to take an interest in their everlasting welfare'. Whereupon, Samuel Gurney had tea and cakes handed around and those attending had the opportunity to ask questions. 'Everyone wants to know what relation to one another we are', young Elizabeth wrote.

And how do we travel? And where have we been to? Then all about our Aunt's private history. Where does she live? Is she married? Are they Quakers? And then the astonishment is vast when I tell them of five and twenty grandchildren. This seems to add to the respect paid to her.[14]

From Berlin, most of the party travelled on to Dresden where there were more prisons and palaces to visit, more grand dukes and diplomats to confer with, and committees to establish. Samuel Gurney expressed himself perpetually amazed at the opulent existence of the princelings of Europe: 'I cannot conceive how these little sovereigns live in such palaces, and maintain such state!' Coburg, he pointed out, had a population of about 150,000 souls but a palace nearly as big as Windsor Castle.

After Dresden, it was on to Leipzig, Frankfurt, Weimar, Gotha and Mainz. At Erfurth, they walked in Martin Luther's footsteps at the Augustinian convent where his career first began. The convent had been converted to a school, run by two of Luther's descendants, and the old schoolmaster 'seemed as though he could not sufficiently appreciate the honour of having Mrs Fry on his arm, of whom he had read about for more than 20 years'.

On their return to Frankfurt, Fry was again feeling the strain. 'Our Aunt was so very ill on our arrival here, and has continued so unwell since we arrived, that our visit to this fine town has not been very agreeable to us', Elizabeth Gurney wrote on 4 May. But a boat trip down the Rhine from Mainz provided a welcome diversion. 'Our Aunt's books were greedily snatched up and read by everyone in the boat; some of the sailors forming groups and reading aloud to those who could not read.'

And then it was on to Düsseldorf. There had been an active ladies' committee at the Düsseldorf prison for several years, and Fry was keen to compare notes. There was also the opportunity to visit the old Trappist monastery at Düsselthal, which had been converted by Count Adalbert von der Recke, at his own expense, into a home for orphaned and destitute children. The count and his wife ran and funded the home themselves and were delighted to receive a 'liberal donation' to their cause from Samuel Gurney.[15]

Perhaps the most important day trip from Düsseldorf was to Pastor Fliedner's charitable establishment at Kaiserswerth on the Rhine. Fliedner was a great admirer of Fry, whom he had met on a fund-raising visit to London as a young man. Many of her Newgate principles had been incorporated into his establishment, which had grown to include a small hospital and nursing training school for Protestant deaconesses. Dressed in their distinctive uniform of blue print dresses and white caps, these women were sent out to all parts of the country to nurse the poor sick.

They appeared a capital set of women, and were pleased when they saw our great interest in them. Our Aunt had them assembled after dinner at the Pastor's house, and he interpreted to them her beautiful address giving them excellent hints on nursing the sick . . . Christian manners of gentleness and evenness of temper form a real nurse [she said]: this had been her experience and she felt sure from their looks and manners it had been theirs also.[16]

If Fliedner had been inspired by Fry's Newgate model, Fry would in turn be inspired by Fliedner's Kaiserswerth initiative when, not long afterwards, her own thoughts turned to a training school for nurses.

The tour was nearly over. From Düsseldorf, the party travelled to Liège by coach and, when the coach broke down through sheer wear, onwards by train to catch the boat at Antwerp from where they enjoyed a calm passage back to London, arriving on 14 May.

They were not so lucky with the weather on their overnight sailing back to the Continent in July the following year. This time the party comprised Fry, her brother Joseph back from America, his daughter Anna and, once again, the chronicler of the group, Samuel Gurney's daughter Elizabeth, who continued her meticulous account of their travels and sent detailed, gossipy letters back to Britain to be circulated among the various branches of the family. By now the younger members of the party were accustomed to being merely 'the hem of Aunt's garment', dragooned into roles as personal assistants and private secretaries, although they were not alone in this: 'It is droll to see how Aunt makes *all* work, whoever they may be'.

On this occasion the North Sea crossing was so stormy that even Joseph, who had sailed the Atlantic, said that he had never seen a ship 'in such fearful breakers'. 'Aunt Fry', who was naturally terrified of the sea anyway, was 'rolling about on her bunk' and at one point 'turned extremely faint'. But by breakfast time, they were safely installed in a hotel in Rotterdam and ready to launch themselves on another relentless round of campaigning 'amidst all the turmoils of high life and low life, between dungeons and palaces'.

Within days they were granted an audience in Amsterdam with King William, who showed a keen interest in Fry's private life: in particular, if she had so many children, how could she leave them to attend to prisons? Fry was equally direct. As the King made to leave, she expressed the wish that his reign

be marked by three things: that the prisons be so improved that punishment may tend to the reformation of the prisoners, that the scriptures may be freely read in all your schools, and that every slave in the dominion may be freed.[17]

Slavery was ended by Britain in 1834 but not by Holland until 1863, and the following day abolition was back on the agenda at a 'capital slavery evening . . . where Uncle Joseph told his tale most clearly. Many stiff Dutch slave owners present but all seemed interested and they lingered late in discoursing the matter with him.'

During the daytime, while other party members amused themselves with trips around the harbour, to the zoo, and attending concerts, Fry's time was taken up with

> visiting prisons, bedlam, workhouses . . . and sad were the tales of misery and wretchedness that she told us of on our return. The madhouse no better . . . the lunatics chained, kept in dungeons and hardly clothed.[18]

Meanwhile, Joseph Gurney continued to foot all the bills, as Samuel had done on the previous year's trip. In addition to the travel, accommodation, food and excursions, he funded couriers, interpreters and other helpers, as his niece noted.

> We always have a commissionaire in every town to do all our business and run messages. Also a neat carriage [and six horses] so then we are well provided for. Nothing can exceed Uncle's *extravagance* almost it amounts to, about these and all sorts of luxuries. In fact, we are living *en Prince* and Anna and I are growing quite fat on eating so much and walking so little.[19]

On 4 August, they left Amsterdam by coach for Germany – an uncomfortable experience over sandy terrain turned to axle-deep mud by recent rain, and Fry again unwell. *En route*, the carriage spring broke. They were forced to interrupt the journey for the night since 'we did not like to trust ourselves to these dreadful roads after dusk, and Aunt was not strong enough to run any risk of the carriage's wholly breaking down'.

When they did at last reach Bremen, Fry remained ill for several days and 'rather low', barely able to venture out on a planned workhouse visit. 'I do not think she is much amiss', her niece recorded,

> but she is so unwise about eating and drinking . . . We are constantly applying to Uncle Buxton's bottles [of Bordeaux, donated for the trip]. I tell Aunt that with them as carnal, and her Bible as spiritual, food, she might travel over the Arabian deserts.[20]

With Fry still weak, it fell to Joseph Gurney to take charge at impromptu Bible readings, Meetings and prisoner addresses 'while Aunt stands by and *looks* sermons to them'. And he was an indulgent an uncle, as ever: 'he does not care the smallest about cost so long as we are all comfortable'.

One of the drawbacks of Fry's international fame was the lack of privacy. The newspapers were full of details of their schedule, and they were recognized wherever they went. 'We are received so hospitably wherever we go . . . Mrs Fry is such a passport. It is marvellous, to be sure, to think how she is known everywhere'. But Elizabeth Gurney sometimes longed for an escape. She noted that many people were in prison in Germany for distributing tracts. The Fry party were also distributing tracts.

> We hope that we shall be also [imprisoned]. It would be so entertaining only one of us must stay out, so that we might go and please for Aunt Fry that she may be allowed porter and beef.[21]

On the journey from Bremen to Hamburg, they were also bothered by crowds. The trip across the mouth of the Elbe would have been delightful

> had not the steamer been very full of people who were all so eager after Mrs Fry and her books that there was no bearing them, and for decency's sake we had to take refuge in the coach at last, locking the door lest the crowd should even enter the carriage on their rude curiosity.[22]

Hamburg proved a much more productive stay than Bremen. On 18 August, the party visited three prisons and one orphanage, and took part in a ladies' committee meeting. It was

> a hard day's work, considering that our resting times between at the hotel were wholly engaged with callers . . . As usual we have seen a strange variety of good clergymen, rich merchants, influential senators, worldly men and agreeable young ladies . . . the word *rest* is not to be found in our dictionary at Hamburg. Happily, Aunt Fry is better.[23]

The next day, they visited a children's home and trade school for 50 boys and girls, a large hospital and an asylum for the poor. A dinner party the same evening was expected to be an intimate affair, but they arrived to find about 80 people seated in rows, waiting for a speech from Fry and her brother.

There was nothing to be done but speak in such a case, and I am sure, had they had days to prepare, they could not have given more elegant or good discourses – Uncle on Wilberforce's life, Aunt stirring up the ladies to do good works. People listened with the most breathless attention.[24]

The next day was their last in Hamburg and it ended with a public meeting attended by hundreds, all of whom were provided with refreshments afterwards. Fry recounted yet again her Newgate experiences, followed by a report on what she had found in the prisons in Hamburg; Joseph Gurney did his slavery speech. Afterwards, there was ice-cream and cakes for 50 personal friends before the two young cousins set about packing everything away for a 'disagreeably' early start for Copenhagen the following day.

This is no light task, what with important papers and quantities of books, and the elders so tired they can do nothing but drink *vin de Bordeaux* and go to bed. Anna and I find it a good hour's work. However, this comes under the immediate office of Aide de Camps. Which is our peculiar office.[25]

When it came to settling up with the hotel for their stay in Hamburg, even Joseph Gurney was surprised. 'Uncle was shocked at the bill; but I asked, what could he have expected, considering the style we had lived in, and having so many take their meals with us?'

The journey to Copenhagen was via Kiel, where their carriage was loaded on to the steamer across the Baltic Sea, which, again being caught in a 'furious thunder storm', was as rough a crossing as the North Sea had been. Just before reaching Copenhagen, it being Sunday, Joseph Gurney assembled the company on deck for a morning service and sermon. Immediately on their arrival in the Danish capital, the British *chargé d'affaires* came on board with a letter of welcome from the Queen and the message that she had booked accommodation for them at the Hôtel d'Angleterre at her own expense. Gurney accepted the booking graciously, but insisted that he would pay the bill. The Queen had also invited Fry to visit her as soon as she was settled; later the entire party were to go to the royal country residence to be introduced to King Christian, 'having in the meantime visited the prisons, that Aunt may lay her story before the King'.[26] She also offered Fry the use of a room at the palace if she wished to hold any large meetings.

Being favoured by the Queen of Denmark was a mixed blessing, since her

liberal views were not necessarily shared either by the 'bigoted old king' or by his
subjects, and Fry and Gurney failed to draw the usual crowds.

> Every body thinks that being so taken up by her, we want no more; [but] we have
> found it difficult to make much access. Anybody else would have been satisfied with
> the numbers . . . but if people do not *flock*, then they [Fry and Gurney] are not satisfied.
> The religious party here is quite sad. *Parties* I ought to say, so that if you are a friend to
> one party, you must expect to be in disrepute with the others. I never knew it so strong
> anywhere. The non-liberty of *conscience* and *press* being the evident cause.[27]

The next day was spent entirely in visiting prisons and thus 'more useful than
agreeable' to the younger members of the party.

> But I think, on the whole, they were better than Aunt expected, though we saw two
> poor men who had quite lost their senses from grief. The most sad sight though was two
> Baptist ministers . . . brothers, each in separate cells . . . imprisoned entirely from their
> religious views.[28]

Throughout their travels, the party seemed to operate in relative harmony.
'We are very happy', Elizabeth Gurney wrote home to her mother. 'Uncle now
and then gets a little nervous because the fleas bite him, or Aunt has poor nights
because the blankets and sheets are not wide enough to cover her – but this is
the extent of our miseries.'[29]

By mid-September the party were in Silesia, on the border with Bohemia.
Wherever they went, they visited prisons, orphanages and asylums. And wherever they went, they were fêted by the minor royalty of the German states. The
King and Queen of Prussia and their family were particularly attentive. But Fry
was tired to the point of collapse.

> She had suffered much from toothache, and was so stiff that she was almost helpless. It
> was quite a trial for us. Most of the day she was on a bed that we have arranged for her
> in the carriage, with Uncle and Anna outside. She was very low about herself, which cast
> a gloom over the whole party.[30]

The last major stage of the tour was to be Dresden. It was not a happy ending.
Their coach broke down on the way, and 'seating Aunt in a cart of the country,
we brought her jolting along' to a local inn which was 'more a hovel than a

Gasthof'. And then, 'to please the Queen [of Prussia], we are going 30 miles out of our way to visit a prison. This is quite a cross to us . . . but if we will have to do with Kings and Queens, we must bear the consequence.'

Finally, on their departure from Dresden, Elizabeth Gurney wrote that 'the Queen kissed Aunt again and again and again, and most affectionately kissed us also. The King called her his dearest and most Christian friend.' This intimacy, deferential though it was, with the Prussian royal family made a deep impression on the young Quaker woman.

> I cannot say we were *sociable* with them, that does not the least express it. *They* were the Royal Family, *we* the poor English travellers all the time. But we *loved* each other none the less for that, though it was love mingled with great respect.[31]

The journey was nearly over. Despite the excitements, Elizabeth Gurney found that 'our journey has been rather dragging, and Aunt has been so very poorly that we doubted how we should get on at all, and we have been delayed by it'. Notwithstanding all setbacks, the party arrived safely back in England on 2 October 1841 after an absence of just over two months.

PART FOUR

The final years

11

Nursing before Nightingale

On her visit to Kaiserswerth in 1840, Fry had been deeply impressed by Pastor Fliedner's establishment, with its small hospital, nurse training school, and its practice of sending nurses into the community to care for the sick who could not afford private nurses. All this had planted the seed of an idea.

It is a little-known fact that, when Florence Nightingale set off for the Crimea, she invited a nursing institute founded by Fry to send nurses to help her. She also invited the All Saints' Sisterhood, founded in 1851, to provide nurses; but both declined, on the grounds that their nurses would be subject to Nightingale's jurisdiction, rather than to that of their own committees.[1]

In the popular imagination, Florence Nightingale is credited with being the pioneer of professional nursing in Britain. The extensive publicity given to her work at the military hospital at Scutari during the Crimean War of the mid-1850s – the campaign needed a hero – established her as a contemporary icon who combined traditional womanly virtues with courage and determination. In the absence of significant military success, Nightingale became the convenient focus of public attention. The pioneering *London Illustrated News* – which outsold even the *Times* during that period, thanks largely to its coverage of the Crimean War in pictures – celebrated her as the angelic 'lady of the lamp', a soubriquet eagerly taken up by other publications. Staffordshire potteries cast her image by the thousands and American poet Henry Wadsworth Longfellow immortalized her in verse.

Despite Nightingale's deserved greater fame, it was Elizabeth Fry, 'the angel of the prisons', who in 1840 established in London the country's first school for nurses, the Institution of Nursing Sisters.[2] It would be another 20 years before the heroine of Scutari opened her own Nightingale School of Nursing at St Thomas's Hospital.[3]

Fry was no stranger to nursing. As a sickly child, she had been on the receiving end of much of it, suffering badly from anxiety and 'nervous prostration'. She was a martyr to toothache all her life – leeches applied to the gums she found particularly unpleasant – yet still preferred laudanum and gin to the prospect of extraction. The mother of 11 children, she suffered repeatedly – although not with every birth – from pregnancy sickness and post-natal depression. From childhood, she had a recurring cough which caused her to spit a little blood from time to time. Two of her sisters appear to have died from pulmonary tuberculosis, although, since the tubercule bacillus was not identified until the 1880s, the condition would have been known by a different name.

But Fry was also on the dispensing side of nursing as well. As a young woman, she regularly visited the ill and dying in her locality; and she nursed family servants when they were sick. As a young wife, she had undertaken an ambitious programme of smallpox inoculation in the neighbourhood, administering all the treatment herself. Throughout her life, despite her often frenetic schedule of public duties, she was frequently on call for members of her large, extended family who needed her nursing skills. Her niece Priscilla Buxton, who was cared for by Fry when she was dangerously ill, described her aunt's sick-room skills: 'her very presence and aspect . . . perfectly calming, possessing an authority mixed with soothing tenderness, quieting both body and mind, and never shrinking from the humblest services'.

Fry's first-aid skills were also said to be impressive: on one occasion she tended the devastating head injuries of a man who had been run over by his own cart, to the point of replacing the lacerated skin over his broken skull, until his family came to collect him.

Fry had always maintained a keen interest in hospitals, from an early age. Whenever she inspected a prison, she would, where possible, include a visit to local hospitals, workhouses and asylums in order to ascertain the conditions under which the poor and unfortunate were confined. In 1827, she wrote in *Observations* that 'during the last ten years much attention has been bestowed by women on the female inmates of our prisons . . . but a similar care is also required for our hospitals, our lunatic asylums and our prisons'.

It was unsurprising, therefore, that in 1840, when her prison reform activities had almost run their course at home – and her campaigning activities in Continental Europe were already achieving much of what could be expected of them – that her thoughts turned to the question of professional training for nurses. Specifically, she was concerned with providing trained nurses for the less well-off, thereby achieving two objectives with one initiative: raising nursing standards, and making nursing care available to those in need, even if they could not afford it.

The Kaiserswerth visit was central to her motivation. She had gone there at the prompting of Christian Bunsen, by now Prussian ambassador to London, whose own daughter would attend a training course there, as would Nightingale herself in 1851, with Bunsen's encouragement.

In 1824, Pastor Fliedner, then just 24 years old, had travelled throughout Holland and England in an attempt to raise funds to support a church in the small Kaiserswerth community which had fallen on hard times following the collapse of the local industry. *En route* he met Fry, and was deeply moved by her conviction that prisons were schools for vice when they ought to be schools for reformation. On his return home, he formed the first German society for improving prison discipline, along Fry principles. He also established a small penitentiary in the summer house in his garden in 1833, initially with just one female criminal and one volunteer. The penitentiary became a halfway house for women recently released from prison, and who expressed a willingness to reform and be trained in domestic service. They could be accepted only with a certificate from a prison chaplain confirming their good intent. Over the next few months, Fliedner received nine more penitents, eight of whom had been in prison more than once. He was in no doubt about the debt he owed to Fry.

Of all my contemporaries, none has exercised a like influence on my heart and life . . . In January 1824, I had the privilege of witnessing the effects of Mrs Fry's wonder-working visits among the miserable prisoners of Newgate. On my return to my fatherland, my object was to found [a prison association] having ramifications in all the provinces of Germany. In this I was greatly assisted by the advice and experience afforded me by this eminent servant of God.

During my second stay in England, in 1834, I had the happiness . . . of spending a day with Mrs Fry, at her own home, and also of accompanying her on one of her visits of mercy to Newgate. By this means, I was enabled to see and admire her, in her domestic as well as public character.

Thus may my happiness be estimated when, in 1840, Mrs Fry came in person to see and rejoice over the growing establishment of Kaiserswerth. She saw the whole house, going into every room, and minutely examining each detail, and then delivered to the inmates a deeply interesting discourse. Many were the tears shed . . . and not in vain. To the 'helping sisters' of the institution she gave much motherly advice, and told the results of her own labours.

After dinner, she permitted us to share with her the rich fruits of her varied experiences, thus giving us counsel and help of the most valuable kind. She examined with me the rules and regulations of the household, with which she expressed herself greatly satisfied ... The remembrance of that spirit of active self-denying love is one of the sweetest consolations which I possess, amid the trials and difficulties which every such institution must possess.[4]

The Kaiserswerth project had begun in 1833 as a small penitentiary for released female prisoners; but by 1840 it had grown to include, as well as the nursing institute, an infant school, a hospital, an orphanage and a teacher-training college.[5] And all were organized according to the Fry model that Fliedner had observed in operation at Newgate. Within weeks, Fry was returning the compliment. Because of Fry's many other commitments, the project was largely supervised by her sister-in-law Elizabeth Gurney, with assistance from Fry's daughters.

In July 1840, the Institution for Nursing Sisters opened its doors at Raven Row, Whitechapel, London. (Later it would move to Devonshire Street, Bishopsgate.) Its first probationer was one Judith Wade, who began her training at the adjacent London Hospital on 26 August. The institute was located close to the London Hospital because there were already strong Quaker ties with the hospital where various Frys and Gurneys served on the board of governors or other committees. Over the years, other trainees would attend at Guy's, St Georges's, King's College and St Thomas's. Typically, Fry had mustered some heavyweight support for her project. Its royal patron was the dowager Queen Adelaide, who had been instrumental in introducing Fry to Queen Victoria. Her secretary wrote to Fry: 'Her majesty commands me to state with what sincere pleasure she will place her name in your society. Her majesty adds that you may call upon her as an extra nurse if short-handed.' The dowager promised an annual subscription of £10 'to your excellent and most useful institution.'[6] Other patrons included the Duchess of Gloucester – the Gloucesters were always stalwart supporters of Fry's work – the Bishop of London, the Marchioness of Cholmondley, Harriet, Duchess of Sutherland (Mistress of the Robes to Queen Victoria), the Dowager Lady Grey and several members of the extensive Fry and Gurney families.

The institution, which combined a training establishment with a nurses' home, was run by a salaried superintendent. Trainees were expected to bring to the task a 'religious spirit as well as aptitude and intelligence'.

By the rules of the institution, Christian women of various denominations are admitted to join its ranks. No direct system of religious instruction is pursued, although the sisters are required to attend family and public worship when in the [patient's] house. They are engaged to read the Scriptures to the patients, and to endeavour to promote their spiritual welfare, as well as to labour for their bodily comfort, and there have been instances in which these efforts have appeared blessed to the souls of those under their charge. Whilst at the home, the sisters visit and nurse the sick poor in its neighbourhood.[7]

This was a dramatic departure from the image of the average nurse as characterized by the unscrupulous, alcoholic, barely trained nurse Sarah Gamp introduced to the reading public by Charles Dickens in *Martin Chuzzelwit* in 1843 as 'a fair representation of the hired attendant on the poor in sickness'. Dickens was appalled that it was left to private persons to alleviate the situation, and thought it 'not least among the instances of their mismanagement . . . that the hospitals [of London] with their means and funds, should have left it to private humanity and enterprise to enter on an attempt to improve that class of person – since, greatly improved through the agency of good women'.[8]

Fry trainees were required to be of good character – references were rigorously pursued – and to be 'desirous of devoting their time to the glory of God and to the mitigation of human suffering'. They needed to be able to read and write, own a copy of the Bible and be prepared to attend up to two religious services a day. They had to be unmarried or widowed. In exchange, they were given free board and lodging, two weeks' holiday a year, a small allowance to free them from financial worries, and a uniform comprising dark brown print dresses, voluminous aprons and a Quaker-like cap in muslin. It was a modified version of the blue uniform worn by the Kaiserswerth deaconess nursing sisters, introduced there partly as a means of visually setting them apart from Catholic nuns – hitherto the main providers of nursing care in the community – and thereby avoiding any anti-Catholic sentiment. The uniform was unpopular from the start with Fry nurses, since 'only a fur tippet or cuffs were allowed as adornments . . . lace, embroidery and ornaments were specifically forbidden . . . no ribbons . . . and the wearing of mourning was prohibited'. One probationer at least was dismissed because she failed to take the uniform code seriously.

The initial probationers' training included three-month placements in selected hospitals (later extended to three years), working on the medical, surgical and obstetric wards, where their services were offered free of charge.

If this seems very short, it was probably the maximum time that hospitals were prepared to put up with having inexperienced young women under their feet. Their presence was not universally welcomed at first.

> I must confess that when they first came I was not at all in favour of the arrangement, as I feared inconvenience would arise from interference with the ward duties, which I consider it is always the duty of the medical officer to promote; but my fears on this point have entirely passed away. The women are attentive and observant . . . and on the best possible terms with the sisters of the wards. When considered qualified, they return to the Institution house where they continue under the control of the Lady Superintendent until appointed as required and applied for.[9]

The school began with an intake of 12, which rose to 100 at its peak. When their hospital training and a probationary period were completed, the certified nursing sisters were paid an annual stipend and given a three-year contract. (Later, they would be guaranteed a pension as well.) They offered a pool of professional nursing skills that people could hire to care for them in their own homes at a relatively modest cost. From the very beginning, the service was aimed at the less well-off. Fry's mission was 'to benefit people of limited income [by supplying] fully trained nurses at a fee much lower than charged by any other institution' and, in special cases of extreme poverty, the fee would be further reduced. Since these charges were 'barely remunerative', donations were invited from members of the public. Sometimes nurses were provided free of charge in very needy cases, or where the beneficiary was a charity.

The institution was at pains to point out that these lower charges did not imply an inferior service; quite the contrary.

> The object of the Institution being to supply fully trained nurses to those who require skilled nurses but who, owing to limited means, are unable to afford the standard fees charges by other private institutions, the committee rely on the kind cooperation of the medical professions, of other nursing institutions, and all those to whom the Institution may become known, to ensure that the services of the staff reach those to whom they are intended.
>
> Owing to the erroneous opinion which is frequently expressed and in justice to the nursing staff, the committee desire it to be understood that all . . . are fully competent to undertake the nursing of all acute cases of illness, and that the lower fee does not imply a lower standard of professional skill.

Fry nursing standards were the highest in the field. While most nurses were sent to private homes and charities, a few were seconded to help in hospitals, at a commercial rate. But the hospitals were required to satisfy certain minimum standards, and an inspection would be carried out by the institute's committee prior to nurses being allocated. If the result was unsatisfactory, the request was turned down. This was the case in 1842 with the London Hospital which, despite having helped to pioneer Fry nurse probationer training, was refused any more trained sisters because of its unsanitary state, and the fact that overcrowding was so bad that it hampered recovery. Remedial measures were recommended, including: whitewashing the wards; ensuring that the annual ward cleaning was properly carried out; and repainting woodwork inside and outside which had suffered years of neglect. As a result of this unfavourable audit, the institute severed its links with the London Hospital in favour of nearby Guy's Hospital.[10]

While Nightingale's fame as a nursing pioneer may have eclipsed that of Fry, there was never any doubt in professional medical circles where the credit was due, even as late as the end of the nineteenth century. In 1897, the year of Queen Victoria's Diamond Jubilee, there was a flurry of articles in various nursing and medical journals seeking to identify a connection between their own profession and the sixtieth anniversary of the monarch's accession. 'Mrs Fry, the founder of modern nursing' boasted the *British Medical Journal* (*BMJ*) in its 'Queen's commemoration number' in an article entitled 'The nursing of the sick under Queen Victoria'.[11]

The article acknowledged the importance of the Kaiserswerth project, and the significance of Fry's connection with it, as a result of which

Mrs Fry, the founder of modern nursing, whose work led her among all forms of suffering, was moved to make some attempts at organised nursing of the sick poor in London; hitherto the sick had been in the hands of the unprincipled and irresponsible attendants so graphically described by Charles Dickens.[12]

Fry's Whitechapel school it called

the first nursing institution [which] marks the origin of that movement which has attained to such proportions in our own times. It started from the Quaker lady whose name has hitherto been almost exclusively claimed by the prisoners, but she must now be accepted as the founder of modern nursing.

The *BMJ* went further. It saw in the establishment of professional nursing training a more general reflection of the spirit of the times and a clear sign that women wanted more out of life than 'the vacuity of a purposeless existence'; but still they placed that desire within an acceptable religious context.

> At the same time, that revival in the Church generally known as the Oxford movement was awakening in the hearts of earnest women a desire for definite religious work; this found its fulfilment for many in the English sisterhoods; and, for those for whom the severe and dedicated life of the religious was not possible, in a life devoted to the care and nursing of the sick. As soon as the pioneers of the movement had demonstrated the possibility of a woman working in the wards of a hospital and still retaining her womanliness and modesty, such women turned to nursing the poor in hospitals. They in their turn were followed by the many who, from stress of circumstances, have to earn their bread, and this large class quickly discerned an advantageous opening in the unoccupied field of sick nursing. These breadwinners have in their turn been succeeded by their fashionable sisters, of whom many had sought to relieve the vacuity of a purposeless life by the variety and excitement of a nurse's training.[13]

The *BMJ* also identified a growing requirement in British society for a better class of nurse, and what one might call a more wholesome, more compassionate, holistic approach to nursing.

> In enumerating the religious and social influences at work among women, we must not forget that in the medical profession there was arising a demand for a higher class of women to tend at the bedside, and this demand has naturally had its influence in creating the supply. For in the thirties, there was a stir along the line of the medical profession, prompted by investigations into the conditions under which the sick were treated, and into the circumstances surrounding the wounded on the field of battle. The object lessons of the battlefield and of the field hospitals were pointing to the moral that there was a grievous waste of human life from causes which were within the control of man, and the more thoughtful were gradually awakening to the limitless resources of nature and to the wonderful recuperative powers of the body – forces which might be turned to good account by the physician or surgeon in their fight with disease or death.[14]

The physician at the bedside and the surgeon in the operating theatre had come to realize that, if they were to do the best possible for their patients, they needed gentle, skilful and sympathetic nurses whose attentions to the patient would accelerate the healing process.

> In other words, the old hospital methods, which had accepted any rough, incapable and sometimes disreputable female as an attendant on the sick, were found to be insufficient both from the scientific and the humanitarian point of view, and the leading members of the medical profession were taking counsel with the leading philanthropists in search of a remedy.[15]

Exit Dickens' grotesque, Sarah Gamp; enter the Fry nurses. But the transition was an uphill struggle as the journal *Nursing Record and Hospital World* pointed out in its own celebration issue published to commemorate Queen Victoria's Diamond Jubilee in 1897. It, too, recalled the dire conditions that prevailed in the field when Victoria ascended to the throne 'when there was neither skilled nursing, nor trained nurses, as we at the present day understand those terms'.

> The type of woman – dirty, disreputable and drunken – who devoted herself to attendance upon the sick because she was considered fit for nothing else, has been depicted by the novelists of the day in a manner which, even if exaggerated, was recognised at the time to be deserved, and sufficiently scathing to prove that the nurse of the day was not only ignorant, but dangerous to the sick upon whom she was supposed to attend. The immortal character of Sarah Gamp was sufficient to stamp the 'nurse', during the first third of this century, as a person who disgraced one of the noblest callings to which womenkind can devote themselves.[16]

The journal is quite clear that this situation was redeemed by Elizabeth Fry, 'who must always be looked upon as the real pioneer of nursing in this country'.

> She recognised the necessity for providing more skilled and trustworthy attendants for the sick . . . and in order to carry this into effect, that most benevolent and far-sighted woman inaugurated the Institution of Nursing Sisters . . . Mrs Fry's idea evidently was to provide women of character and efficiency, and, in fact, her organisation was the first in this country to place the great department of Private Nursing upon a proper basis. The workers of that day, as depicted in the pages of Dickens, Thackeray, and others, are represented as so hard and cruel that the very name of 'nurse' was held in horror and contempt. It was therefore not an easy task which Mrs Fry undertook, and she probably went as far as the circumstances of the time permitted.

The only exception one could find with this eulogy was that the *Nursing Record* implied that Fry trained nurses for 'the sick of the richer classes'. This was emphatically not the case. Her institution may have provided a nurse for Queen Adelaide, but it also raised funds from the public at large to enable it to subsidize nurses for deserving cases or organizations that could ill afford the required fees. The dowager Queen had the services of Fry nurse Harriet Rowe for two weeks at a cost of £25, the same as the Manchester Royal Infirmary paid for a year.

Following the establishment of a training school for 'Fry nurses', a number of successful Protestant sisterhoods were founded throughout Europe, devoting themselves to hospital nursing. At least one – the Établissement des Soeurs de Santé Protestantes, founded in Paris in 1841 – acknowledged that it took its inspiration from the institution that Fry had established.

Fry remained president of the committee that supervised the nursing institution until her death in 1845. The last committee meeting she attended was in 1843. In later years, the institute moved from Devonshire Square to South Kensington. The last recorded committee meeting minutes were in December 1939, shortly after the beginning of World War Two. At the end of the war, in 1945, the institution's assets were transferred to the Queen's Nursing Institute. Today, this organization is a charity dedicated to improving patient care by supporting the 100,000 community nurses and midwives in England, Wales and Northern Ireland, and representing them at national policy level.

12

'Into the valley of old age'

During the years of her Continental campaigning, Fry had always secretly enjoyed rubbing shoulders with the sovereigns of Europe, and the Prussian royal family in particular. But by 1842, now 62 years of age, she was simply too frail to undertake any more serious travel. As luck would have it, however, the new King of Prussia was visiting London in January that year to stand as godfather to the infant Prince of Wales. Fry was invited by the King to join the christening party at a lunchtime reception hosted by the Lord Mayor at the Mansion House on 30 January following the baptism service at St Paul's Cathedral. Since it was a Sunday, she had some reservations, which she aired at the reception.

> We had much deeply interesting conversation on various important subjects of mutual interest. We spoke of the christening. I dwelt on its pomp as undesirable; then upon Episcopacy and its danger; on prisons, . . . on the Sabbath. I entreated the Lord Mayor to have no toasts, to which he acceded, and the King approved; but it was no light or easy matter. I rejoice to believe my efforts were right. I told the King my objection to anything of that kind on that day; indeed I expressed my disapprobation of them altogether.

Undeterred, the King arranged to meet Fry the following day at Newgate, and to join her for lunch afterwards at Upton Lane. For Fry, it would be 'a day never to be forgotten while memory lasts'.

> We set off about eleven o'clock . . . to meet the King of Prussia at Newgate . . . We waited so long for the King that I feared he might never come; however, at last he arrived, and the Lady Mayoress and I, accompanied by the Sheriffs, went to meet the King at the door of the prison. He seemed much pleased to meet our little party, and, after taking a little refreshment, he gave me his arm, and we proceeded into the prison and up to one of the long wards, where everything was prepared: the poor women round a table, about sixty of them, many of our Ladies' Committee and some others.

> After we were seated, the King on my right, the Lady Mayoress on my left, I expressed my desire that the attention of none, particularly the poor prisoners, might be diverted from attending to our reading by the company there.

And then, Fry began to read some passages from the Bible, after which she knelt down to pray 'before this most curious, interesting and mixed company'. She prayed for the conversion of prisoners, for the work of those in authority over them, for the welfare of the King of Prussia and his country, and for salvation for all those present. 'The King then gave me his arm and we walked together.' Some difficulties of protocol had been raised about the King's going to Upton House, 'but he chose to persevere'. As he arrived, Fry

> went down to meet him at his carriage-door, with my husband and seven of our sons and sons-in-law. I then walked with him into the drawing-room, where all was in beautiful order – neat and adorned with flowers. I presented to the King our eight daughters and daughters-in-law (Rachel only away), our seven sons and eldest grandson, my brother and sister Buxton . . . and my sister Elizabeth Fry – my brother and sister Gurney he had known before – and afterwards presented 25 of our grandchildren. We had a solemn silence before our meal, which was handsome and fit for a King, yet not extravagant, everything most complete and nice.
>
> I sat by the King, who appeared to enjoy his dinner, perfectly at his ease and very happy with us. We went into the drawing-room after another solemn silence, and a few words which I uttered in prayer for the King and Queen. We found a deputation of Friends with an address to read to him. This was done; the King appeared to feel it much. We then had to part. The King expressed his desire that blessings might continue to rest on our house.

Fry continued in indifferent health. Her brother-in-law Samuel Hoare, husband of Louisa, offered the loan of a hilltop house that he owned at Cromer in Norfolk, the scene of many happy childhood memories. Initially feeling 'poorly part of every night', and in a state where even a 'grasshopper becomes a burden', she slowly regained some strength during her two-month summer stay. Eager as ever for a good cause to espouse, she became involved in establishing a library for local fishermen, 'to draw them from the public-house and its attendant evils', and a local district visiting society.

Her repeated debilitating bouts of illness during the 1841 Continental tour should have persuaded Fry that she simply no longer had the stamina for such enterprises, even when accompanied by several members of her family. And indeed, on New Year's Day 1843, she admitted that she was feeling tired. 'Mine is rather a rapid descent into the valley of old age', she admitted in her diary. Nevertheless, she was determined – indeed, she felt it was her duty – to visit France one last time, and to check on what progress had been made at the institutions she had inspected previously. Her particular wish was to consolidate the contacts she had made in Paris. Her brother Joseph also had business of his own to do in Paris, and brought with him his new, third wife Eliza. Josiah Forster joined the party, too. In April they set off.

Channel crossings at that time of year can be notoriously rough, and the weather was so severe that there was some debate on landing at Boulogne as to whether or not Fry was strong enough to continue. But press on they did, arriving two days later at Amiens. At Clermont-en-Oise, the ladies of the party were allowed to inspect the Great Central Prison for women, designed to contain 1,200 inmates but at the time only holding a comfortable 900. Run by 27 nuns, it was supervised by an intelligent, robust and enlightened Mother Superior who expressed to them her great fear of the effect of 'the abuses to which the solitary system is liable, and the silent system also, when carried to extremes'. The prisoners worked in 'large cheerful rooms' under the close inspection of the nuns 'who relieve the monotony by not infrequently uniting in singing hymns'. Before she left, Fry addressed the women, telling them of all that had been achieved at Newgate by simply applying the message of the gospels, and encouraged them to do the same.

One evening, a dinner was held in honour of Fry and her friends by the Foreign Minister, François Guizot. Until recently, Guizot had, for a short while, been the ambassador to London; a few years later, he would briefly be the Prime Minister of France, until the 1848 Revolution. He encouraged Fry to 'speak to him on the subjects which had so long been near her heart', and in the course of the evening they talked 'of crime and its causes, its consequences, the measures to be adopted for its prevention; of the treatment of criminals, of education and of scriptural instruction'.

In early May, France celebrated the great festival known as the Fête du Roi. 'There is something in the French very attractive to me', Fry wrote in her diary. 'Their lively yet sober habits, their politeness to one another – indeed they are particularly agreeable.'

For the rest of their stay, there were many more religious gatherings, great and small, and more interviews with members of the royal family. Much to her satisfaction, Fry discovered that since her last inspection many measures had been introduced for the improvement of French prisons. Indeed, a Bill had been put before Parliament which sought to reconcile the 'requirements of humanity with the interests of the community at large'. It recommended a range of improvements to the existing system, and proposed, as had been done in Britain, bringing all prisons throughout the kingdom under the direct, centralized authority of the Ministry of the Interior.

In proposing the Bill, Interior Minister Charles Duchâtel declared that its object was 'not entirely to sequestrate the prisoner, or to confine him to absolute solitude', unlike the American system.

> We want to exclude convicts from the society of their fellow prisoners, to keep them free from bad examples, and wicked associations; but we want at the same time to multiply around them moral and honest connections. Besides their being visited by the director of the jail, they will be in frequent communication with the teacher and the medical attendant. The chaplain, or the ministers of several denominations acknowledged by the State, will have easy access to the cells at the hours appointed by the prison regulations . . . the infection of bad example and contaminating influence will be removed.[1]

While in Paris, Fry also visited an asylum for female Protestants, run by the Sisters of Charity. Although it had only been recently established, Fry was 'deeply impressed with its promises of usefulness'. Its ambitious plans (which were largely realized, as a letter to Fry's daughters after her death confirmed) included a crèche with eight cots, a home for up to 150 infants, a school for up to 120 girls, with the opportunity for 30 apprenticeships. There would also be a 25-room refuge for penitent women, a house of correction for another 30, a three-ward hospital for 30 people (men, women and children), an infirmary for children suffering from scrofula (a form of tuberculosis), and six convalescent rooms. Two Sunday schools were to be established, and a meeting room with a capacity for 300 people was to be provided for regular worship. A vaccination programme was made available on a daily basis, as well as free medical attention for local people. Deaconesses from the order would regularly visit the poor of the neighbourhood to bring them spiritual and material help. So famous did the Sisters of Charity's Paris project become, that it prompted John Stuart Mill to write an article for the *Edinburgh Review*.

Fry celebrated the week of her sixty-third birthday with a private audience, together with her brother and his wife, with King Louis Philippe, the Queen and Princess Adelaide, the King's sister and adviser.

Before leaving Paris for the last time, Fry paid one last call to St Lazare. This institution was her French Newgate, and her failure to make a difference there was upsetting. What she found on her final visit was

> such a scene of disorder and deep evil as I have seldom witnessed – gambling, romp-ing, screaming. With much difficulty we collected four Protestant prisoners, and read with them. I spoke to those poor disorderly women who appeared attentive and showed some feeling. I have represented to many in authority the sad evils of this prison, and have pleaded with them for reform, for religious care, and for scriptural instruction.

The quality of prisons was as variable in France as it had been in England; but it was a major disappointment to her that she had not succeeded in doing anything to improve conditions at Paris's main female prison, where the Archbishop of Paris had ruled, from the start, that her recommendations should not be imple-mented, and her ministrations confined to non-Roman Catholics.

At the end of May, it was time for the party to head home, loaded down with gifts from their French friends. But it was a solemn time, 'little knowing whether we should see each other's faces again'.

The year 1844 dawned as a time of 'sorrow upon sorrow' for Fry. Within a few months she lost a sister-in-law, two grandchildren, a son-in-law and, worst of all, her son William. Utterly broken in spirit, and in serious ill-health, she struggled to maintain some semblance of normality in everyday life. 'I am very poorly, very low and flat . . . the effect of William's death is hardly to be told', she wrote in October to her brother Samuel's wife, Elizabeth Gurney. 'The trial is almost inexpressible.'

She wrote what would be her last letter to the committee of the Ladies' British Society, confirming her ongoing commitment to their cause.

> Amidst many sorrows, that have been permitted for me to pass through, and bodily suffering, I still feel a deep and lively interest in the cause of poor prisoners; and earnest is my prayer that the God of all grace may be very near to help you to be steadfast in the important Christian work of seeking to win the poor wanderers to return, repent and live.[2]

In private, the sorrows continued to pile up and 'the grave once more (and so soon) opened amongst us' when her niece Catherine, daughter of her late sister Louisa, died shortly after the death of her infant son. Then came the crushing news of the death on 19 February of her dear friend Thomas Fowell Buxton, husband of her sister Hannah, heir to William Wilberforce in the anti-slavery movement, and an equally staunch supporter of prison reform. So close were Fry and Fowell that she even fancied she had anticipated his decline. To his daughter, her niece Priscilla Buxton, she wrote: 'Strange to say, before your note came, I had been so much with you in spirit, that I was ready to believe thy dearest father was sinking. I have felt such unity with him spiritually.' Perhaps sensing that her own end was not far away, Fry was moved by a powerful desire to spend some time at Earlham where, as a girl, she had been so happy, and where dear Fowell himself had been like an adopted son. And so it was arranged, and she spent several weeks at her old childhood home, revisiting old memories, before she returned to Upton Lane. On New Year's Eve, she wrote again to Priscilla.

> How weighty to come to the close of this year, wherein so much has passed . . . I desire your prayers, for my estate is a very low one . . . I write sadly, as it is difficult to do it, my hands are so much affected by my general state of health.

As winter gave way to spring, Fry's spirits revived to some degree and she took a closer interest in everyday events. She was brought downstairs in a chair and wheeled from room to room. She went to Meeting most Sundays and Friends continued to visit. To one, she confided that her life had been one of 'great vicissitude'.

> Mine has been a hidden path, hidden from every human eye. I have had deep humiliations to pass through . . . I have wandered in the wilderness in a solitary way, and found no city to dwell in . . . I have passed through many and great dangers . . . I have been tried with the applause of the world, and none know how great a trial that has been, and the deep humiliations of it . . . The more I have been made much of by the world, the more I have been inwardly humbled.

In the summer of 1845, Fry's youngest son Daniel was married. On 3 June, she attended her last annual meeting of the British Ladies' Society. Out of consideration for her frailty, and to spare her fatigue, the delegates convened at a Meeting House close to her home.

The large number of Friends who gathered round her upon that occasion, proved how gladly they came to her, when she could no longer with ease be conveyed to them. The enfeebled state of her bodily frame seemed to have left the powers of her mind unshackled, and she took, though in a sitting posture, almost her usual part. She urged, with increased pathos and affection, the objects of philanthropy and Christian benevolence with which her life had been identified.[3]

As she left the meeting, Fry had the satisfaction of knowing that the prison reform initiatives with which she and her lady visitors had been involved were doing well.

Newgate, Bridewell, the Millbank prison, the Giltspur Street Compter, White Cross Street Prison, Tothill Fields Prison, and Cold Bath Fields Prison, were all in a state of comparative order; some exceedingly well arranged; and the female convicts, in all, more or less visited and cared for by ladies – varying according to their circumstances and requirings; and the prisons generally throughout England much improved.[4]

Shortly afterwards the family took a house at Ramsgate in Kent, so that Fry could benefit from the sea air. On the packet-boat to Ramsgate, she was so frail that it required four men to carry her on board in an invalid chair. This did not prevent her from distributing to fellow passengers some of the religious books and tracts that she had brought with her in a big case. On her arrival in Ramsgate, she also took great pains to disseminate Bibles and tracts among the crews of foreign and domestic vessels that frequented the harbour; she even persuaded the Foreign Bible Society to fund this initiative.

Nevertheless, she continued to feel worse than ever, 'more poorly than usual', in fact. Not that this prevented her from finding work to do, wherever and whenever the opportunity presented itself. When she was wheeled along the pier, she would hand out religious tracts to the sailors she met. She would chat to them and their families, and enquire about the success of the coastguard libraries that she had helped to establish. At home, family members came to keep her company; the widow and children of her recently deceased son William were a particular delight and comfort; and young Willie Fry, her dear grandson – and the image of his father at the same age – was on hand to read the Bible to her every morning.

I feel myself much broken, and finding that neither sea air nor any other thing appears much to raise me up; I do feel that while here (I mean this life), a great desire to be as much as I can with those most dear to me. My heart overflows with love . . . I feel certainly very poorly and unless there be some revival more than I now feel, I think that you cannot expect, that you will very long have a mother to come to.

Fry's last diary entry was written on 16 September 1845. The following day, her recently widowed sister Hannah (Lady Buxton) and daughter Richenda visited, followed by Fry's youngest son Daniel and his new bride. Grandchildren came and went. More family members came when it became clear that more nursing was needed. For by now there was a worrying new symptom – recurrent severe headaches. To anyone who would listen, Fry kept repeating: 'Are we now all ready? Are we prepared?'

'Afflictions abound', she wrote, as her health continued to fail and her diary entries became almost illegible. She fretted over one son far away in Madeira, and felt 'rather blanked' when another was unable to visit one week. There was a sense that time was running out. At the beginning of October, Fry wrote to her youngest daughter Louisa, expressing the hope to see her sooner rather than later. 'I feel so shaken and so broke down, that I wish to see as much of my beloved children as I can; my love is very strong, and my flesh is very weak.' Despite her obvious suffering, she never seemed impatient to depart this life. Whether this was through fear of the end – although her faith was strong – or through a desire simply to hold on as long as she still thought she could be useful, she expressed herself content to 'stay the Lord's time'.

The weekend before she died, Fry began to appear distracted, distant to those around her. The headaches she had been experiencing became extreme. She barely noticed when the grandchildren came to read the Bible to her, and absent-mindedly asked twice for her favourite psalm to be read. It was Psalm 27, a psalm of David, and it begins: 'The Lord is my light and my salvation'. Guests arrived for lunch but Fry appeared so unwell that they stayed only a short while. In the afternoon she collapsed in her room, while trying to move from the sofa to a chair by the fire. Although only able with difficulty to hold herself upright, she struggled through dinner but collapsed again twice during the evening, and was carried to bed. Doctors attended regularly during the next 24 hours but she was so ill and worn out that there was little they could do. Members of the family came and went. The next evening, after making her comfortable for the night, her daughters left her in the care of her husband Joseph who remained by her side throughout the hours of darkness, as he had done throughout her illness. It was a long night. Although her mind seemed receptive to the passages of Scripture that were read to her, her body remained powerless and her speech became increasingly indistinct.

At nine o'clock on the Sunday morning, she slipped into unconsciousness and it seemed clear that the end was near. While those of her children who were in the house prepared themselves to face the inevitable, a messenger was dispatched to summon as many of the others who might yet have time to say goodbye before the end. Another agonizing day and night followed. After midnight, Fry's breathing became increasingly difficult. Over the next few hours, it turned into a continuous convulsive spasm until at last, shortly before four o'clock on Monday 13 October, the end came. The night had reportedly been dark and glowering, but the dawn that broke over Ramsgate that morning was said to be glorious.

By the evening of the day she died, most of Fry's children and many other friends and relatives had called to pay their last respects at Ramsgate, where her body was to remain for the next six days in the care of her eldest son and son-in-law. The funeral was set for noon the following Monday 20 October at the Friends' Meeting House at Barking, where she had first been appointed a minister 34 years earlier. Among the first from outside the circle of family and friends to offer condolences was a deputation of seamen from the local coast-guards. They wanted to know what gesture they could make in honour of their late benefactress. It was agreed that, until the funeral, the flag of the Ramsgate coastguards would fly at half-mast. It is what they would have done had the Queen died, they said.

The following Sunday, the hearse carrying Fry's body left Ramsgate and travelled quietly through the night, arriving at seven o'clock at Upton House, the home where she had spent many happy years and where she would spend a few more hours before the funeral.

At a quarter to eleven, the cortège set off from Upton House for Barking. Four men walked ahead of the hearse, which was followed by 39 carriages carrying family, friends, neighbours and distinguished acquaintances. The procession was over half a mile long. Thousands of well-wishers stood in silence along the route to pay their respects. It took over two hours for the cortège to cover the four miles to the Friends' burial ground, where another 50 carriages and their passengers had been waiting since early morning. Barking had never seen a funeral like it.

According to Quaker custom, there is no prescribed service for burying the dead, which is carried out in a strictly unostentatious manner. The crowds observed a deep silence until Joseph Gurney stood up to speak of his sister. Others shared their memories and thoughts, and then it was all over, and Elizabeth Fry was laid to rest beside her infant daughter.

An era was coming to an end. William Savery and Deborah Darby had long since passed away. Joseph Lancaster died in poverty in New York. William Allen had died two years before Fry, and Fowell Buxton just a few months previously. Joseph Gurney died two years later, and within a decade William Forster and Stephen Grellet would also be gone. Many of the philanthropic initiatives that they had begun, devoted their lives to, and funded at their own expense, were now being managed by the state.

In June 1846, eight months after Elizabeth Fry's death, a meeting was held in the Egyptian Hall of the Mansion House, with the Lord Mayor of London in the chair. Ostensibly, its aim was to raise funds for an appropriate memorial; but it soon took on the nature of a memorial service, a very un-Quaker-like gesture. There had been suggestions that a statue should be erected in either Westminster Abbey or St Paul's Cathedral, where there was already a statue of prisoner reformer, John Howard. But many people felt that a more practical memorial would better honour Fry's particular type of active benevolence. And what could be more appropriate than to establish the Elizabeth Fry Refuge, a hostel that would provide food and temporary lodging for destitute women on their release from London's prisons?[5]

The panel of experts who came together to commend the plan to the meeting – and to encourage donations – included Lord Ashley (later Lord Shaftesbury, one of the century's greatest reformers), Christian von Bunsen, Edward Parry and the Bishop of Norwich.[6] All had a close connection with Fry. Lord Ashley, who had recently been appointed permanent chairman of the new Lunacy Commission, had been discussing his work with her until the very end. Christian von Bunsen, the Prussian ambassador, was a good friend; his son Ernest married Fry's niece Elizabeth Gurney (daughter of Samuel) just weeks before Fry's death. Edward Parry was an Arctic explorer and had been governor of a model convict settlement at Port Stephens in New South Wales. A former assistant poor-law commissioner for Norfolk, he also sat on Fry's coastguard library committee and would soon become captain superintendent of the Haslar Royal Naval Hospital in Hampshire. He married into Fry's extended family when he wed the widow of her nephew, Samuel Hoare.

Lord Ashley told the audience at the Mansion House that the idea of a refuge was 'in perfect harmony with her life, her character, her feelings'. Such a memorial was far better than the erection of mere statues or monuments. It would perpetuate the nation's gratitude by confirming for future generations 'the sympathy which they entertain for her righteous endeavours' in reforming prisoners and improving prison management; endeavours to which she had dedicated nearly 30 years of her life. Christian von Bunsen added praise for Fry's campaigning work in Continental Europe, and the success she had achieved abroad in improving conditions in prisons, schools, hospitals and workhouses. The Bishop of Norwich described her as 'the friend of the poor and needy, when no other means of succour remained'. Though she was not of his Church, he reminded the audience that there was 'a church far beyond, and superior to ours, which contained in its circle all that was great and splendid in gospel morality'.

The panel explained that the plan was to find premises that would house 600–700 women for a few days or weeks 'until they could be restored to their friends, or placed in some honest pursuit; or, failing these resources, may be passed to their parishes and so escape the temptations that cold and hunger hold out to destitute creatures, to commit crimes, which too often render them again the inmates of a gaol'. Members of Fry's ladies' committees had already agreed to take responsibility for the internal management of the institution; and members of the public were invited to contribute to procure a building and establish an endowment to fund the institution. For this, some £15,000 was required, of which nearly one-third had already been pledged privately. Royal donors included Queen Victoria, Prince Albert, the dowager Queen Adelaide, the Queen of the French and the Duchess of Orléans, and Fry's old friend, the King of Prussia.

The project met with popular approval, funds were raised and, in 1849, the Elizabeth Fry Institute for the Reformation of Women Prisoners was opened at Mare Street, Hackney.[7]

Her friends may have insisted that a monument was an inadequate memorial compared with a women's refuge. But Fry got her statue as well, in the end. When the central criminal courts at the Old Bailey were refurbished in 1913, a marble sculpture of Elizabeth Fry, commissioned from artist Alfred Drury, was erected on the second gallery overlooking the Great Hall.[8] Fry is shown in typical Quaker costume, complete with muslin bonnet. Two bronze reliefs, one at each side, illustrate two visits by her to Newgate prison. One shows Fry and her sister-in-law Anna Buxton surrounded by drunken and dishevelled women on their very first visit. The other shows a much older Fry giving a lesson to an orderly group of female prisoners, while a group of men look on. The men have been identified as Thomas Fowell Buxton, Fry's brother-in-law, prisoner reformer and abolitionist colleague of William Wilberforce; her brothers Samuel Gurney and Joseph John Gurney, both of them deeply involved in philanthropic reform in the early nineteenth century; and the Bishop of Gloucester. The statue is believed to be based on a painting by George Richmond (1809–96), and the panels on a painting by Jerry Barrett (1824–1906).

The marble figure, without the bronze side panels, was exhibited at the Royal Academy in 1912. It was apparently commissioned by a Miss P. J. Fletcher of The Keep, Maidstone, but the donor's identity was kept secret until the statue was installed at the Old Bailey on 21 May 1914, Fry's birthday. The original plan was that it should be installed in Millbank Gardens, on the site of the old Milbank prison, but it was decided that an outdoor location would be detrimental to the material. The inauguration event at the Old Bailey was ticket-only, in order to prevent its being hijacked by suffragettes. The Old Bailey is, of course, located on the site of Newgate prison, where Fry's story first began.

13

Epilogue

The early nineteenth century witnessed a great surge of Quaker involvement in a wide range of humanitarian issues: anti-slavery, prisons, education, hospitals, workhouses, orphanages, asylums, libraries, self-help societies and many others.[1] Their contribution in these areas was out of all proportion to their numbers. In 1800, there were 20,000 Quakers, just 2 per cent of the total church-going population; by 1850, that had dropped to 15,000.[2] But their influence was everywhere. It was said, for example, of Fry's friends Grellet and Allen that they 'probably did not narrowly distinguish between one good cause and another . . . they could not see *any* wrong without desiring to correct it'.[3] This echoes a motto of Fry's own: 'whatever thy hand findeth to do, do it with thy might'. To some extent, then, she was a product of her time; a time when enlightened private philanthropists took responsibility for righting public ills before the state took over.

This 'professionalization of government' meant that, in addition to the Prison Acts of 1823 and 1835, there were, during Fry's career alone, four major Factory Acts and seven Local Government and Public Health Acts; the rate increased exponentially during the latter half of the century. Private patronage was already on the wane.

> Government was now, through the agency of its inspectors and commissioners, a regulator, co-ordinator and, within limits, director of business of Poor Law and prisons, factories and coalmines [and many other areas of endeavour].[4]

Nonetheless, the rate at which Fry brought about change, specifically in the treatment of women prisoners – both in practical measures and in policy – was astonishing. A renowned nineteenth-century prison inspector and Newgate chronicler – and one not particularly convinced by her concept of redemption – conceded nevertheless that it was truly remarkable what a difference she made at the prison, and how quickly.

What Mrs Fry accomplished against tremendous odds is one of the brightest facts in the whole history of philanthropy. How she persevered in spite of prediction of certain failure; how she won the cooperation of lukewarm officials; how she provided the manual labour for which these poor idle hands were eager, and presently transformed a filthy den of corruption into a clean whitewashed workroom, in which sat rows of women, recently so desperate and degraded, stitching and sewing orderly and silent: these [were] extraordinary results.[5]

Newgate, of course, was not the whole story, just its beginning. Over the years, a pattern emerged to Fry's career that she neither planned nor anticipated. The Newgate project – and her experience with the 1818 Select Committee on London prisons – opened her eyes to the extent of what was still needed in terms of prison reform, and how little concrete information was available. So she widened her brief to take in most other major gaols in Britain, including Ireland and the Channel Islands. At her interview in 1835 by the Select Committee on prisons in England and Wales, she was able to offer probably a wider range of experience of contemporary prison conditions than anyone. Once the 1823 Gaols Act and the 1835 Prisons Act had enshrined in law many of her recommendations, and as management of British prisons devolved increasingly to central government, she turned her sights to Continental Western Europe. Her fame having preceded her – and her letters of introduction being second to none – there was no difficulty in gaining access to people of influence abroad. With increasing age, when foreign travel was no longer an option, she turned her attention to more local projects, but she never let up.

How did she achieve such success? Her two elder daughters, who compiled her memoir, said she approached all men as equals; she talked to prisoners and princes with the same quiet respect. Others said her voice had a 'witchery' about it that reduced to tears even those who spoke no English.

Fry's prison reform cause had great merit, and most of those who flocked to hear her speak would have been genuine supporters; others would have come out of curiosity to see this tall, stately woman, with her magical voice and strange costume, doing what women of the time never usually did in public. Her presence was clearly enthralling. George Campbell, Duke of Argyll, liberal politician and writer, described the mesmerizing effect her presence had on people. She was for him a figure who left a deep impression on her time and a lasting blessing to the generations following . . . The story of her entering, alone and entirely undefended, into a prison reserved for abandoned and vicious women of whom even the keepers were so afraid that they never could go except in company, is a story which used to thrill me with admiration and astonishment. It was a great pleasure, therefore, to meet this illustrious woman. She was the only really very great human being I have ever met, with whom it was impossible to be disappointed. She was, in the fullest sense of the word, a majestic woman. She was already advanced in years, and had a very tall and stately figure. But it was her countenance that was so striking. Her features were handsome in the sense of being well-proportioned, but they were not in the usual sense beautiful. Her eyes were not large, or brilliant, or transparent. They were only calm, and wise, and steady. But over the whole countenance there was an ineffable expression of sweetness, dignity and power. It was impossible not to feel some awe before her, as before some superior being. I understood in a moment the story of the prison. She needed no defence but that of her own noble and almost divine countenance . . . It is a rare thing indeed, in this poor world of ours, to see any man or woman whose personality responds perfectly to the ideal conception formed of an heroic character and an heroic life.[6]

Fry was an expert in the art of delegation. Her niece, Elizabeth Gurney, who travelled with her on the Continent, commented how marvellous it was that Aunt Fry got everybody to work for her. Her daughter Rachel added that she had a remarkable knack of adaptation, the ability to 'find the right person for the right thing: this led to many valuable appointments, both at home and abroad, and to placing numerous persons in situations exactly suited to their talents'.[7] Above all, Fry was persistent, relentless even, in the pursuit of her objectives. She was, as Florence Nightingale once described herself, 'a well-connected female nuisance'. Her brother Joseph wrote:

She almost always obtained her object. One of the qualities which tended powerfully to this result was her patience – her indomitable perseverance. She was never one of those who embraced a philanthropic object warmly, and as readily forgot it. But month after month, and year after year, she laboured in any plan of mercy which she had thought it her duty to undertake; and she never forsook it in her heart or feeling, even when her health failed, or other circumstances, not under her control, closed the door for a time on her personal exertions.[8]

The cost of those 'personal exertions' to her constitution, which had never been particularly robust, quite apart from the 11 children she bore in 21 years, was considerable. She once told a Bible Society meeting that she was 'morning, noon and night under a deep impression of my responsibility to others'.[9] She was frequently prone to physical and nervous exhaustion, particularly on the campaign trail, when she was mobbed by fans. She was always ambivalent about her celebrity status, but accepted that it was part of what furthered the cause of prison reform. She regularly felt unequal to the task of addressing – or being followed by – large, heaving masses of people. Meeting the great and good, however, she relished – but then felt guilty at the vanity of enjoying such attention.

If there was a personal cost to be paid for her career, her husband and children shared it; for it is an inescapable fact that Fry neglected her family in the pursuit of her public good works. Certainly there was a tradition of Quaker ministers, men and women, spending long periods away from home, even thousands of miles away, travelling 'in the ministry'. Stephen Grellet spent nearly ten years on the road; Deborah Darby was away for three years at a stretch. However, even the Society of Friends, which had appointed Fry as a minister, and continued to issue certificates giving her permission to go on missionary work (to which she then added her prison reform agenda), admonished her in the early days for the degree to which she put work before family. As her celebrity increased, one can only assume that the publicity her tours attracted were in the Society's interest as well.

In the early days, Hannah More wrote in Fry's defence: 'If she stole some hours from the family to visit the prison, she stole some hours from sleep to attend to the family'.[10] But in later years, it was months rather than hours that she stole.

> The 'concern' of Quaker women, often with large families, which took them on ministerial journeys thousands of miles away from their husbands and children, astonished the world at large, but was accepted in their community and fully understood. Deborah Darby found also in Coalbrookdale that 'as we are comfortable amongst ourselves, it makes us not much dependent on those not with us for our consolation, which is a blessing'.[11]

The Quaker community may have been accepting and understanding of female ministers. The reality was, of course, that Darby was fleeing an unsatisfactory marriage to a possibly mentally ill husband. Darby was a great influence on Fry in her youth. Fry's marriage, one suspects, was also less than she had hoped for. The ministry offered her an escape as well as a socially acceptable vehicle for her prison reform activities. And her family was not universally understanding. In her diary, she admits that her husband resented the time she spent on public duties; in turn, she resented the fact that he resented it; and her eldest daughters Katherine and Rachel, in their memoirs written two years after Fry's death, simply wondered why it was thus. When she left to visit Ireland, leaving them with various relatives, they wrote:

> Most painful was it for [the children] to part with her; nor was the trial lessened by some of her children as they advanced in life, not being altogether satisfied as to those engagements, or able to comprehend how a career so peculiar could be consistent with their mother's domestic duties.[12]

Rachel, in a second memoir published in 1856, added that it would be untrue to say that their mother

> took any pleasure in domestic concerns . . . She would not have chosen for her own pleasure, the oversight of either house or table; and when in later life circumstances rendered care and economy a duty, it was a great relief to her to be able to depute the charge of household affairs to her eldest daughter.[13]

This impression, that Fry put public life before family life, lingered down through the generations. As a boy, her great-great-nephew, the writer Percy Lubbock, used to spend his summers visiting his grandparents at Earlham, Fry's childhood home. He described the portrait by George Richmond of 'Aunt Fry', 'old, portly and immensely majestic', that hung in a corner of the drawing-room, 'looking very stately'.

> She looked as if she had accomplished her good works with a high hand. And, mixed with legitimate pride in her fame, there survived in the family some tradition that she was more interested in her grand European activities than in her nearest and homeliest duties . . . She became a character that perhaps, to her family, seemed strangely public. And in our grandmother's voice, as she spoke to us of Aunt Fry, there might be a hint of such an idea, quickly covered with admiring veneration.[14]

Fry has been credited with being the first woman to bring private good works into the public domain. She claimed that it was not a role she particularly relished, were it not for the good she could see being achieved. In May 1828, by which time she had been seriously involved with prison reform for over a decade, she described her attendance at an early meeting of the British Ladies' Society.

> It was a very numerous assemblage of ladies, many of them of high rank. I had much to
> do in it from time to time . . . I went away low and humbled at the conspicuous part I
> had to take, not doubting that it would bring me into evil report as well as good report;
> and feeling lest the secretaries might feel my doing so much, and their doing so little.

'I trust good was done', she added. 'But I may set my seal to this – that public services are fearful services, and none but those engaged in them know how much those are spared who do so privately.' But she accepted that a vocation was a vocation, for 'if the Master calls us to public duty, it is not only well but honourable'.

Finally, can Fry be called an early feminist? Certainly the debate for the advancement of women's rights, particularly in education, had been stimulated by the feminist philosopher Mary Wollstonecraft in 1792 with the publication of *A Vindication of the Rights of Woman*. So the context already existed for a feminist interpretation of Fry's public career. And the Great Reform Act of 1832 gave limited voting rights at local level to some women who owned property (mainly widows). But it would be another 40 years before the establishment of the National Society for Women's Suffrage began to agitate for equal rights.

Fry had a unique advantage in being a Quaker, in that such women enjoyed more equal rights than most; within the Society of Friends, from their earliest days, women had been accepted as ministers. So Fry had no need to fight in that respect for equal status and the independence that went with it: being a minister gave her the freedom legitimately and respectably to pursue activities, under the cloak of religion, which would have been impossible for non-Quaker women. Fry also came from a rich and influential family with top-level connections that gave her an entrée to opportunities closed to others; she was, in that sense, already more equal than most. Even after her husband's bankruptcy, the generosity of her brothers ensured that there was always the funding for her projects and campaigns.

Certainly, Fry brought female philanthropy decisively out of the private sphere, and into the public arena. But personally, she regarded this as more a

responsibility than a privilege, less an advocacy of women's rights than an extension of their duties. In the introduction to *Observations*, her handbook on the
good management of female prisoners, she wrote about the 'duty and privilege'
of women's role in society.

> I rejoice to see the day in which so many women of every rank, instead of spending their
> time in trifling and unprofitable pursuits, are engaged in works of usefulness and char-
> ity. Earnestly it is to be desired that the number of these valuable labourers in the cause
> of virtue and humanity may be increased, and that all of us may be made sensible of the
> infinite importance of redeeming the time, of turning our talents to account.
>
> Far be it from me to attempt to persuade women to forsake their right province. My
> only desire is, that they should *fill that province well*; and, although their calling, in many
> respects, materially differs from that of the other sex, and may not perhaps be so exalted
> a one – yet a minute's observation will prove that, if adequately fulfilled, it has nearly, if
> not quite, an equal influence on society at large.
>
> No person will deny the importance attached to the character and conduct of a
> woman, in all her domestic and social relations, when she is filling the station of a
> daughter, a sister, a wife, a mother, or a mistress of a family. But it is a dangerous error
> to suppose that the duties of females end here. Their gentleness, their natural sympathy
> with the afflicted, their quickness of discernment, their openness to religious impres-
> sions, are points of character (not unusually to be found in our sex) which evidently
> qualify them, within their own peculiar province, for a far more extensive field of
> usefulness.[15]

Fry's straightforward, practical approach to the needs of female prisoners is as
relevant today as it was two centuries ago. The following words are taken from
the 2007 report for the government by Baroness Jean Corston on the particular
vulnerability of women and young girls. But they could have been Fry's own.
Corston, like Fry, said that she would 'above all, never forget my first sight of a
baby in prison'.[16] She added:

> The criminal justice system is a complex institution and it is tempting to think that
> solutions to its problems must also be complex. But grasping the simple fact that
> women are different from men can go a very long way to bringing about change by
> focussing on basic and achievable factors that reduce emotional distress . . . promoting
> meaningful activity, providing structure and routine and rules for living; encouraging
> women to help each other; helping them to feel more in control of their lives; providing

a normalising environment; promoting social inclusion, health and recovery . . . This is a human rights approach to prison management. It is also common sense![17]

Corston stressed that women have been 'marginalised within a system designed by men for men for far too long, and called for a "champion" to ensure that their needs are properly recognised and met'.[18] Elizabeth Fry was just such a champion.

Shortly after Fry's death, a gift arrived for her from Australia. It was a calabash – or ornamental gourd – from the garden of a woman called Hester who had been one of Fry's Newgate protégées and a convict on the transport ship *Brothers* in 1823. She sent it as 'a simple tribute of affectionate remembrance'.

Hester had been chosen by her fellow prisoners at Newgate to act as their school mistress. In recognition of her services, Fry had given her a pound of sugar and half a pound of tea for the voyage out to New South Wales, in addition to the patchwork quilt kit and other comforts routinely provided to every departing female convict. At the time of Fry's death, of which she was not aware, Hester reported that she had been happily married in Australia for 20 years, was 'very comfortably established', and was now able to buy her tea 'by the chest'. She had kept for herself the patchwork quilt she made on the outward voyage.[19]

Hester's story encapsulated everything that Fry had strived to achieve for the Newgate women and, indeed, for prisoners everywhere: redemption, rehabilitation and self-respect.

Chronology

1770	Captain James Cook 'discovers' Botany Bay, Australia.
1776	American War of Independence ends practice of transporting British convicts across the Atlantic. Convicts begin to be kept on 'prison hulks', anchored mainly in the rivers Thames and Medway.
1777	Prison reformer John Howard publishes *The State of Prisons in England and Wales with Preliminary Observations, and an Account of Some Foreign Prisons.*
1780	Elizabeth Fry (née Gurney) born at Gurney Court, Magdalen Street, Norwich.
	Newgate prison, as well as the Clink and Fleet prisons, devastated in the anti-Catholic Gordon Riots.
1782	Newgate and Fleet prisons rebuilt.
1786	Gurney family moves to Earlham Hall, Norwich.
1787	First British convict fleet sets sail for Botany Bay, Australia; 192 of the convicts are women.
1790	Death of John Howard.
1792	Death of Fry's mother, Catherine Gurney.
1797	Fry meets American Quaker minister, William Savery.
	Fry meets British Quaker minister, Deborah Darby.
	Fry becomes 'plain' Quaker.
1800	Fry marries plain Quaker Joseph Fry, banker and tea merchant; moves to St Mildred's Court, Poultry, London.
1801	Birth of daughter Katherine.
1803	Birth of daughter Rachel.
1804	Birth of son John.
	Death of mother-in-law, Elizabeth Fry.
1806	Birth of son William.

1808   Birth of daughter Richenda.
          Death of father-in-law, William Storrs Fry.
1809   Death of father, John Gurney.
          Birth of son Joseph.
          Elizabeth and Joseph Fry and family move to Plashet House, East
          Ham.
1811   Birth of daughter Elizabeth.
          Fry is appointed a Quaker minister.
1812   Birth of daughter Hannah.
1813   Fry's first visit to Newgate women's wing.
          First financial crisis in Fry businesses.
1814   Birth of daughter Louisa.
          Death of brother John.
1815   Death of daughter Elizabeth.
1816   Birth of son Samuel.
          Fry launches the Newgate experiment.
1817   Fry gives Newgate evidence to House of Commons' Select
          Committee on prisons in London and Southwark.
          Fry's first campaign/prison inspection tour of Scotland and the
          north of England, with brother Joseph Gurney.
          Fry introduces female transportee support system.
1819   John Joseph Gurney publishes, in collaboration with Fry, *Notes
          on a Visit Made to Some of the Prisons in Scotland and the North
          of England, in Company with Elizabeth Fry, with Some General
          Observations on the Subject of Prison Discipline*.
1821   London's Millbank penitentiary is completed, based on Jeremy
          Bentham's 'panopticon' principle; later becomes holding prison for
          transportees.
1822   Death of sister Priscilla.
          Birth of eleventh and final child, Daniel; birth of first grandchild
          on same day.
1823   Gaols Act introduced by Home Secretary, Sir Robert Peel; lack
          of funding or provision for an inspectorate largely impedes its
          implementation.
1825   Second financial crisis in Fry businesses.
1826   Third financial crisis in Fry businesses; Gurney brothers act as
          receivers.

1827	Fry's first prison inspection tour of Ireland, with brother Joseph Gurney.
	Fry publishes *Observations of the Visiting, Superintendence and Government of Female Prisoners*.
1828	Fry and Gurney produce 'Report addressed to the Marquess Wellesley, Lord Lieutenant of Ireland by E. F. and J. J. G., respecting their late visit to that country'.
1828–29	Bankruptcy of Joseph Fry, and his Quaker 'disownment' until 1838; Gurney brothers take Fry business in hand.
1829	Fry family leaves Plashet for a smaller house.
1831	Fry publishes *Texts for Every Day in the Year, Principally Practical and Devotional*.
1833	Fry's first prison inspection tour of Channel Islands.
1834	Fry's second prison inspection tour of Scotland.
	Fry establishes network of libraries for coastguards.
1835	Fry gives evidence to House of Lords' Select Committee on prisons in England and Wales.
	Prisons Act provides for national inspectorate and standardized regulations.
1836	Fry's second prison inspection tour of Ireland.
	Fry's second prison inspection tour of Channel Islands.
1837	Establishment of Britain's first women-only prison at Grange Gorman Lane in Dublin; matron appointed on Fry's recommendation.
1838	Fry's first Continental prison inspection tour – France.
	Fry's third prison inspection tour of Scotland.
1839	Fry's second Continental prison tour – France, Switzerland, Germany.
1840	Fry's third Continental prison tour – Holland, Belgium and Germany – including visit to Kaiserswerth Institute and training school for nurses.
	Fry establishes Institution for Nursing Sisters in London.
1841	Fry's fourth Continental tour – Holland, Germany and Denmark.
1842	Pentonville prison completed, based on 'separate' principle.
1843	Fry's fifth and final Continental prison inspection tour – France.
1845	Fry dies at Ramsgate.

1849   The Elizabeth Fry Institute for the Reformation of Women
         Prisoners opens at Mare Street, Hackney, as a memorial.
1853   Penal Servitude Act substitutes periods of confinement and hard
         labour for transportation.
1868   Transportation to Australian colonies ceases.
1913   Statue of Elizabeth Fry is erected at the Old Bailey, site of the
         Newgate prison.

Notes

Notes to Chapter 1: A Norfolk childhood

1 'At length I became as rich as the Gurneys' was the boast of the Learned Judge in Gilbert and Sullivan's *Trial by Jury*. The operetta opened at the Royalty Theatre on 25 March 1875.
2 Earlham Hall became part of East Anglia University.
3 Percy Lubbock, *Earlham* (London, 1922), p. 46. Lubbock (1879–1965) was a great-great-nephew of Elizabeth Fry.
4 For a medical analysis of the available evidence, see T. R. Miles and Richard Huntsman, 'The stupidity of Elizabeth Fry – was it dyslexia?', *British Journal of General Practice*, December 2002.
5 Her periods of illness were also a way of achieving some solitude in a household where many children would share a bedroom.
6 Augustus J. C. Hare, *The Gurneys of Earlham* (London, 1897), i, pp. 37–8.
7 Ibid., i, p. 34.
8 Ibid., i, p. 41.

Notes to Chapter 2: Awakenings

1 Augustus J. C. Hare, *The Gurneys of Earlham* (London, 1897) i, p. 51.
2 Ibid., i, p. 57.
3 Ibid., i, p. 73.
4 Ibid., i, p. 96.
5 Francis Taylor, *The Life of William Savery* (New York and Philadelphia, 1925), p. 432.
6 Hare, *The Gurneys*, i, p. 75.
7 Benjamin Seebohm (ed.), *Memoirs of the Life and Gospel Labours of Stephen Grellet* (London, 1860), p. 15.
8 Hare, *The Gurneys*, i, p. 85.
9 Edward H. Milligan, *Biographical Dictionary of British Quakers in Commerce and Industry* (York, 2007), pp. 190–1.
10 Hare, *The Gurneys*, i, p. 108.

Notes to Chapter 3: Marriage and ministry

1   London Debtors Prisoners Act 1804.
2   So called because the method was to insert under the skin on the arm of the child a pustule removed from the body of another.
3   The Circassia region, where the practice originated, was famous for supplying the great harems of the Middle East.
4   *Plain Dealer*, no. xxx, 3 July 1724.
5   Voltaire (François-Marie Arouet), 'On inoculation', *Letters Concerning the English Nation* (London, 1926), pp. 57–64. Four other letters in the collection are on the subject of Quakers.
6   Annual Register 1762, p. 78.
7   Hannah Ransome Geldart, *Memorials of Samuel Gurney* (Philadelphia, 1859), p. 20.
8   MSS Brit. Emp. 558, f. 1 (Rhodes House, Bodleian Library).
9   Quoted in David E. Swift, *Joseph John Gurney: Banker, Reformer, Quaker* (Connecticut, 1962), p. 22.
10 Augustus J. C. Hare, *The Gurneys of Earlham* (London, 1897), i, p. 172.
11 A note found in between the pages of Fry's journals for mid-1812, quoted in Katherine Fry and Rachel Cresswell, *Memoir of the Life of Elizabeth Fry* (London, 1847) i, p. 188.
12 William Forster (1784–1854) married Anna Buxton, sister of Fry's brother-in-law Thomas Fowell Buxton, MP, abolitionist and prison reformer. Anna was the first woman to visit Newgate with Fry.
13 Benjamin Seebohm (ed.), *Memoirs of the Life and Gospel Labours of Stephen Grellet* (London, 1870), p. 97.
14 Ibid., p. 97.
15 Ibid., p. 98.

Notes to Chapter 4: Howard's inheritor

1   Also Hooton and Hooten.
2   Emily Manners, 'Elizabeth Hooton: first Quaker woman preacher (1600–1672)' (London, 1914), p. 10. Published as Supplement 12 to the *Journal of the Friends Historical Society*. The language and spelling of the original have been simplified.
3   Manners, 'Hooton', p. 15.
4   Ibid.
5   Ibid.
6   Cartel ships were neutral vessels commissioned in time of war specifically to exchange prisoners, or to carry proposals between the warring parties. They were not permitted to be armed, except for a single gun with which they might send signals.
7   John Howard, *The State of Prisons in England and Wales with Preliminary Observations, and an Account of Some Foreign Prisons* (Warrington, 1777).
8   Ibid., p. 2.
9   Ibid., p. 2.

10 Ibid., p. 3.
11 Ibid., p. 3.
12 Ibid., p. 5.
13 Ibid., p. 5.
14 Ibid., p. 16.

Notes to Chapter 5: 'Hell above ground'

1 Dickens also included a complete essay on Newgate in his *Sketches by Boz* (1836), in which he suggests that he had 'a great respect for Mrs Fry'. *Oliver Twist* was published in 1838, and *A Tale of Two Cities* in 1859.
2 The 1818 (275) House of Commons' Select Committee report on the state of prisons in the City of London.
3 For a vivid account of the Gordon Riots, see Christopher Hibbert, *King Mob: The Story of Lord George Gordon and the Riots of 1780* (London, 1958).
4 Surprisingly, most of the 2,000 were rearrested without much difficulty in the days following the riots and were housed in specially erected temporary sheds.
5 Meetings were held at his house but he never joined the movement.
6 His grandmother Priscilla (née Bell) was the sister of Fry's mother Catherine.
7 The tale is told in full in Abby Ashby and Audrey Jones, *The Shrigley Abduction* (Stroud, 2004).
8 The jury may have been disinclined to show much sympathy to Edward Wakefield on the grounds that this was not the first such romantic escapade in which he had been involved. In 1816, at the age of 20, he had eloped to Edinburgh and married 17-year-old Eliza Pattle, a ward in chancery who was due to inherit £30,000 on her twenty-first birthday. Influential family friends persuaded the Pattle family to accept the union. However, Eliza died shortly after giving birth to their second child, and just days before her twenty-first birthday; her inheritance therefore stayed with the Pattles.
9 Edward Gibbon Wakefield, *Facts Relating to the Punishment of Death in the Metropolis* (London, 1831).
10 Quoted in Ashby and Jones, *The Shrigley Abduction*, p. 176.
11 See, in particular, Paul Bloomfield, *Edward Gibbon Wakefield: Builder of the British Commonwealth* (London, 1961).
12 Mrs Francis Cresswell, *A Memoir of Elizabeth Fry* (London, 1856), p. 112.
13 Ibid., p. 117.
14 Fry's cousin, colonialist Edward Gibbon Wakefield, on hearing this, suggested that a better idea would be for Botany Bay to be 'done away with'.
15 Thomas Fowell Buxton, *An Enquiry Whether Crime and Misery Are Produced or Prevented by Our Present System of Prison Discipline* (London, 1818), p. 109.
16 Augustus Hare, *The Gurneys of Earlham* (London, 1897), i, pp. 282–3.
17 Ibid., i, pp. 283–4.
18 Ibid., i, p. 284.
19 Ibid., i, p. 286.

20   The 1818 report, p. 34.
21   Ibid., p. 35.
22   Ibid.
23   Ibid.
24   Ibid., p. 36.
25   Ibid.
26   Ibid., p. 37.
27   Ibid., p. 38.
28   Ibid., p. 40.
29   Ibid.
30   Ibid., p. 41.

Notes to Chapter 6: Exiles to a distant land

1   Elizabeth Fry, *Observations on the Visiting, Superintendence and Government of Female Prisoners* (London, 1827). Fry's views on capital punishment are recorded on pp. 71–6.
2   Ibid.
3   Ibid.
4   He would have achieved much more, but for his sudden suicide, following the unexpected death of his wife.
5   Samuel Romilly, *Memoirs* (London, 1840), iii, pp. 332–3, quoted in Leon Radzinowicz, *A History of English Criminal Law and Its Administration from 1750* (London, 1948), i, p. 544.
6   The debtors included former remand prisoners who had ultimately been found innocent of any criminal charges, but who had incurred living costs while in prison awaiting trial – costs they then could not pay.
7   The Act substituted four years' penal servitude for seven years' transportation, thus confirming the view, long held by some, that transportation was the soft option. Long-term transportation was retained for certain offences until it was abolished completely by a further Act of Parliament in 1857.
8   Magwitch, Pip's benefactor in Dickens' *Great Expectations*, was an escapee from one such prison hulk on the Medway.
9   The fastest journey recorded by a convict ship was 127 days for the *Matilda* in 1791. See Alan Brooke and David Brandon, *Bound for Botany Bay: British Convict Voyages to Australia* (Richmond, 2005), p. 47.
10 See Robert Hughes, *The Fatal Shore* (London, 1987), and Brooke and Brandon, *Bound for Botany Bay*, which includes an invaluable bibliography of primary sources in the British National Archive.
11 Quoted in Brooke and Brandon, *Bound for Botany Bay*, p. 244.
12 The surgeon-superintendents were chosen from unemployed naval surgeons, who were plentiful in times of peace. They were effectively in charge of the convicts' welfare. See Brooke and Brandon, *Bound for Botany Bay*, pp. 168–71.
13 Fry's optimism that these young women had the chance of a decent and productive future

is borne out by a Royal Commission of 1820 which found that native-born Australians – by-and-large the convicts' children – turned out to be the most law-abiding of citizens.

14 Quoted in Brooke and Brandon, *Bound for Botany Bay*, p. 206.

15 Thomas Timpson, *Memoirs of Mrs Elizabeth Fry, including a History of Her Labours in Promoting the Reformation of Female Prisoners, and the Improvement of British Seamen* (London, 1847), pp. 36–7. Rev. Timpson was a great practical supporter of Fry's work, sat on her committees, and was Honorary Secretary to the British and Foreign Sailors' Society.

16 Timpson, *Memoirs*, p. 124.

17 Brooke and Brandon, *Bound for Botany Bay*, p. 238.

18 Charlotte Anley, *Prisoners of Australia* (London, 1841), p. 8.

19 Ibid., p. 9.

20 Ibid., p. 16.

21 Ibid., p. 22.

22 Ibid., p. 23.

23 Ibid., p. 28.

24 The Cascades female factory opened in 1828 and served until 1856 as an establishment where transported women convicts would serve a sentence, wait to be assigned or hired, or await confinement. It also served later as a regular gaol, hospital, boys' reformatory and training school, lunatic asylum and contagious diseases unit, until its closure in 1904.

25 Some time later the quilt was returned to England, apparently to be presented to Fry, although there is no record of her having received it. Its fate during the next century and a half is unknown. It was discovered in an attic in Edinburgh in late 1987.

26 For a full technical description of the coverlet, see <www.nga.gov.au.RajahQuilt>. The quilt is a major focus of the Gallery's Australian Textiles collection but, due to its size, fragility and the light-sensitive nature of its materials, it is only made available for viewing once a year. It was given to the Gallery by former editor of *The Australian* newspaper, Les Hollings, and the Australian Textiles Fund in 1989.

27 Penny Russell, '"Her Excellency": Lady Franklin, female convicts and the problem of authority in Van Diemen's Land', Journal of Australian Studies, no. 53, 1997.

28 Timpson, *Memoirs*, pp. 139–43.

29 Brooke and Brandon, *Bound for Botany Bay*, p. 217.

Notes to Chapter 7: Celebrity and crash

1 Hansard, xxxvii, 50, 14 April 1818.

2 *Journal of the Friends Historical Society*, vol. 38, 1946, pp. 21–3.

3 Quoted in Mrs Francis Cresswell, *A Memoir of Elizabeth Fry* (London, 1856), p. 167.

4 Sidney Smith, 'Prisons', *Edinburgh Review* (1822), pp. 359, 374.

5 William Roberts, *Memoirs of the Life and Correspondence of Mrs Hannah More* (London 1834), iv, pp. 30–1.

6 George Byron, *Don Juan*, canto 10, verse 85

7 MSS Brit. Emp. s. 559

8 Joseph John Gurney, *Notes on a Visit Made to Some of the Prisons in Scotland and the North*

of England, in Company with Elizabeth Fry, with Some General Observations on the Subject of Prison Discipline (London 1819), pp. iv–vi.

9 Quoted in Cresswell, *A Memoir*, p. 167.

10 Joseph John Gurney, *Memoirs of Joseph John Gurney*, ed. Joseph Bevan Braithwaite (Norwich, 1854), i, p. 299.

11 Hannah Ransome Geldart, *Memorials of Samuel Gurney* (Philadelphia, 1859), p. 41.

12 Quoted in M. G. Jones, *Hannah More* (Cambridge, 1952), p. 215.

13 Gurney, *Memoirs*, i, p. 319.

14 Ibid., p. 329.

15 Ibid., p. 339.

16 Ibid., p. 348

17 Ibid., p. 356.

18 Quoted in Maria Luddy, *Women and Philanthropy in Nineteenth-Century Ireland* (Cambridge, 1995), p. 158.

19 L. S. Pressnell, *Country Banking in the Industrial Revolution* (Oxford, 1956), p. 113.

20 Quoted in David E. Swift, *Joseph John Gurney: Banker, Reformer, Quaker* (Connecticut, 1962), p. 85.

21 Among his many philanthropic activities, Wilberforce was also a founding member of the Church Missionary Society, which sent chaplains to Australia. The best known of these was Samuel Marsden of Parramatta.

22 MSS Brit. Emp. s. 558.

Notes to Chapter 8: A manifesto for reform

1 Elizabeth Fry, *Observations on the Visiting, Superintendence and Government of Female Prisoners* (London, 1827), p. 4.

2 Ibid., p. 4.

3 Ibid., p. 6.

4 Ibid., p. 7.

5 Ibid., p. 7.

6 Ibid., p. 20.

7 Ibid., p. 22.

8 Ibid., p. 24.

9 Ibid., p. 26.

10 Ibid., p. 29.

11 Ibid., p. 48.

12 Ibid., p. 65.

13 Ibid., p. 69.

14 Ibid., p. 70.

Notes to Chapter 9: Recovery

1   Mrs Francis Cresswell, *A Memoir of Elizabeth Fry* (London, 1856), p. 174.
2   Katherine Fry and Rachel Cresswell, *Memoir of the Life of Elizabeth Fry* (London, 1847), ii, p. 122–6.
3   Or almost £250,000, at today's value.
4   Charles Dickens, 'A visit to Newgate', *Sketches by Boz*, first published 1839 (Penguin, 1995) p. 239.
5   The 1835 Report of the House of Lords' Select Committee on the present state of the several gaols and houses of correction in England and Wales, p. 80.
6   Ibid., p. 327.
7   Ibid., p. 329.
8   Ibid., p. 332.
9   Ibid., p. 334.
10 Ibid., p. 334.
11 Ibid., p. 336.
12 Fry and Cresswell, *Memoir*, ii, p. 186.
13 Ibid., p. 187.

Notes to Chapter 10: Continental campaigns

1   Quoted in Augustus Hare, *The Gurneys of Earlham* (London, 1897), ii, p. 101.
2   Letter from Priscilla Buxton to her brother Fowell; an account of Fry's first French journey as told at a family party. MSS Brit. Emp. s. 559.
3   Bunsen's son Ernest married Fry's niece Elizabeth Gurney in August 1845.
4   Once the home of Sir Thomas More, fifteenth-century Crosby Hall was moved stone by stone to Cheyne Walk, Chelsea, in 1910, to rescue it from proposed demolition. It is now a private house. The sale of prisoners' work and books raised over £1,000.
5   Frances Bunsen, *A Memoir of Baron Bunsen* (London 1868), i, p. 510.
6   Ibid., i, p. 516.
7   Ibid., i, p. 517.
8   Allen & Hanbury was acquired in 1958 by Glaxo Laboratories, which retained 'Allen & Hanbury' as a brand name.
9   Elizabeth Gurney, *Elizabeth Fry's Journeys on the Continent, 1840–1841* (London, 1931), p. 44.
10 Ibid., p. 55.
11 Ibid., p. 58.
12 Ibid., pp. 58–9.
13 Ibid., p. 66.
14 Ibid., p. 67.
15 The spirit of von der Recke is continued today by a charitable trust bearing his name.
16 Gurney, *Journeys*, p. 100.
17 Ibid., pp. 119–20.

18   Ibid., p. 122.
19   Ibid., p. 127.
20   Ibid., pp. 136–7.
21   Ibid., p. 138.
22   Ibid., p. 146.
23   Ibid., p. 148.
24   Ibid., p. 150.
25   Ibid., p. 152.
26   Ibid., p. 156.
27   Ibid., p. 160.
28   Ibid., p. 160.
29   Ibid., p. 161.
30   Ibid., p. 180.
31   Ibid., p. 192.

Notes to Chapter 11: Nursing before Nightingale

1   Mark Bostridge, *Florence Nightingale: The Woman and Her Legend* (Penguin/Viking, 2009), p. 207.
2   The organization was originally to be called The Protestant Sisters of Charity, but the Anglican establishment objected.
3   Fry nurses also served in the Boer War and World War One.
4   Katherine Fry and Rachel Cresswell, *Memoir of the Life of Elizabeth Fry* (London, 1847), ii, pp. 357–9.
5   By the time Nightingale visited Kaiserswerth, the hospital had no fewer than a hundred beds.
6   History of the Institution of Nursing Sisters. Wellcome Institute, SA/QNI/W6.
7   Mrs Francis Cresswell, *A Memoir of Elizabeth Fry* (London, 1856), p. 465.
8   Charles Dickens, *Martin Chuzzlewit* (London, 1843–44), Preface, vi.
9   John South, *Facts Relating to Hospital Nurses* (London, 1857), pp. 25–6.
10   There is some suggestion that the hospital was, in fact, trying to poach Fry nurses by paying them directly.
11   *British Medical Journal*, 19 June 1897, pp. 1644–8.
12   Ibid.
13   Ibid.
14   Ibid.
15   Ibid.
16   *The Nursing Record and Hospital World* (London, 1897), vol. 18, p. 493.

Notes to Chapter 12: 'Into the valley of old age'

1   Katherine Fry and Rachel Cresswell, *Memoir of the Life of Elizabeth Fry* (London, 1847), ii, p. 464.
2   Ibid., ii, p. 504.
3   From the minutes of the Society's committee meeting on 3 November 1845, quoted in Mrs Francis Cresswell, *A Memoir of Elizabeth Fry* (London, 1856), pp. 566–7.
4   Ibid., p. 567.
5   For a fuller account of the meeting, see Thomas Timpson, *Memoirs of Elizabeth Fry* (London, 1847), pp. 332–40.
6   Anthony Ashley-Cooper (1801–85), politician and philanthropist, later the seventh earl of Shaftesbury; Christian, Baron von Bunsen (1791–1860), diplomat and scholar; Edward Parry (1790–1855), Arctic explorer and administrator. As a commissioner of the Australian Agricultural Company, Parry had been in charge of the penal colony at Port Stephens in Australia, regarded as a model settlement. Like Bunsen, he married into Fry's extended family when he wed the widow of the son of Louisa Hoare (née Gurney).
7   The ledgers for the institute are kept in Hackney Council archives. The institute moved to Islington in 1913, where the operation still continued in 2008 as part of the local probation service.
8   Alfred Briscoe Drury (1856–1944), best known for his architectural and public space sculpture.

Notes to Chapter 13: Epilogue

1   In 1812, another Quaker philanthropist, James Neild, an international campaigner against imprisonment for debt in particular, had published a report, *The State of the Prisons in England, Scotland and Wales*.
2   Eric Evans, *The Forging of the Modern State: Early Industrial Britain, 1783–1870* (London, 1996), p. 445.
3   William Wistar Comfort, *Stephen Grellet 1773–1855* (New York, 1942), p. 189.
4   Evans, *The Forging of the Modern State*, pp. 444, 299.
5   Arthur Griffiths, *The Chronicles of Newgate* (London, 1883). Griffiths had also been a governor at Chatham convict prison, Millbank and Wormwood Scrubs. He was involved on the fringe of the 'Jack the Ripper' murders.
6   George Douglas, *Autobiography and Memoirs*, quoted in *Journal of Friends Historical Society* (York, 1907), iv, p. 33.
7   Mrs Francis Cresswell, *A Memoir of Mrs Fry* (London, 1856), p. 210.
8   Augustus J. C. Hare, *The Gurneys of Earlham* (London, 1897), i, p. 302.
9   Joseph John Gurney, *Memoirs of Joseph John Gurney* (Norwich, 1854), i, p. 383.
10   Hannah More, *Moral Sketches of Prevailing Opinions and Manners, Foreign and Domestic* (London, 1820), p. 213.
11   Comfort, *Stephen Grellet*, p. 4.

12   Katherine Fry and Rachel Cresswell, *Memoirs of the Life of Elizabeth Fry* (London, 1847), i, p. 499.

13   Cresswell, *A Memoir*, p. 95.

14   Percy Lubbock, *Earlham* (London, 1922), p. 10.

15   Elizabeth Fry, *Observations on the Visiting, Superintendence and Government of Female Prisoners* (London, 1827), p. 2.

16   The Corston Report: A Review of Women with Particular Vulnerabilities in the Criminal Justice System (HMSO: London, 2007).

17   The Corston Report, p. 18.

18   The Corston Report, p. 2.

19   Cresswell, *A Memoir*, p. 208.

Bibliography

ARCHIVE SOURCES

The diaries of Elizabeth Fry (Friends' Meeting House Library, Euston, London; and Norfolk Record Office, Norwich).

The 1818 (275) House of Commons' Select Committee report on the state of prisons in the City of London.

The 1835 (438) (439) (440) (441) House of Lords' Select Committee report on the present state of the several gaols and houses of correction in England and Wales.

History of the Institution of Nursing Sisters. Wellcome Institute, SA/QNI/W6.

MSS Brit. Emp. s. 444, 547, 558, 559 (Rhodes House, Bodleian Library, Oxford).

PRIMARY SOURCES

Anley, Charlotte, *Prisoners of Australia* (London, 1841).

Breay, Margaret, 'Nursing in the Victorian era', *The Nursing Record and Hospital World* (1897) 18, pp. 493–502.

British Medical Journal (1897), i, pp. 1644–8.

Brown, J., *Memoirs of the Public and Private Life of John Howard, the Philanthropist* (London, 1818).

Bunsen, Frances, *A Memoir of Baron Bunsen* (London, 1868), 2 vols.

Buxton, Charles (ed.), *Memoirs of Sir Thomas Fowell Buxton* (London, 1849).

Buxton, Thomas Fowell, *An Enquiry Whether Crime and Misery Are Produced or Prevented by Our Present System of Prison Discipline* (London, 1818).

—*The African Slave Trade and Its Remedy* (London, 1840).

Cresswell, Mrs Francis, *A Memoir of Elizabeth Fry* (London, 1856).

Dickens, Charles, 'A visit to Newgate', *Sketches by Boz*, first published 1836 (London, 1995).

Dixon, Hepworth, *John Howard and the Prison-World of Europe* (London, 1849).

Fry, Elizabeth, *Observations on the Visiting, Superintendence and Government of Female Prisoners* (London, 1827).

—*Texts for Every Day in the Year, Principally Practical and Devotional* (Philadelphia, 1851), first published 1831.

Fry, Katherine, and Rachel Cresswell, *Memoir of the Life of Elizabeth Fry* (London, 1847).

Geldart, Hannah Ransome, *Memorials of Samuel Gurney* (Philadelphia, 1859).

Griffiths, Arthur, *The Chronicles of Newgate* (London, 1883).

Gurney, Elizabeth, *Elizabeth Fry's Journeys on the Continent 1840–1841* (London, 1931).

Gurney, Joseph John, *Notes on a Visit Made to Some of the Prisons in Scotland and the North of England, in Company with Elizabeth Fry, with Some General Observations on the Subject of Prison Discipline* (London, 1819).

—*Memoirs of Joseph John Gurney*, ed. Joseph Bevan Braithwaite (Norwich, 1854).

Halsband, Robert (ed.), *The Complete Letters of Lady Mary Wortley Montagu* (Oxford, 1967), 3 vols.

Hansard, vol. xxxviii (April 1818).

Hare, Augustus J. C., *The Gurneys of Earlham* (London, 1897), 2 vols.

Howard, John, *The State of Prisons in England and Wales with Preliminary Observations, and an Account of Some Foreign Prisons* (Warrington, 1777).

Lubbock, Percy, *Earlham* (London, 1922).

The Manchester Guardian, 23 February 1826.

Mayhew, Henry, and John Binney, *The Criminal Prisons of London and Scenes from London Life* (New York, 1968), first published London, 1862.

More, Hannah, *Moral Sketches of Prevailing Opinions and Manners, Foreign and Domestic* (London, 1820).

The Newgate Calendar, ed. Norman Birkett (London, 1951), first published 1774.

Nightingale, Florence, *The Institution of Kaiserswerth on the Rhine for the Practical Training of Deaconesses, under the Direction of the Rev. Pastor*

Fliedner, Embracing the Support and Care of a Hospital, Infant and Industrial Schools, and a Female Penitentiary (London, 1851).

—*Notes on Nursing: What It Is and What It Is Not* (London, 1859).

The Nursing Record and Hospital World (London, 1897), vol. 18, pp. 493–502.

Raffles, Sophia, *Memoir of the Life and Public Services of Sir Thomas Stamford Raffles* (London, 1835), 2 vols.

Reid, Thomas, *Two Voyages to New South Wales and Van Diemen's Land, with a Description of the Present Condition of the Colony* (London, 1822).

Roberts, William, *Memoirs of the Life and Correspondence of Mrs Hannah More* (London, 1834), 4 vols.

Seebohm, Benjamin (ed.), *Memoirs of the Life and Gospel Labours of Stephen Grellet* (London, 1870).

Smith, Sidney, 'Prisons', *Edinburgh Review* (1822).

South, John, *Facts Relating to Hospital Nurses* (London, 1857).

Timpson, Thomas, *Memoirs of Elizabeth Fry*, including a History of Her Labours in Promoting the Reformation of Female Prisoners, and the Improvement of British Seamen (London, 1847).

Trench, Melesina, 'Elizabeth Fry at Newgate', *The Journal of the Friends Historical Society* (London, 1946), vol. 38, article dating from 1820.

Voltaire (François-Marie Arouet), *Letters Concerning the English Nation* (London, 1926), first published 1734.

Wakefield, Edward Gibbon, *Facts Relating to the Punishment of Death in the Metropolis* (London, 1831).

SECONDARY SOURCES

Ashby, A., and A. Jones, *The Shrigley Abduction* (Stroud, 2004).

Bardens, Dennis, *Elizabeth Fry: Britain's Second Lady on the Five Pound Note* (London, 2004).

Bloomfield, Paul, *Edward Gibbon Wakefield: Builder of the British Commonwealth* (London, 1961).

Bostridge, Mark, *Florence Nightingale: The Woman and Her Legend* (London, 2008).

Brailsford, Mabel, *Quaker Women 1650–1690* (London, 1915).

Braithwaite, William, *The Second Period of Quakerism* (London, 1919).

Brooke, Alan, and David Brandon, *Bound for Botany Bay: British Convict Voyages to Australia* (Richmond, 2005).

Clark, Manning, *History of Australia*, ed. Michael Cathcart (London, 1993).

Collins, Philip, *Dickens and Crime* (London, 1962).

Comfort, William Wistar, *Stephen Grellet 1773–1855* (New York, 1942).

Cooper, R. A., 'Jeremy Bentham, Elizabeth Fry and prison reform', *Journal of the History of Ideas* (1981), 42, pp. 675–90.

Cornish, W. R., *Crime and Law in Nineteenth Century Britain* (Dublin, 1978).

The Corston Report: A Review of Women with Particular Vulnerabilities in the Criminal Justice System (London, 2007).

The Cumberland News, 19 May 2006.

Damousi, Joy, *Depraved and Disorderly: Female Convicts, Sexuality and Gender in Colonial Australia* (Cambridge, 1997).

Dobash, Russell P., R. Emerson Dobash, and Sue Gutteridge, *The Imprisonment of Women* (Oxford, 1986).

Evans, Eric, *The Forging of the Modern State: Early Industrial Britain, 1783–1870* (London, 1996).

Freeman, John (ed.), *Prisons Past and Future, in Commemoration of the Bi-centenary of John Howard's 'The State of the Prisons'* (London, 1978).

Fry, Elizabeth, *A Brief Memoir of Elizabeth Fry* (Montana, 2004).

Grünhut, Max, *Penal Reform: A Comparative Study* (Oxford, 1948).

Hatton, Jean, *Betsy: The Dramatic Biography of Prison Reformer, Elizabeth Fry* (Oxford, 2005).

Hibbert, Christopher, *King Mob: The Story of Lord George Gordon and the Riots of 1780* (London, 1958).

Howard, David, *John Howard: Prison Reformer* (London, 1958).

Hughes, Robert, *The Fatal Shore* (London, 1987).

Huntsman, R. G., Mary Bruin, and Deborah Holttum, 'Twixt candle and lamp: the contribution of Elizabeth Fry and the Institution of Nursing Sisters to nursing reform', *Medical History* (2002), 46, pp. 351–80.

Ignatieff, Michael, *A Just Measure of Pain: The Penitentiary in the Industrial Revolution 1750–1850* (London, 1978).

Isichei, Elizabeth, *Victorian Quakers* (Oxford, 1970).

James, David W., *Crime and Punishment in Nineteenth Century England* (London, 1975).

Jones, M. G., *Hannah More* (Cambridge, 1952).

Kent, John, *Elizabeth Fry* (London, 1962).

Labouchere, Rachel, *Deborah Darby* (York, 1993).

Larson, Rebecca, *Daughters of Light: Quaker Women Preaching and Prophesying in the Colonies and Abroad, 1700–1775* (New York, 1999).

Lewis, Georgina King, *Elizabeth Fry* (London, 1909).

Lloyd, Lewis, *Australians from Wales* (Gwynedd, 1988).

Luddy, Maria, *Women and Philanthropy in Nineteenth-Century Ireland* (Cambridge, 1995).

Manners, Emily, 'Elizabeth Hooton: first Quaker woman preacher (1600–1672)', *The Journal of the Friends Historical Society* (London, 1914), supp. 12.

Milligan, Edwards H., *Bibliographical Dictionary of British Quakers in Commerce and Industry* (York, 2007).

Mottram, R. H., *Buxton the Liberator* (London, n.d.).

Nadel, George, *Australia's Colonial Culture: Ideas, Men and Institutions in Mid-Nineteenth Century Eastern Australia* (Melbourne, 1957).

Pitman, E. R., *Elizabeth Fry* (London, 1889).

Pressnell, L. S., *Country Banking in the Industrial Revolution* (Oxford, 1956).

Priestley, Philip, *Victorian Prison Lives* (London, 1999).

Radzinowicz, Leon, *A History of Criminal Law and Its Administration from 1750* (London, 1948), i, 'The movement for reform'.

Ramsbotham, David, *Prison-gate: The Shocking State of Britain's Prisons and the Need for Visionary Change* (London, 2003).

Reay, Barry, *The Quakers and the English Revolution* (New York, 1991).

Rose, June, *Elizabeth Fry* (London, 1980).

Russell, Penny, '"Her Excellency": Lady Franklin, female convicts and the problem of authority in Van Diemen's Land', *Journal of Australian Studies* (1997), 53.

Salt, Annette, *These Outcast Women: The Parramatta Female Factory 1821–1848* (Sydney, 1984).

Shaw, A. G. L., *Convicts and the Colonies* (London, 1996).

A Short History of the Institute of Nursing Sisters (London, 1934). [Held in the archive of the Wellcome Institute, London.]

Skidmore, Gil, *Elizabeth Fry: A Quaker Life – Selected Letters and Writings* (Altamira, 2005).

Stott, Anne, *Hannah More: The First Victorian* (Oxford, 2003).

Summers, Anne, *Female Lives, Moral States: Women, Religion and Public Life in Britain 1800–1936* (Newbury, 2000).

Swift, David E., *Joseph John Gurney: Banker, Reformer, Quaker* (Connecticut, 1962).

Taylor, Francis, *The Life of William Savery* (New York and Philadelphia, 1925).

Trevett, Christine, *Seventeenth Century Women and Quakerism* (New York, 1991).

—*Women's Speaking Justified* (New York, 1999).

Walvin, James, *The Quakers: Money and Morals* (London, 1997).

Ward-Jackson, Philip, *Public Sculpture of the City of London* (Liverpool, 2003).

Whitney, Janet, *Elizabeth Fry: Quaker Heroine* (London, 1937).

Williams, Katherine, 'From Sarah Gamp to Florence Nightingale', in Celia Davies (ed.), *Rewriting Nursing History* (London, 1980), pp. 41–75.

Women and Girls in the Penal System (London, 2006) Howard League for Prison Reform, Prison Information Bulletin 2.

Acknowledgments

I am very grateful for the help of many librarians: at the Friends' Meeting House at Euston, particularly Jennifer Milligan and Joanna Clarke; at the Bodleian Library at Oxford, particularly Lucy McCann at Rhodes House; at the Norfolk Record Office at Norwich; at Lancaster University, which has an extensive Quaker book collection, including a microfiche facsimile of most of Fry's diaries; and at the Wellcome Trust Library in London, which holds the minute books of the committee of Fry's Institution of Nursing Sisters.

Tony Morris, then at Continuum, first launched me on a life of Fry, and Robin Baird-Smith, my editor at Continuum, steered the project to its conclusion, ably supported by Rhodri Mogford. I am deeply indebted to Alan Brooke, co-author with David Brandon of *Bound for Botany Bay: British Convict Voyages to Australia*, on which I relied heavily for the chapter on transportation, and who made very useful suggestions. Officials at the Old Bailey helped by providing photographic access to the Fry statue there; the Guildhall Art Gallery identified other Fry-related images; and Geoffrey Fisher, at the Conway Library of the Courtauld Institute, located important photographs. Nick Nicholson of the National Gallery of Australia provided a picture of the *Rajah* quilt, the only such item known with certainty to have been made by Fry-sponsored convict women on their way to Australia; the image of this quilt, scheduled to be shown in an exhibition at the Victoria and Albert Museum in 2010, appears for the first time in a Fry biography.

Friends, family and neighbours too numerous to mention kept me going; they know who they are, and I thank them all. Specifically, I should like to thank Jean Gilliland, whose research at the Bodleian Library was an enormous help; also Bill Pritchard and Jo Wilkinson, who were always willing to take time off from their own busy writing schedules to offer support and suggestions; Jo also compiled the index. My children Ben, Rachel and Miriam, and my friend Chris Hodkinson, have, as ever, been a tower of strength; hardly ever, in three years, have their eyes glazed over when the words 'prison reform' were mentioned.

Index

Aberdeen Bridewell 104, 106
Aberfeldy 138
Ackworth school 23
Adelaide, Princess 191
Adelaide, Queen 134, 180, 186, 197
Albert of Saxe-Coburg-Gotha 162, 197
alcohol 75, 148
all-female prisons 146–7
All Saints' Sisterhood 177
Allen & Hanbury 163, 217n. 8
Allen, William 151, 163, 196, 199
Althrop, Lord 137
America
    Joseph Gurney's ministry 149–50
    transportation to 83, 84
Amiens 189
Amphitrite, convict ship 135
Amsterdam 164, 168
Anley, Charlotte 91–4
anti-slavery campaigning 138
Antwerp 168
Armagh 111
Ashley, Lord (Anthony Ashley-Cooper, later
    Lord Shaftesbury) 196–7, 219n. 6
Association for Bettering the Condition of
    Female Prisoners 114
Association for the Improvement of Prisons
    and Prison Discipline 114
Association for the Improvement of the
    Female Prisoners at Newgate 64, 66
Athenaeum 62
Australia
all-female prisons 146
    chaplains sent to 216n. 21

matrons 143–4
transportation of women 86–91
transportation to 83–6
Avignon 158

bagnes 159–60
Ballborough 111
Ballitore 112–13
Ballnasloe 112
Balloch 139
Barclay, Robert 4
Barol, Marquise de 133
Barrett, Jerry 198
Bedford prison 52–3
Belfast 111
Belgium 163
Bell, Andrew 127
Bell, Priscilla (Fry's aunt) 213n. 6
Béranger, Alphonse de 155
Berlin 133, 165
Berlin, Rudolf 6
Berne 162
Bible readings 99–100, 108, 111–12, 133–4,
    197
Bible Society 41, 70
Birr 112
Blackfriars Bridewell 56
Bolland, Mary 70
Borough Compter prison 57, 70
Boston, USA 51
Botany Bay 65, 73, 85
Boulogne 189
Bourhill, Rebecca 141
Boyle 112

Bradshaw, Lucy 151, 163
Bramerton 4
Bremen 169–70
Brest, France 52
Bridewell prison 53–4, 193
Brighton 136
British and Foreign Sailors' Society 137
British and Foreign School Society 163
British Ladies' Society for Visiting Prisons
    121, 191, 192–3, 204
British Medical Journal (*BMJ*) 183–5
Brothers, convict ship 206
Bruges 163
Brussels 163
Bunsen, Christian von 153–4, 179, 196, 197,
    219n. 6
Bunsen, Ernest von 196, 217n. 3
Buxton, Anna (Fry's sister-in-law) 45, 197,
    212n. 12
Buxton, Hannah, née Gurney (Lady Buxton,
    Fry's sister) 34, 36, 37, 38, 194
Buxton, Priscilla (Fry's niece) 117, 153, 178,
    192
Buxton, Thomas Fowell 36, 63, 65, 70, 138,
    192, 196, 198
Byron, Lord George 102

Cambridge, USA 51
Camisards 158
Campbell, George, Duke of Argyll 200–1
capital punishment 62, 81–3, 107, 113, 125,
    133
Cardington, Shropshire 52
Carlow 111, 112
Caroline Amalie, Queen of Denmark 171–2
Carpaix, France 52
Carrick on Suir 112
cartel ships 52, 212n. 6
Casanova, Giovanni Giacomo 61
Cascades female factory 90, 91, 94, 215n. 24
Catholic Relief Act (1778) 60
Chalons-sur-Saône 157
Channel Islands 134–5, 147–8
charitable works 35, 122

Charles II 51
Charlotte Augusta, Princess of Wales 32
Charlotte, Queen of England 102–3
Chatham convict prison 219n. 5
Chelsea, refuge for young girls 162
Chesterton, George 102
child management 42
Chiswick, asylum for women 141
Cholmondley, Marchioness of 180
Christian, King of Denmark 171
Christiantown 111
Church Missionary Society 216n. 21
classification of prisoners 127–8
Clerkenwell Bridewell 57
Clermont-en-Oise 189
Clonmel 112
Coalbrookdale 17–18, 19–20, 202
coastguard library project 136–8, 196
Coburg 167
Cold Bath Fields prison 102, 146, 193
Coleraine 112
Cologne 162
colonization 62
Commissioners of Sick and Wounded
    Seamen 52
committees, use of 123–4
Conciergerie 151
convict ships 87, 96, 129, 140, 206
    see also individual ships
Cook, James 85
Cootehill 111
Cope, Matthew 140
Copenhagen 171
Corporation of the City of London 69
Corston, Jean, Baroness 205–6
Cromer 188
Cromwell, Oliver 49–50
Crosby Hall 153, 217n. 4

Darby, Abraham 18
Darby, Deborah 18–21, 43, 196, 202–3
Darby, Samuel 18, 19–20
Darby, Sarah 18
Darling, Ralph 91

debtors 83, 214n. 6
Defoe, Daniel 61
Denmark 171–2
Denmark, Prince and Princess Royal of 107
Dickens, Charles 83, 183, 185, 213n. 1
    Martin Chuzzlewit 181
    Sketches by Boz 102, 139–40
    A Tale of Two Cities 59
disease 54, 55, 57
District Visiting Societies 108
Dover, USA 51
Dresden 166–7, 172–3
Drury, Alfred 197, 219n. 8
Dublin 113, 114
Dublin House of Industry 110
Dublin Newgate 110–11
Duchâtel, Charles 190
Dumaresq, Edward 91
Dumaresq, Frances 91
Dunbarton 139
Dunkeld 138
Durham House of Correction 106
Durham Old Gaol 106
Düsseldorf 167
Düsselthal, Trappist monastery 167
dyslexia 6, 121

Earlham Hall 4–5, 12, 14, 16–17, 21, 39, 103,
    115, 192, 203, 211n. 2
Earlham (Lubbock) 211n. 3
East India Company 84
East Indies, transportation to 83
Edenderry 111
Edinburgh 23, 104, 139
Edinburgh Review 85–6, 190
education of girls 7–8
    see also schools
Elisabeth Ludovika, Queen of Prussia 172–3
Elizabeth Fry Institute for the Reformation of
    Women Prisoners 197
Elizabeth Fry Refuge 196–7
employment for prisoners 129, 141–2, 142
Erfurth 167
Ernest Augustus, Duke of Cumberland 165

Établissement des Soeurs de Santé
    Protestantes 186
Europe, continental
    first tour of 163–8
    second tour of 168–73
Evans, William 88–9

feminism 204–5
Ferguson, Charles 94, 95–6
Fête du Roi 189
Fleet prison 59
Fletcher, P.J. 198
Fliedner, Pastor 167–8, 177, 179–80
Fontainebleau 157
Foreign Bible Society 193
Forster, Josiah 151, 154, 157, 158, 160, 163,
    189
Forster, William 43, 196, 212n. 12
Fox, George 3, 49, 51
France
    first tour of 151–3
    Protestant Church 162
    second tour of 154–61
    third tour of 189–91
Frankfurt 162, 166, 167
Franklin, John 94, 95
Franklin, Lady 94, 95
Frazer, Catherine 140
Friedrich Wilhelm III 165, 197
Friedrich Wilhelm IV 153, 172–3, 187
Friends' Meeting House, Barking 195
Fry family 25, 45–6, 108–9, 180, 188
Fry, Daniel (Fry's son) 107, 192, 194
Fry, Elizabeth (Fry's daughter) 41, 46
Fry, Elizabeth (Fry's mother-in-law) 24, 35
Fry, Hannah (Fry's daughter) 42, 63
Fry, John (Fry's brother-in-law) 36
Fry, John (Fry's son) 35, 45, 62
Fry, Joseph (Fry's husband) 30, 31, 36, 38, 42,
    115, 149, 150, 151, 154, 160, 163, 194
    courtship of Fry 24–6, 27–8
Fry, Joseph (Fry's son) 39, 63
Fry, Katherine (Fry's daughter) 31–2, 63, 103,
    149, 203

Fry, Louisa (Fry's daughter) 46, 63, 194
Fry, Rachel (Fry's daughter) 34, 63, 103, 107, 115, 201, 203
Fry, Richenda (Fry' sister) 14, 21
Fry, Richenda (Fry's daughter) 37, 63, 194
Fry, Samuel (Fry's son) 46, 63
Fry, William (Fry's brother-in-law) 45
Fry, William (Fry's son) 36, 45, 62, 149, 191
Fry, William Storrs (Fry's father-in-law) 24, 38
Fry, Willie (Fry's grandson) 193–4
Fry's diary 115
    faith 8–9, 39–40
    family 150
    fears 5–6
    health 34, 35, 46, 112
    homecoming 147
    journeys 104
    marriage 25–6, 36–7
    ministry 41, 42, 64–5, 150, 152
    observations on life 12–13, 15–16, 37, 109, 192, 194
    public speaking 36, 40–1, 99
    relations with others 30
    the Sabbath 187
    servants 38
    unfulfillment 30–1
    vanity 134

galley slaves 159–60
Gaol Committee of the City of London 63
gaol-distemper 54
Gaols Act (1823) 135, 141, 142, 144, 147, 165, 200
Garland Grove, convict ship 96
garnish 49, 51, 53
Geneva 161–2
George Hibbert, convict ship 143
George I, King of England 32
George, Prince of Wales 16
Germany 164–8, 169–71
Géronda, Joseph-Marie de 155, 157
Ghent 163
Giltspur Street Compter 193

Glasgow 139
Glasgow Bridewell 104–6
Gloucester, Bishop of 198
Gordon-Lennox, Charles, Duke of Richmond 140
Gordon, Lord George 60–1
Gordon Riots 59–61
Gotha 167
Gouda 164
Grange Gorman Lane Prison, Dublin 145–7
Great Lisbon Earthquake 52
Great Reform Act (1832) 204
Grellet, Joseph 19, 161
Grellet, Stephen 19, 21, 43–4,163, 196, 199, 202
Grenoble 160–1
Grey, George 150
Grey, Mary, Dowager Lady Grey 180
Griffiths, Arthur 199–200, 219n. 5
Grindrod, Eliza 96
Guernsey 135
Guizot, François 189
Gurney family 3–4, 11–12, 14, 25, 115, 180, 188
Gurney, Anna (Fry's niece) 104–6, 168
Gurney, Catherine (Fry's mother) 3, 4, 7–8, 9, 213n. 6
Gurney, Daniel (Fry's brother) 7
Gurney, Eliza (Fry's sister-in-law) 189
Gurney, Elizabeth (Fry's cousin) 36
Gurney, Elizabeth (Fry's niece) 196, 201, 217n. 3
    record of first European tour 163–8
    record of second European tour 168–73
Gurney, Elizabeth (Fry's sister) 116
Gurney, Elizabeth (Fry's sister-in-law) 42, 150, 180, 191
Gurney, John (Fry's brother) 24, 37, 46
Gurney, John (Fry's father) 9, 10, 15, 17, 20, 23, 24, 26–7, 39
Gurney, Joseph Bevan (Fry's cousin) 26
Gurney, Joseph (Fry's uncle) 14, 39, 169
Gurney, Joseph (later Joseph John, Fry's brother) 34, 37, 41, 45, 103, 108, 114, 116,

157, 163, 168, 170, 171, 189, 196, 198, 201
American ministry 149–50
Ireland tour 109–14
Notes on a Visit Made to Some of the Prisons in Scotland and the North of England 106
Gurney, Katherine (Kitty, Fry's sister) 7, 9, 22, 63, 103, 115
Gurney, Louisa 11, 12, 14–15
Gurney, Mary (Fry's sister-in-law) 103
Gurney, Priscilla (Fry's sister) 37, 39, 41, 107, 116
Gurney, Priscilla Hannah (Fry's cousin) 17–18
Gurney, Rachel (Fry's sister) 9, 22, 63, 115
Gurney, Richenda (Fry's sister) 14, 21–2
Gurney, Samuel (Fry's brother) 34, 45, 109, 116, 150, 163, 164, 166, 167, 198
Guy's Hospital 180, 183

Haddington 106
hair-cutting 128
Hamburg 170–1
Hampton, John 96
Hampton, USA 51
handmill, the 141
Hanover 164–5
Harriet, Duchess of Sutherland 180
Haslar Royal Naval Hospital 136, 196
Hawkins, Bisset 147–8
Hayter, George 94
Hayter, Kezia 94, 95
Henry II, King of England 59
Herm 135
Hester, Fry's protégée 206
Hoare, Catherine (Fry's niece) 192
Hoare, Louisa, née Fry (Fry's sister-in-law) 36
Hoare, Louisa, née Gurney 219n. 6
Hoare, Samuel (Fry's brother-in-law) 36, 63, 188, 196
Holland 163–4, 168–9
Hollings, Les 215n. 26
Hootten, Elizabeth 49–52

hospitals 155
see also individual hospitals
Hôtel Dieu 155
Howard, John 49, 52–7, 59, 85–6, 103, 141, 145, 164, 196
The State of Prisons in England and Wales with Preliminary Observations, and an Account of Some Foreign Prisons 56–7
Hull, Henry 41
Hunter, John 33

imprisonment as punishment 83
Institution of Nursing Sisters 177, 185
Inverary 139
Ireland 114, 144
first tour of 109–14
second tour of 145–7
Irving, Lydia 88–9
Islington school 35–6

Jenner, Edward 33
Jersey 134–5, 148
Julius, Nicolaus 133

Kaiserswerth 167–8, 177, 179, 180, 181, 218n. 5
Kells 111
Kiel 171
Kilmainham prison 110
Kilmuck 104
King's Bench prison 57
King's College Hospital 180
Kirkdale House of Correction 133

La Force prison for men 151
La Perrache 158
La Trappe, monks of 156
Ladies' Newgate Association 65
Ladies' Society for the Reformation of Female Prisoners 94
Lady of the Lake, convict ship 88–9
Lancaster, Joseph 127, 155, 163, 196
Launceston, female factory 90
Lausanne 162

Leiningen, Countess of *see* Victoria, Duchess of Kent
Leipzig 167
Leopold, King of Belgium 163
Leuwarden 163–4
Leyden 164
libraries
    coastguard project 136–8, 196
    fishermen 188
Liège 168
Lincoln Castle prison 50–1
Lisburn 111
Livesay, Captain 89
Loch Awe 139
Loch Katrine 139
Loch Lomond 139
Loch Tay 138
London, Bishop of 180
London Hospital 183
London Illustrated News 177
Londonderry 111
Longfellow, Henry Wadsworth 177
Louis Philippe, King of the French 191
Lubbock, Percy 203, 211n. 3
Ludwigsburg 162
Lunacy Commission 196
Lurgan 111
Luss 139
Luther, Martin 167
Lyons 157

Mackintosh, James 107
Mainz 167
Maison Centrale, women's prison 160
Maison d'Arrêt 158
Maison Pénitentiaire, Geneva 161–2
Manchester Royal Infirmary 186
Mansion House 196–7
Marie-Amelie, Queen of the French 197
Marie Antoinette 151
Marriage Act (1753) 28
Marsden, Samuel 90–1, 216n. 21
Marseilles 159
Marshalsea prison 57, 83

Martineau, Harriet 12
Mary, Duchess of Gloucester 134, 180
matrons 69, 126, 142–4, 146
Melun 157
Mill, John Stuart 190
Millbank penitentiary 73, 144–5, 193, 198, 219n. 5
missionaries 89
monitors 124, 127–8
Montagu, Mary Wortley 32
Montauban, Protestant training college 160
Montpellier 160
More, Hannah 101–2, 109, 202
Morpeth, Lord 150
Mountmellick 112

National Society for Women's Suffrage 204
Neild, James 3–4, 219n. 1
New Prison, Clerkenwell 56–7
Newgate experiment 65, 72–3
Newgate prison 57, 59, 79–80, 197, 198, 199–200
Newgate prison, women's wing 44–5, 57, 62–5, 71, 107, 117, 166, 179, 187–8, 193
    accommodation 74
    alcohol banned 75
    bedding 77
    children 64, 70–1
    clothing allowance 75–6
    employment of prisoners 142
    Friday Bible readings 99–100, 108
    health and diet 74–5
    hygiene and sanitation 76–7
    improved treatment of women 139–40
    inadequacies of 145
    management of women by women 77
    matrons 69
    overcrowding 78
    punishment of prisoners 74
    religious education 142
    reward system 74
    school established 64, 71
    Stephen Grellet visits 43–4
    visitors to 67–9

Newgate Rules 66–7, 105
Nightingale, Florence 26, 177, 179, 201, 218n. 5
Nightingale School of Nursing 177
Nîmes 158–9
Normanby, Marquis of 146
Norwich 3
Norwich, Bishop of 196, 197
nurses and nursing 38, 177–8
    holistic approach 184–5
    professional training 178–9, 180–2
    provision of service 182
    'Sarah Gamp' type 181, 185
    standards 183
    uniforms 181
Nursing Record and Hospital World 185–6

Oates, Titus 61
Oban 139
Observations on the Visiting, Superintendence and Government of Female Prisoners (Fry) 121, 133, 146, 178, 205
Old Bailey, Fry's statue 197–8
Orléans, Duchess of 197
Overend, Gurney & Co. 116
Oxford movement 184

Paris 133, 151–2, 154–7, 190–1
Paris, Archbishop of 157, 191
Parramatta female factory 90–4, 216n. 21
Parry, Edward 137, 138, 196, 219n. 6
Pastoret, Marquise de 133
Pattle, Eliza 213n. 8
Peel, Robert 133, 137
Penal Servitude Act (1853) 83, 97, 214n. 7
Penn, William 61
Pentonville prison 97
Pharmaceutical Society 163
Philadelphia, USA 18–19
Pirie, Jane 140
Plain Dealer 32
Plashet 29, 30, 33, 38–9, 41–2, 106–8, 115–16, 117
Plymouth 136

Poissy, central prison 151
Popham, Alexander 54
Port Stevens, New South Wales 196, 219n. 6
Potsdam 133
Poultry Compter prison 29
Preston House of Correction 106
prison hulks 57, 84, 214n. 8
Prisons Act (1835) 145, 147, 200
Project Newgate *see* Newgate experiment
prostitution 88, 91
Protestant Association 60
Protestant Church, France 162
Pryor, Elizabeth 88–9, 140, 143–4
Psalm 27 194
Pyrmont 164

Quakers
    burial of dead 195–6
    businesses 4
    communities 4
    humanitarian issues 199
    imprisonment of 49
    marriage 28
    ministry 202–3
    and transportation 84
    women's rights 204
    see also Society of Friends
Quarterly Review 86
Queen's Nursing Institute 186
quilts 94–5, 129–30, 206, 215n. 25, 215n. 26

Rajah, convict ship 94–5
Rajah, quilt 94–5, 215n. 25, 215n. 26
Ramsgate, Kent 193, 195
Rawlins, Marian 146–7
Recke, Count Adalbert von der 167, 217n. 15
Reid, Thomas 86
religion 13
religious education 73, 128–9, 142
remand prisoners 53, 67, 76, 79, 127, 156–7, 214n. 6
reward systems 74, 125
Rhode Island, USA 51
Richard Dixon and Co. 65

Richard, William 85
Richmond Bridewell 110
Richmond General Penitentiary 110, 145–7
Richmond, George 198, 203
Richmond Lunatic Asylum 110
Roman Catholic Church
    nuns and nursing 181
    resistance from 111–12, 113, 114, 157,
        181, 191
    and women prisoners 122
Romilly, Samuel 82, 99, 107
Roscommon 112
Roscrea 112
Rotterdam 163, 168
Rowe, Harriet 186
Royal Academy 198
Royal Lancastrian Society 163
Royal Pharmaceutical Society 163
Royal Victoria Asylum 141
Russell, Lord John 148
Russell, Lord William 165

St George's Hospital 180
St Germain military prison 151
St Joseph, order of 158
St Lazare women's prison 151, 152, 157, 191
St Mildred's Court, Cheapside 29, 33–4,
    115–16, 154
St Petersburg 133
St Thomas's Hospital 180
Sâlpetrière Hospital 151
Sark 135
Saunders, John 89
Savery, William 13–16, 18–19, 20, 21, 43, 196
Savoy prison 57
School of Discipline, for young girls, Chelsea
    141
schools 22, 26–7, 41
    Ackworth school 23
    Islington 35–6
    Newgate prison 64, 71
    Whitechapel 183
Scotland and North of England
    first tour of 103–6

second tour of 138–9
    third tour of 149
Scutari, military hospital 177
Seebohm, Benjamin 164
Seebohm family 164
Select Committee on prisons in England and
    Wales (1835) 140–5, 200
Select Committee on London prisons (1818)
    69–80, 82, 99, 200
sentences, mitigation of 74, 83, 125
sexes, separation of 57, 63, 126–7, 144, 146–7
Shaw, Mrs Benjamin 141
Sheepwash 23
Shrigley Abduction 61–2
Sidmouth, Lord 74, 83, 103
Silesia 172
Sir George Seymour, convict ship 96
Sisters of Charity 190
Skelton, Harriet 103
slavery, abolition of 138, 169
Sligo 112
smallpox inoculation 32–3, 41, 178, 212n. 2
Smith, Sydney 86, 100–1
social cleansing 84
Society for the Reformation of Juvenile
    Offenders 70
Society for the Reformation of Prison
    Discipline 63, 70
Society of Friends 3, 115, 116, 117, 158, 202,
    204
    see also Quakers
solitary confinement 125, 155–7
Spring-Rice Thomas (later Lord Monteagle)
    146
Stuttgart 162
surgeon-superintendents 86, 90, 214n. 12
Suringar, Willem Hendrick 163
Switzerland, tour of 161–2

Tasmania *see* Van Diemen's Land
Tasmanian Ladies' Society 95
Thackeray, William Makepeace 185
The Grove 14
Thomas, C.B. 68–9

Thun 162
Timpson, Thomas 137, 215n. 15
Tothill Fields Bridewell 57, 193
Toulon 159–60
Toulouse 160
Tower Hamlets gaol 57
transportation 62, 73–4, 130, 140, 144–5, 206, 214n. 7
  to America 83, 84
  to Australia 83–6
  to East Indies 83
  end of 96–7
  use of matrons 143–4
  see also convict ships
treadmill, the 127, 141
Trench, Melesina 100
Trial by Jury (Gilbert and Sullivan) 211n.1
Trim 111
Tronchin, Colonel 161
Turin 133
Turner, Ellen 62

untried prisoners *see* remand prisoners
Upper Goat Lane meeting House 3, 13
Upton House 188, 195
Upton Lane, Essex 117, 153, 162, 187, 192
Utrecht 164

Van Diemen's Land 85, 86–96
Victoria, Duchess of Kent 134, 163
Victoria, Queen 162, 165, 197
  as Princess 134
Voltaire (François-Marie Arouet) 32–3, 212n. 5

Wade, Judith 180
Wakefield, Edward Gibbon 61–2, 213n. 8, 213n. 14
Wakefield, William 62
Wandsworth 24

Waterford 112
Weimar 167
Wellesley, Marquess 113, 114
Westminster Gatehouse, prison 57
Wexford 113
White Cross Street Prison 193
Whitechapel, school 183
Whittington, Richard 'Dick' 59
Wilberforce, William 36, 70, 99, 117–18, 138, 198, 216n. 21
Wild, Jonathan 61
Wilhelm, Princess 165–6
William Frederick, Duke of Gloucester 11–12, 103
William, King of Holland 168
Wollstonecraft, Mary 204
women
  roles in society 205
  suited to visiting 130–1
women prisoners
  charitable activities 122
  clothing allowance 75–6, 128
  codes of conduct 124–5
  and committees 123–4
  improved treatment of 139–40
  management by women 77, 121–3, 126, 142–4
  personal numbers 128
  release of 130
  transportation to Australia 86–91
  transportation to Van Diemen's Land 91–6
Wood, Sir Matthew 69
Wormwood Scrubs 219n. 5

York 23
York Castle prison 49–50
Young, Rebecca 18–19, 20

Zurich 162
Zwolle 164